Natural Resources: Exploitation, Depletion and Conservation

Natural Resources: Exploitation, Depletion and Conservation

Katherine Potter

Callisto Reference

www.callistoreference.com

Callisto Reference,
118-35 Queens Blvd., Suite 400,
Forest Hills, NY 11375, USA

Visit us on the World Wide Web at:
www.callistoreference.com

ISBN: 978-1-64116-612-6 (Hardback)

Cataloging-in-Publication Data

Natural resources : exploitation, depletion and conservation / Katherine Potter.
p. cm.
Includes bibliographical references and index.
ISBN 978-1-64116-612-6
1. Natural resources. 2. Conservation of natural resources. 3. Environmental protection.
4. Natural resources--Management. I. Potter, Katherine.

S944 .N38 2021
333.7--dc23

TABLE OF CONTENTS

PREFACE

This book is a culmination of my many years of practice in this field. I attribute the success of this book to my support group. I would like to thank my parents who have showered me with unconditional love and support and my peers and professors for their constant guidance.

The resources that exist naturally and without actions of humankind are known as natural resources. Some of the varied natural resources that are available on Earth are sunlight, water, land and atmosphere as well as all crops, vegetation and animal life. They can also exist in another form that needs to be processed to obtain the resource such as metal ores, petroleum, rare earth metals and various forms of energy. They can be classified in different ways such as origin and stage of development. On the basis of origin, they are classified as biotic and abiotic resources. They can also be categorized as potential resources, actual resources, reserve resources and stock resources, on the basis of their stage of development. Using natural resources for economic growth, generally at the cost of environmental degradation is referred to as exploitation of natural resources. The consumption of a resource faster than it can be replenished is known as depletion. The practices involved in the protection and restoration of natural resources are referred to as natural resource conservation. The topics included in this textbook on natural resources are of utmost significance and bound to provide incredible insights to readers. Some of the diverse topics covered in this book address the varied branches that fall under this category. It will provide comprehensive knowledge to the readers.

The details of chapters are provided below for a progressive learning:

Chapter - Introduction

The resources that exist naturally, without any human actions are known as natural resources. They are broadly categorized as renewable and non-renewable resources. Some of the important resources are air, water, coal, oil and natural gas. This is an introductory chapter which will introduce briefly all the significant aspects of natural resources.

Chapter - Types of Natural Resources

Natural resources are categorized on the basis of their origin, stages of development and renewability. Based on source of origin, natural resources divided into two types, biotic and abiotic. They are also categorized as renewable and non-renewable on the basis of their renewability. This chapter has been carefully written to provide an easy understanding of these types of natural resources.

Chapter - Exploitation of Natural Resources

The exploitation of natural resources can lead to various consequences that can arise from the careless and excessive consumption of these resources. Some of the consequences are deforestation, soil erosion, desertification, natural disasters and increase in greenhouse gas emissions. The topics elaborated in this chapter will help in gaining a better perspective about these impacts of exploitation of natural resources.

Chapter - Depletion of Natural Resources

The consumption of a resource faster than it can be replenished can lead to resource depletion. Some of the natural resources which are being depleted are oil, gas, groundwater, freshwater and ozone. The chapter closely examines the key aspects related to the depletion of these natural resources to provide an extensive understanding of the subject.

Chapter - Conservation of Natural Resources

Natural resources can be conserved by using various methods such as using alternative energy sources, rainwater harvesting, switching to biofuel, reducing the use of plastics, using hybrid vehicles, etc. This chapter discusses in detail these practices and concepts related to conservation of natural resources.

Chapter - Environmental Protection and Natural Resource Management

The practice of protecting the natural environment by individuals, organizations and governments is termed as environmental protection. Natural resource management involves the management of natural resources such soil, water, land, etc. All the diverse principles of environmental protection and natural resource management have been carefully analyzed in this chapter.

Katherine Potter

Introduction

1 CHAPTER

The resources that exist naturally, without any human actions are known as natural resources. They are broadly categorized as renewable and non-renewable resources. Some of the important resources are air, water, coal, oil and natural gas. This is an introductory chapter which will introduce briefly all the significant aspects of natural resources.

NATURAL RESOURCES

Natural resource is any naturally occurring substance or feature of the environment (physical or biological) that, while not created by human effort, can be exploited by humans to satisfy their needs or wants. There are different schools of thought on whether economic value is a necessary condition for something to be classified as a natural resource, a distinction that can have legal ramifications.

Atlantic salmon, Salmo salar, a renewable, biotic natural resource.

Examples of natural resources include fossil fuels (crude oil, coal, etc.), minerals (diamonds, copper, etc.), salmon, and timber. Trees in a park that provide aesthetic beauty can be considered natural resources among those who do not limit the term to the presence of economic product value.

Resources such as fossil fuels and minerals are considered "non-renewable resources" since they are irreversibly depleted as they are extracted for use. Other resources, such as fish and timber, are "renewable resources" and will be replenished if managed well.

Some natural resources, such as oil and natural gas reserves, may be associated with particular properties. Other resources, such as whales, migratory birds or fish, or clean air are not fixed to particular properties. According to economic theory, the private ownership of natural resources tends to produce more efficient extraction and consumption because of the profit motive, which leads to realistic pricing and careful management. On the other hand, when natural resources are not privately owned, there is a greater tendency for their being over-exploited, as individual parties compete for them. This overuse, sometimes to the point of destruction, has been termed the "tragedy of the commons." However, in both cases, there is danger of inefficiency and over-harvesting of the natural resources when individual parties, in their exploitation or use of the natural resources, fail to consider the broader needs of others in society or the needs of future generations.

A well-known paradox is the fact that abundant natural resources, under some defined circumstances, may actually correlate with poor state development, such as seen in the Democratic Republic of Congo or Nigeria. This is known as the "resource curse."

Diamonds are naturally existing and serve a human want: a natural resource.

There are two basic conditions for a substance or feature to be classified as a natural resource. First, the resource must exist naturally in the environment; that is, not synthetically produced by human beings, such as in a laboratory or factory. Crude oil, timber, deer, and sailfish fit that requirement, whereas genetically engineered bacteria or computers do not. A naturally occurring commodity typically is classified as a natural resource when it is extracted or purified from its natural state rather than being created. Second, the resource must be able to be exploited by humans to directly satisfy a need or want. Copper, tuna, and air fulfill such a requirement (with air supplying a need, as a condition for life), whereas an infectious parasite or mosquito does not (although the parasite or mosquito may provide an indirect benefit as part of nature, such as part of food chains).

A silver nugget. Silver is an economically valuable, non-renewable natural resource.

Some authorities hold that for a substance or feature to be classified as a natural resource, it must offer potential or actual economic value, creating wealth. This was an original definition provided in the 6th edition of *Black's Law Dictionary*: "any material in its native state which when extracted has economic value." Others do not limit the term to those resources having economic product value, but also include supplying a non-economic value. Resources such as oil, coal, wood, water power, and arable land clearly can be seen as providing potential economic value. These are considered natural resources by all parties. The second, broader concept also includes such features as climate and trees planted in a park. While not considered to have any direct economic value, they do provide important non-economic values. A climate may be seen as part of one's enjoyment of nature and tourism, while trees in a park provide aesthetic values.

This distinction is reflected in the two divergent definitions of natural resource found in the 7th edition of *Black's Law Dictionary*: (1) "any material from nature having potential economic value or providing for the sustenance of life; and (2) Environmental features that serve a community's well-being or recreational interests, such as parks."

It is a distinction that has important legal ramifications. For example, in a legal case considering the trees and wildlife on Fairfield University in Connecticut (USA), an Appellate Court held that natural resources must have economic value. However, this decision was subsequently overturned by the Connecticut Supreme Court, which stated "the view that the term natural resources is confined to the limited economic product value standard is nowhere expressed in our legislative history. To the contrary, the legislative history of the act is antithetical to that conclusion". Judge Barry Schaller, a dissenting view on the Appellate Court decision, also advanced this view in embracing a broader view of natural resources as "a complex of interrelated elements existing in a state of ecological balance, which must be preserved for life to survive on the planet". As an example, one can note that the loss of wetlands can greatly impact the quality of life on the planet, yet have historically been drained or otherwise destroyed in order to use the land for more economically viable uses, such as residential, commercial, or agricultural uses.

A natural resource industry is one in which the primary activity involves extraction and/or purification of the natural resource, instead of creation of the commodity. Examples of natural resource industries include crude oil extraction and processing, fishing, and forestry. Agriculture is not considered a natural resource industry.

Examples of Natural Resources

The natural resource of wind powers these 5MW wind turbines on this wind farm 28 km off the coast of Belgium.

Examples of resources supplied by nature:

- Fossil fuels (petroleum, natural gas, coal),
- Minerals (diamonds, gold, copper, silver),
- Natural vegetation, forests, timber,
- Animals (salmon, whales, deer, etc.),
- Air, wind,
- Water, water power, wetlands, watercourses, lakes,
- Sunlight,
- Soil, topsoil.

Note that while soil is itself considered a natural resource, heavily worked agricultural lands, with their input of fertilizer, pesticides, herbicides, and so forth, are often not considered to be natural resources. In one legal case, the Connecticut Supreme Court specifically held that agricultural lands are not natural resources. It further noted that the associated air and water are natural resources (ones not owned by anyone).

Classification

Natural resources can be classified according to several methods:

Renewable versus Non-renewable

Tuna, a renewable natural resource (Thunnus albacares).

Renewable resources are those physical or biotic resources that are used by people but can be replenished in a timely manner. For example, forests, fish stocks (such as salmon or tuna), water, and agricultural crops can be replenished over time, with forests taking a longer time than fish or water, and agricultural crops replenished over a short time period.

Renewable resources can further be sub-divided into two additional categories:

- Plentiful: This sub-category includes those natural resources that are plentiful and continuously available; they are not affected by human consumption. Examples include sunlight (solar energy), air, and wind.
- Limited: This sub-category includes those natural resources that are limited and can be depleted by human use, but also can be replenished or reproduced relatively quickly. Examples include animal life (fish, deer, etc.), plants, agricultural crops, water, and forests.

El Chino open-pit copper mine in New Mexico.
Copper is a non-renewable natural resource.

- Non-renewable natural resources: Non-renewable resources are those limited in amount that cannot be replenished in a timely manner or feasibly and are essentially irreplaceable once extracted. For example, minerals and fossils fuels are formed over very long geologic periods. Since their rate of formation is very slow, they cannot be replenished once they get depleted. Examples of non-renewable natural resources include petroleum, natural gas, gold, silver, diamonds, and copper.

Biotic versus Abiotic

- Biotic natural resources: Biotic natural resources are those obtained from living sources, such as from trees and their products (apples, coconuts, timber, etc.), agricultural crops, birds and their products (feathers, meat, etc.), fish, marine organisms, and so forth. In addition, fossil fuels such as coal and petroleum are classified as biotic because they derive from organic matter, with coal believed to have formed from land plants and petroleum from plankton.
- Abiotic natural resources: Abiotic natural resources are those obtained from non-living sources. For example, minerals (gold, copper, silver, iron, etc.), as well as air,land and water, are classifed as abiotic natural resources.

Resource Curse

The "resource curse" is an observation that countries with an abundance of point-source, non-renewable natural resources (such as oil and minerals), and that have a high level of export dependence on such resources, tend to have poorer economic performances (less economic growth) and worse development outcomes (undemocratic, corrupt, and/or ineffective governance) than states that have fewer natural resources.

For example, 18 of the 20th largest oil exporters in 2000 had undemocratic governments, and many oil-exporting countries were highly indebted. Nigeria is rich in oil but is among the poorest states. The Democratic Republic of Congo is rich in many minerals, such as tin, copper, cadmium, diamonds, and gold and yet is poor and with many governance issues.

The proposed causes for such a phenomena are many. Conflict over resources (separatist and inter-governmental conflicts), revenue volatility (fluctuating prices), lack of government incentive to build up infrastructure, and lack of economic and human resource diversification (because of dependence of natural resources due to their high profitability) are some of the explanations. In addition, when the government does not have to rely on taxes for revenue, then the citizens have less incentive to demand efficient, responsive government than the highly taxed citizens of other countries, who are strongly motivated to be watchful of how the government spends its money. Money from sales of natural resources also provide rulers with the means to control the armed forces and buy favors. Governments may also borrow based on the resource potential, and can fall into debt when the price of the commodity drops.

In addition to these causes that are internal to the nation, there also are external factors involving foreign powers (governments, individuals, or corporations) exploiting the resources. For example, King Leopold II of Belgium looted the region of the present-day Democratic Republic of Congo for its rubber, enslaving, maiming, and killing much of the native population in the process.

Here are the top 10 natural resources in the world, how they are already in danger from the current demands placed on them; and how conservationism can help to manage these resources so they don't disappear. Using alternate resources is one thing that will help; creating better resource management plans is what will also help to preserve these resources for the future.

Water

While the earth may be mostly water, only about 2-1/2 percent of it is fresh water. Of that 2.5%, even less is considered to be potable. Potable water is water that is considered to be safe to drink and cook with. While many countries are working to build water treatment plants, the fact is that due to changes in the climate the amount of rain and ice melts from winter have dropped off and lowered the reserve supplies of freshwater to be treated. There are initiatives to educate and regulate the use of water in the world, as well as exploration into the technology of water farming in arid countries too.

Air

Clean air is necessary for the existence of life on this planet. It is essential for the existence of plants, animals and wildlife. It is important to reduce air pollution as polluted air degrades the environment and can enter our body and can cause health related problems. There are number of ways to keep the air clean and reduce air pollution like riding bus instead of using your own vehicle, carpooling etc.

Coal

Coal is estimated to be able to last less than 200 more years. One of the issues is that as countries such as China increase their demands on the coal supply it will dwindle faster. Coal is also the major source of air pollutant in the world so there is much discussion about regulating its usage. The problem is it is one of the cheapest sources of fuel for industrial applications.

Oil

The general estimate is that with the projected rate of consumption of oil supplies and known resources that there is enough to last for 30 40 more years. While many in the oil industry are pushing to be allowed to frack and drill in protected areas to look for undiscovered oil fields, little has been done to address the question of what will happen to the Earth's crust when the fields are empty and there are large empty cavities beneath the Earth. Even if new fields and methods of oil extraction are discovered, geologists project that it would be impossible for the Earth to have an unlimited supply of oil. It takes millions of years for oil to be created; there is no way of speeding up that process.

Natural Gas

Natural gas reserves are doing only slightly better than oil, it is estimated that there is enough to last for 60 years. Gas is a much cleaner fuel source than oil, which has led to an increased level of consumption of it as an alternative fuel, but it still stands to run out quickly.

Phosphorus

Phosphorus comes from phosphate rock and is used to grow all of our food and crops. Unfortunately, phosphate rock is only found in three places on Earth – the US, China and Morocco. The projected lifespan of the current known resources is about a 100 years. There has not been significant research in developing new and safe fertilizers that can be effective replacements for phosphorus.

Other Minerals

Other minerals like gypsum, bauxite, phosphate, bentonite, mica, titanium, zirconium are found in sea beds along the coastal plains. Rare earth elements like scandium and terbium are two of the earth powerful minerals that are used in wind turbines and electronic circuits in smartphones. Coastal plains contains deposits of potassium carbonate and rare elements like cerium and neodymium.

Iron

Iron is also in limited supply. It is made from elements such as silica which then have to be heated to create the pig iron that industrialization depends on. Iron was the most important natural resource on earth during ancient ages. It allowed people at that time to build stronger weapons, better transportation and taller buildings. Both iron and steel are still used in modern day industries.

Soil

Another important natural resource is soil. Soil is composed of many different particles and nutrients in the soil helps plants grow. Apart from this, soil can also be used to provide shelter. A pile of garbage along with some soil when placed in worm compost bin, creates nutrient rich soil that helps in growth of plants and makes them healthy.

Forests and Timber

As the world gets more modern and population grows, there is more of a demand for housing and construction projects. This reduces open green spaces. Forests are necessary to preserve the ecology of the world that supports all of the natural resources and life. Forests also play a critical role in providing clean air and the lumber that builds the homes.

Apart from the ones listed above, rocks and sediments, rivers and lakes, mountains, farmland, wetlands, coastal shores, clays, sand, copper, manganese and stone are some of the other natural resources.

Types of Natural Resources

CHAPTER 2

Natural resources are categorized on the basis of their origin, stages of development and renewability. Based on source of origin, natural resources divided into two types, biotic and abiotic. They are also categorized as renewable and non-renewable on the basis of their renewability. This chapter has been carefully written to provide an easy understanding of these types of natural resources.

The resources that are derived from the natural environment are known as natural resources. Starting from rivers to mountains, stones to minerals, our Mother Earth is abundant with rich resources that have helped a long way for the man made developments. The human race could not have probably thrived without the use of these natural resources. It's surprising but true that every man made product is made up of natural resources to some extent. The natural resources can be classified under various heads depending on their type, source of origin, developing stages and renewability.

Source of Origin

Biotic

The biotic resources are derived from organic and living material. The materials that are obtained from animals and forests can be said as the biotic natural resources. Some of these are the fossil fuels – coal, and petroleum, which originates from the decayed organic matter.

Abiotic

The resources that can be derived from non-living and non-organic materials are known as abiotic resources. Some of the justifying examples are air, fresh water, land, and heavy metals (copper, gold, iron, silver, etc.).

Developing Stages

Potential Resources

The resources that already exist in a region in abundance and used in future catering to the developmental needs are known as potential resources. For instance, if a country has petroleum deposits on the sedimentary rocks, it can be termed as a potential resource until mechanical drilling is done out of the rock and utilised.

Actual Resources

The resources which have already been scrutinized, recognised, surveyed, and are used presently after measuring their quantity and quality are known as actual resources. However, development of these resources depends on the technological inputs.

Reserve Resources

These are sectional parts of the actual resource that has the probabilities of being developed in the future with the help of technology.

Stock Resources

The resource that has been surveyed and still cannot be used due to lack of technology is known as stock resources; one such example is hydrogen.

From Renewability Aspect

Renewable Natural Resources

The resources that can be replenished are known as renewable natural resources. Some examples are air, sunlight, and wind. These resources are continuously available and the quality does not get reduced due to human consumption. One demerit is that renewable resources cannot be rapidly recovered and are vulnerable to complete exhaustion if overused.

Non-renewable Natural Resources

The formation of these resources takes place slowly and also does not form naturally in the environment. These are known to be non-renewable because the rate of human consumption is usually exceeding the rate of creation or recovery. The common examples are minerals and fossil fuels.

However, apart from these classifications, natural resources are also classified into types like Forest resources, Aquatic/Marine resources, Hydro geological resources, Animal resources, Microbial resources, Human resources, Atmospheric resources, Crop resources, Geological resources,

Edaphic resources, Wildlife resources and others. The most common natural resources in use are wind, soil, water, minerals and vegetation.

FROM SOURCE OF ORIGIN

Biotic Resources

Biotic Resources are also known as the living resources. These are the renewable resources and include the plants and animals. The foods, sugars, tea, coffee, medicines are obtained from the plants. The timber is obtained from the tress and is used for the construction, furniture, ships, poles and radio. The wood pulp forms different types of paper. The gums, wool, acetic acid, alcohol, and dry fruits are obtained from the trees. They also provide the shelter and food to the other organisms. They also provide oxygen and affect the weather of a particular area. The plants present on the land and are classified as a forests, croplands, shrubs and grassland. The vegetation affects the soil by preventing soil erosion. The humus is formed by the decayed leaves which provide nutrition to the soil. The spread of deserts is also checked by the plants. In a year the annual production of biomass produced by the marine plants is three hundred twenty five million tones. The total production of biomass is three hundred eighty million tones. The humans mostly depend on the land vegetation for survival. The earth has around 4 million species of plants and a few of them are edible. The conservation of plants must be done.

The pollution in the environment, deforestation, overgrazing, and the formation of cropland causes an adverse effect on the growth of plants. Some of the species of plants get endangered. So, there should be a check on the activities of human. The use of marine plants is multipurpose. The humans must explore the plants and which act as a source of food. The role of animals in the biotic environment is very crucial. They act as a food for the man. The food is provided by the prawns, fish, goat, sheep, and pig and honey Bess. Some of them are used as a mode of transport. They include the camel, horse, asses, horses and mules. Some of them are used as a mode of agriculture operations. They include the cattle and camel's .Some of them is used as a scavenger. They include the jackals and pigs. Some of them are used as pearls. They include the mollusks. The animals maintain the ecosystem. The fecal matter of certain animals is used as manure. The deer and elephant provide the musk and ivory. The wax and lac is provided by the honey bees and lac insect. The pollination and dispersal of seeds and fruits is mainly done by the insects. Some animals are used as a laboratory research model like the guinea pigs, rats and rabbits. The diseases of human beings are cured by the secretion of hormones of some mammals. The conservation of animals must be done. The pollution in the environment, deforestation, killing and the poaching of animals causes an adverse effect on the growth of animals. Some of the species of animals get endangered. So, there should be a check on the activities of human. In the coming 25 years around one fourth of the species of animals are going to disappear. The people must be educated regarding the wild life of animals. The micro organisms as the name suggests consists of small organisms which cannot be seen with the help of a naked eye. They are present almost everywhere on the earth. The Anton van Leeuwenhoek was the first one to discover them. It consists of the bacteria, protozoa, viruses and fungi. The fungi involve the yeast and moulds. Bacteria are present everywhere. The size of bacteria is not static. It is different for every species.

Their size ranges from 0.1 micrometer to 750 micrometer. Bacterial cells vary in shape and they have no definite structure. They can be coccus, bacilli, spirillum, stalked in shape. The fungi are organisms without chlorophyll, have heterotrophic mode of nutrition. They are spore forming, avascular and eukaryotic organism. Their cell wall is made up of chitin. They store their food in the form of glycogen. The fungi form a medicine known as penicillin which is used to treat the bacterial infections. The fungi also acts on the dead organisms and act as a saprophyte. They can create a problem also. The protozoa can act as a harmful as well as beneficial organism. The harmful organisms act to pollute water, decrease the soil fertility and cause certain diseases. They also act as a food for the aquatic animals. The oil deposits are found in association with the skeletal deposits of radiolarian and other organisms. They help to locate the fuel. Almost all the viruses are harmful.

Abiotic Resources

Abiotic resources are resources that are nonliving. These resources fall into the larger category of natural resources, which occur naturally in the environment and are not created or produced by humans or human activity. Human depletion of abiotic resources, such as water, soil, and minerals is a source of concern for humans, as these resources are not easily replenished and are being used above the rate that they can be naturally replaced.

Land

Land is one of the must lucrative abiotic resources for humans, as property costs in urban and suburban development has rapidly increased in price and demand throughout cities and communities across the world. Land degradation as a result of extensive use of fertilizers and chemicals as well as development have rendered large portions of land unusable. Along with environmental harm, land degradation is also a large source of lost revenue.

Water

Water is an abiotic resource that is of need to all living things. Yet, access to clean and safe water remains a challenge for members of developing nations. Even in developed nations, water depletion and pollution remains a concern. In the United States, farm animals require huge amounts of water daily, and farms tend to pollute nearby water sources from fertilizers and animal excrement.

Coal

Coal remains one of the major sources of heat and electrical energy in the world today, and will likely retain that role for decades to come. That being said, coal depletion is an issue that faces much of the world today, as a major source of energy could soon run out. According to David Rutledge, an electrical engineering professor at the California Institute of Technology, the U.S. has about enough coal reserves to last about 120 years.

Oil

Oil is also one of the most valuable natural resources to humans, as cars, planes, ships, trucks, and most other forms of transportation require oil. Oil depletion is therefore a major concern, as oil that took millions of years to form from decomposing plant matter is being extracted and burned in a matter of months. The top four oil consuming nations are the United States, China, Japan, and India.

FROM DEVELOPING STAGES

- Potential resources are known to exist and may be used in the future. For example, petroleum may exist in many parts of India and Kuwait that have sedimentary rocks, but until the time it is actually drilled out and put into use, it remains a potential resource.
- Actual resources are those that have been surveyed, their quantity and quality determined, and are being used in present times. For example, petroleum and natural gas is actively being obtained from the Mumbai High Fields. The development of an actual resource, such as wood processing depends upon the technology available and the cost involved. That part of the actual resource that can be developed profitably with available technology is known as a reserve resource, while that part that can not be developed profitably because of lack of technology is known as a stock resource.

FROM RENEWABILITY ASPECT

Nonrenewable Resources

A nonrenewable resource is a resource of economic value that cannot be readily replaced by natural means on a level equal to its consumption. Most fossil fuels, such as oil, natural gas and coal are considered nonrenewable resources in that their use is not sustainable because their formation takes billions of years.

Types of Nonrenewable Resources

Fuels created from nonrenewable resources are still the primary source of all the power generated in the world, due to their affordability and high energy content. Usually, nonrenewable resources are formed from organic carbon material which, over the course of billions of years, is heated and compressed enough to change form into crude oil and natural gas. Crude oil and natural gas are then used to manufacture everyday forms of fuel, including gasoline, diesel fuel, heating oil and propane.

The term nonrenewable resource also refers to minerals and metals from the earth, such as gold, silver, and iron, which are similarly formed as a long-term result of geological processes such as plate tectonics. These resources are often costly to mine, as they are usually deep within the Earth's crust, but they are much more abundant than fossil fuels. Some types of groundwater are considered to be a nonrenewable resource, if the aquifer is unable to be replenished at the same rate at which it's drained. Also, nuclear materials such as uranium are nonrenewable resources.

Global Impacts of using Nonrenewable Resources

It is widely understood that the burning of fossil fuels has harmful consequences to the environment and contributes to global warming and climate change. For this reason, many organizations have developed alternative energy sources that don't rely on these resources. There are also risks associated with nuclear material, since its radioactive nature makes it toxic, and it must be handled properly. Climate change has been brought to the forefront of international talks in recent years, and the countries involved have made pledges to significantly reduce carbon dioxide emissions and pollution (for example, implementing a Pigovian tax on companies that directly pollute the environment). The first international agreement on fighting climate change was the Kyoto Protocol, adopted in 1997.

Besides the environmental impact of burning fossil fuels, the economic impact of nonrenewable resources can also be damaging. Following the basic premise of supply and demand, as nonrenewable resources become scarcer, the cost to obtain them will continue to rise. Supply for many of these fuels is in danger of running out completely. Eventually, the price will hit a point that end users cannot afford, forcing a move toward alternative energy sources. However, many of these alternative sources require ample time to be put into place, which means their development should begin as early as possible in order to enable a smooth transition to sustainable energy.

The alternative to using nonrenewable resources is to use renewable resources, including such sources as solar and wind power or any source that is essentially unlimited in supply or reusable.

Renewable Resource

A renewable resource is a substance of economic value that can be replaced or replenished in the same or less amount of time than it takes to draw the supply down. Some renewable resources have, essentially, an endless supply such as solar energy, wind energy, and geothermal pressure, whereas other resources are considered renewable even though some time or effort must go into their renewal (e.g., wood, oxygen, leather, and fish). Most precious metals are renewable also. Although precious metals are not naturally replaced, they can be recycled because they are not destroyed during their extraction and use.

Renewable Resources Explained

A renewable resource is different from a nonrenewable resource; a nonrenewable resource is depleted and cannot be recovered once it is used. As the human population continues to grow, the demand for renewable resources increases.

According to the Renewable Resources Coalition, an online publication of recent news, research, and information on renewable energy and green living, overpopulation is one of the main contributors to environmental and natural resource issues.

Types of Renewable Resources

Natural resources are a form of equity, and they are known as natural capital. Biofuel, or energy made from renewable organic products, has gained prevalence in recent years as an alternative energy source to nonrenewable resources such as coal, oil, and natural gas. Although prices are still higher for biofuel, increasing scarcity and the forces of supply and demand will result in higher prices for fossil fuels, which will make the price of biofuel more competitive.

Types of biofuel include biodiesel, an alternative to oil, and green diesel, which is made from algae and other plants. Other renewable resources include oxygen and solar energy. Wind and water are also used to create renewable energy. For example, windmills harness the wind's natural power and turn it into energy.

Global Impact of Renewable Resources

Renewable resources have become a focal point of the environmental movement, both politically and economically. Energy obtained from renewable resources puts much less strain on the limited supply of fossil fuels, which are nonrenewable resources. The problem with using renewable resources on a large scale is that they are costly and, in most cases, more research is needed for their use to be cost-effective.

Adopting sustainable energy is often referred to as "going green" due to the positive impact on the environment. Energy sources such as fossil fuels damage the environment when burned and contribute to global warming. The first major international accord to curb carbon dioxide emissions and global warming was the Kyoto Protocol, signed in 1997. More recently, global powers met in Paris in 2015 to pledge emissions reductions and focus on higher reliance on renewable resources for energy.

To encourage the use of renewable resources, there are many incentives designed to encourage the use of alternative energy. For example, energy taxes place a surcharge on fossil fuels so that the prices of renewable resources are more competitive and people will be more inclined to use renewable energy. Green funds, investment vehicles such as mutual funds, support eco-friendly and sustainable companies by investing in them and helping to promote environmental awareness.

These incentives seem to be having an effect. According to the U.S. Energy Information Administration (EIA), In 2017, renewable energy provided approximately 11 quadrillion British thermal units (Btu). (One quadrillion is 1 followed by 15 zeros.) This amount of energy represented 11% of total U.S. energy consumption. Around 57% of U.S. renewable energy in 2017 was consumed by the electric power sector, and approximately 17% of U.S. electricity generation was from renewable energy sources.

State and federal governments have encouraged more biofuel consumption by imposing requirements and incentives for the use of renewable energy. The EIA anticipates that U.S. renewable energy consumption will continue to increase through 2050.

- Demand for renewable resources increases as the human population continues to grow.
- Energy from renewable resources puts less strain on the limited supply of fossil fuels, which are considered nonrenewable resources.
- Using renewable resources on a large scale is costly, and more research is needed for their use to be cost-effective.

References

- Natural-resources: thenewecologist.com, Retrieved 3 June, 2019
- Wanagopa - nyawakanmiller, G.T. & S. Spoolman (2011). Living in the Environment: Principles, Connections, and Solutions (17th ed.). Belmont, CA: Brooks-Cole. ISBN 0-538-73534-1
- What-are-biotic-resources, biology: thebigger.com, Retrieved 4 July, 2019
- Cullati, Stéphane; Kliegel, Matthias; Widmer, Eric (2018). "Development of reserves over the life course and onset of vulnerability in later life". Nature Human Behaviour. 2 (8): 551–558. Doi:10.1038/s41562-018-0395-3. ISSN 2397-3374
- Definition-of-abiotic-resources: hunker.com, Retrieved 5 August, 2019
- Hut, PM (2008-09-07). "Getting and Estimating Resource Requirements - People". Pmhut.com. Retrieved 2012-01-02
- Nonrenewableresource, terms: investopedia.com, Retrieved 6 January, 2019
- Renewable-resource, terms: investopedia.com, Retrieved 7 February, 2019

Exploitation of Natural Resources

CHAPTER 3

The exploitation of natural resources can lead to various consequences that can arise from the careless and excessive consumption of these resources. Some of the consequences are deforestation, soil erosion, desertification, natural disasters and increase in greenhouse gas emissions. The topics elaborated in this chapter will help in gaining a better perspective about these impacts of exploitation of natural resources.

Exploitation of natural environment or resources is an essential state of human existence, throughout the history of mankind; human have been manipulating natural resources to produce various materials they needed to sustain growing human populations. This likely to refer primarily for economic development and food production but many other entities from the natural environment have been extracted. Natural resources are an important material basis for a stable natural economy and social development. These materials can be divided into two distinctive groups such as the non-renewable: which includes raw minerals and the renewable: such as grasslands and forests. With the increasing rate of industrialization and urbanization mankind's great demands for natural resources and their large scale exploitation as well as their consumption has resulted in deteriorating, weakening and exhaustion of these precious resources.

In the struggle for survival and development, mankind creates a lot of negative impacts on the environment, these impacts ranges from over-exploitation of resources, destruction of ecosystem as well as pollution. Typically the exploitation of nature has been executed in a non-sustainable way, which is causing an increasing concern, as the non-sustainable exploitation of natural resources ultimately threatens the existence of human being itself. One major difficult task faced by both developed and developing countries it to guarantee the lasting utilization of natural resources at the lowest possible environmental cost, while still assuring the economic and social development.

In religious point of view, exploiting natural resource is permissible for mankind to achieve a better living standards as well as their survival at a minimal level. In Genesis, Adam is told by God that he has "domination over the animals of the earth, the birds of the air, and the fish of the sea" and that nature is essentially is there for his purposes. Adam was also told "go forth and multiply" and has dominion over everything. This again makes nature and everything in it compliant to human beings and their wishes, implying that nature exists strictly for their use and has little or no value in itself. However, in the current competitive and leap forward era, humans are exploiting these resources at an alarming rate which will indeed causing these precious resources to deplete in a long run basis.

In addition, in science point of view, the rise to an exploitative attitude toward nature made science and other scientific progress possible. It is no accident that science has progressed by leaps and bounds in the Western world. If nature, and all it contains, is compliant to mankind, or if mankind can make it so by harnessing its powers and using if for their own best interest, then why not do so? As science and technology advanced, nature become more and more compliant to human needs and desires, and the environment and animals were used and exploited without regard to any intrinsic value they might have. After all, mankind are the only beings with intrinsic value, nature has only instrumental value. Nature only has valuable values only as it helps mankind to attain whatever goals they believe are important to them.

Ethical egoism describes an individual's act such as "exploiting natural resource" based on their self interest for the sake of gaining more profits. Moreover, in utilitarianism stand point of view, it illustrate an individual's act for the interest of all which in terms act on behave for the majority which brings benefits, such as exploiting natural resource for the sake of survival and further developments of infrastructure that will bring mankind a step further into the future as well as providing more amenities which enables mankind to have a much more easier lifestyle. Furthermore, in deontology terms of exploiting natural resources are where individual's judgment regarding their act is either right or wrong for themselves. In addition, in Act nonconsequentialism view, only individual acts and situation count morally, which practically illustrate that an individual or corporation may conduct exploitation of natural resource legally as long as the government and other legal policies permits it to do so. Therefore it is permissible for them to continue exploiting natural resources even though it violates ethical rights for the sake to satisfying consumer demands as well as building a better and more advanced civilization for mankind.

RESOURCES UNDER PRESSURE

- Increase in the sophistication of technology enabling natural resources to be extracted quickly and efficiently. E.g., in the past, it could take long hours just to cut down one tree only using saws. Due to increased technology, rates of deforestation have greatly increased.
- The number of humans is increasing. According to the UN, there were 7.6 billion of us in 2017. This number is expected to rise to about 10 billion in 2050 and about 11 billion in 2100.
- Cultures of consumerism. Materialistic views lead to the mining of gold and diamonds to produce jewelry, unnecessary commodities for human life or advancement. Consumerism also leads to extraction of resources for the production of commodities necessary for human life but in amounts excessive of what is needed, because people consume more than is necessary or waste what they have.
- Excessive demand often leads to conflicts due to intense competition. Organizations such as Global Witness and the United Nations have documented the connection.
- Non-equitable distribution of resources.

Consequences of Exploitation of Resources

Natural resources are not limitless, and the following consequences can arise from the careless and excessive consumption of these resources:

- Deforestation

- Desertification
- Extinction of species
- Forced migration
- Soil erosion
- Oil depletion
- Ozone depletion
- Greenhouse gas increase
- Extreme energy
- Water pollution
- Natural hazard/Natural disaster
- Metals and minerals depletion

Effects on Local Communities

Human Resources Macon, Georgia, 1909.

When a mining company enters a developing country in the global south to extract raw materials, advocating the advantages of the industry's presence and minimizing the potential negative effects gain cooperation of the local people. Advantageous factors are primarily in economic development so services that the government could not provide such as health centers, police departments and schools can be established. However, with economic development, money becomes a dominant subject of interest. This can bring about major conflicts that a local community in a developing country has never dealt with before. These conflicts emerge by a change to more egocentric views among the locals influenced by consumerist values.

The effects of the exploitation of natural resources in the local community of a developing country are exhibited in the impacts from the Ok Tedi Mine. After BHP, now BHP Billiton, entered into

Papua New Guinea to exploit copper and gold, the economy of the indigenous peoples boomed. Although their quality of life has improved, initially disputes were common among the locals in terms of land rights and who should be getting the benefits from the mining project. The consequences of the Ok Tedi environmental disaster illustrate the potential negative effects from the exploitation of natural resources. The resulting mining pollution includes toxic contamination of the natural water supply for communities along the Ok Tedi River, causing widespread killing of aquatic life. When a mining company ends a project after extracting the raw materials from an area of a developing country, the local people are left to manage with the environmental damage done to their community and the long run sustainability of the economic benefits stimulated by the mining company's presence becomes a concern.

EXTRACTIVISM

Extractivism is the process of extracting natural resources from the Earth to sell on the world market. It exists in an economy that depends primarily on the extraction or removal of natural resources that are considered valuable for exportation worldwide. Some examples of resources that are obtained through extraction include gold, diamonds, lumber and oil. This economic model has become popular in many Latin American countries but is becoming increasingly prominent in other regions as well.

Many factors are involved in the process of extractivism. These include but are not limited to community members, transnational corporations (TNCs) and the government. Trends have demonstrated that countries do not often extract their own resources; extraction is often led from abroad. These interactions have contributed to extractivism being rooted in the hegemonic order of global capitalism. Extractivism is controversial because it exists at the intersection where economic growth and environmental protection meet. This intersection is known as the green economy. Extractivism has evolved in the wake of neo-liberal economic transitions to become a potential avenue for development to occur. This development occurs through, stabilizing growth rates, increasing direct foreign investment and reducing poverty.

However, while these economic benefits are substantial, extractivism as a development model is often critiqued for failing to deliver the improved living conditions it promises and failing to work collaboratively with already existing programs, therefore inflicting environmental, social and political consequences. These environmental concerns include; climate change, soil depletion, deforestation, loss of food sovereignty, declining biodiversity and contamination of freshwater. Social and political implications include violation of human rights, unsafe labour conditions, unequal wealth distribution and conflict. As a result of this, extractivism remains a prominent debate in policy related discourse because while it delivers high economic gains, it also raises social and environmental concerns. Case studies in Latin America demonstrate these policy gaps.

Extractivism refers to the process of removing large quantities of raw or natural materials, particularly for export. Most extracted resources are exported abroad because there is a lack of demand for these raw materials in their country of origin.

Actors

Transnational corporations (TNCs) are a primary actor in neo-extractivism. Originally, as TNCs began to explore raw material extraction in developing countries they were applauded for taking a risk to extract high-demand resources. TNCs were able to navigate their way into a position where they maintained large amounts of control over various extraction-based industries. This success is credited to the oftentimes weak governance structure of the resource dependent economies where extraction is taking place. Through complex arrangements and agreements, resources have slowly become denationalized. As a result of this, the government has taken a "hands-off" approach, awarding most of the control over resource enclaves and the social responsibility that accompanies them to TNCs. However, the government still plays an important role in leading development by determining which TNCs they allow to extract their resources and how thorough they are when it comes to enforcing certain standards of social responsibility.

Example of mass extraction of trees for lumber, resulting in deforestation.

Resources and Techniques

Some resources that are obtained through extraction include but are not limited to gold, diamonds, oil, lumber and food. This occurs through techniques such as mining, drilling and deforestation. Resources are typically extracted from developing countries as a raw material. This means that it has not been processed or has been processed only slightly. These materials then travel elsewhere to be turned into goods that are for sale on the world market. An example of this would be gold that is mined as a raw mineral and later in the supply chain manufactured into jewellery.

Impacts of Extractivism

Economic Benefits

Neo-extractivism is seen as an opportunity for successful development in many areas of the developing world. Demand for extracted resources on the global market has allowed this industry to expand. Since the year 2000, there has been a substantial rise in global demand and value for raw materials – this has contributed to steadily high prices. Neo-extractivism has therefore been seen as a tool for economically advancing developing countries that are rich in natural resources by participating in this market.

It is argued that the emergence of this industry in the neo-liberal context has allowed extractivism to contribute to stabilizing growth rates, increasing direct foreign investment, diversifying local economies, expanding the middle class and reducing poverty. This is done by using surplus revenue to invest in development projects such as expanding social programs and infrastructure. Overall, extraction based economies are seen as long-term development projects that guarantee a robust economic foundation. It has created a new hegemonic order that closely intertwines with the dominant capitalist system of the world. The green economy has emerged as an economic model in response to the arising tensions between the economy and the environment. Extractivism is one of the many issues that exist at this intersection between the economy and the environment.

Environmental Consequences

One of the main consequences of extractivism is the toll that it takes on the natural environment. Due to the scale extraction takes place on; several renewable resources are becoming non-renewable. This means that the environment is incapable of renewing its resources as quickly as the rate they are extracted at. It is often falsely assumed that technological advancements will enable resources to renew more effectively and as a result make raw material extraction more sustainable. The environment often must compensate for overproduction driven by the need to maximize profits. Global climate change, soil depletion, loss of biodiversity and contamination of fresh water are some of the environmental issues that extractivism contributes to. As well, extraction produces large amounts of waste such as toxic chemicals and heavy metals that are difficult to dispose of properly. To what degree humans have a right to take from the environment for developmental purposes is a topic that continues to be debated.

Social Impacts

In addition to the environmental consequences of extractivism, social impacts arise as well. Local communities are often opposed to extractivism occurring. This is because it often uproots the communities or cause environmental impacts that will affect their quality of life. Indigenous communities tend to be particularly susceptible to the social impacts of extractivism. Indigenous peoples rely on their environment to sustain their lifestyles as well as connect with the land in spiritual ways. This changes game populations, migration patterns for animals, pollutes rivers and much more. Doing so, does not allow Indigenous populations to practice their culture and ways of life because the environment they depend on to hunt, fish etc. is drastically changed. In addition, this destruction hinders the practice of Indigenous culture and creation of knowledge making it more difficult for Indigenous individuals to pass down their traditions to future generations.

While employment opportunities are brought to local communities as a pillar of neo-extractivism projects, the conditions are often unsafe for workers. TNCs can take advantage of more lenient health and safety conditions in developing countries and pay inadequate wages in order to maximize their profits. As well, foreigners usually fill the highest paying managerial positions, leaving local community members to do the most labour intensive jobs. Frequently, the enclaves where extractivism occurs are distanced from government involvement, therefore allowing them to avoid being subjected to the enforcement of national laws to protect citizens. This can result in widespread human rights violations. It is argued that prolonged social transformation cannot thrive on export dependent extractivism alone therefore making neo-extractivism a potentially flawed development method on its own.

Political Implications

The Idle No More campaign began in Canada to build indigenous sovereignty and nationhood and to protect water, air, land and all creation for future generations.

Due to the fact that the state is a prominent actor in the extractivism process it has several political implications. It pushes the state into a position where they are one of the central actors involved in development when recent decades have seen a shift to civil society organizations. As well, the relationship between the State providing the natural resources and the TNCs extracting them can be politically complex sometimes leading to corruption. Likewise, as a result of government involvement, this process as a development project becomes politicized. The increasing demand for raw materials also increases the likelihood of conflict breaking out over natural resources.

Extractivism near or on Indigenous land without the permission of Indigenous peoples begins to threaten the land based self-determination of Indigenous groups. Conflicts between Indigenous peoples, corporations and governments are occurring around the world. Because many of the extractivist practices take place where Indigenous communities are located, the conflicts are making these landscapes politicized and contested. The conflicts are driven because Indigenous lives are put in jeopardy when they are dispossessed, when they lose their livelihoods, when their water and land is polluted and the environment is commodified.

CONSEQUENCES OF EXPLOITATION OF RESOURCES

The way we use resources provokes often irreversible ecological change. Extraction and processing of non-regenerative raw materials are often energy intensive activities involving large scale interventions in ecosystems and the water balance and result in air, soil and water pollution. Even the extraction and production of renewable resources often involve extensive use of energy, materials, chemicals and in some cases water; and all this translates into pollution. Greenfield land is often transformed to create arable land and in some cases whole ecosystems are destroyed in the process.

In short, raw material extraction and processing always impact on the environment, resulting as they do in soil degradation, water shortages, biodiversity loss, damage to ecosystem functions and global warming exacerbation. And that's not all. For the use of products made of raw materials almost always results in greenhouse gas emissions, pollution, ecosystem damage and/or biodiversity loss. Products need energy and water, as well as land for shipping, marketing and use. Improper product use provokes noxious emissions that can end up in our water, soil and air. The very infrastructure elements that we take for granted such as our homes, not to mention countless daily activities, often involve extensive resource use and result in greenfield land being paved over, damage to ecosystems and spoiling the beauty of nature.

And even at the end stage of the supply chain, environmental harm is unavoidable. For example, recycling requires energy, using waste for energy generates greenhouse gases and other pollutants, and greenfield land is permanently occupied by waste dumps. Thus resource use already somewhat exceeds the earth's regenerative capacities by virtue of the fact that non-renewable natural resources are finite and their quality is often mediocre. The increasing pressure on natural resources resulting from steady worldwide population growth may incite competition from other potential uses.

Resource use has Social Consequences too

The myriad social consequences of resource use are related to issues such as the distribution of raw materials, ready access to clean water, and worldwide food security. Per capita use of raw materials in the world's industrial nations is estimated to be four times greater than in less developed countries. However, while the lion's share of value-added from resource use is generated in industrial nations, less developed nations often bear the brunt of the ecological and social impact of raw material production.

Raw Material Production

People in the regions in question report abuses such as severe human rights violations or permanent ecological damage in the wake of raw material extraction, which often provokes health problems resulting from air pollution and drinking water contamination. Other consequences include local populations being driven off their land and forced to settle elsewhere – not to mention growing poverty. In areas that suffer these consequences, efforts on the part of companies that engage in mining and similar operations to institute sustainable development are few and far between. Moreover, in some states profits from raw material production are used to finance armed conflicts. According to UN statistics, natural resources play a key role in 40 percent of all intra-state conflicts.

From a product lifecycle standpoint, we here in Germany are at least partly responsible for such ecological and social outcomes, by virtue of our increasing dependence on imported raw materials and the products made from them. In some cases this also holds true for sustainable raw materials such as the animal feed and energy crops that we use in such abundance and for which large tracts of fertile land are used. Fertilizer and pesticide use to some extent goes unmonitored, and no protective measures are taken. This can have a negative impact on the health of local populations. Displacement and forced resettlement of local populations, as well as land grabbing, can cripple the food supply of local populations, while non-sustainable production methods often provoke soil degradation and water scarcity, and destroy badly needed fertile land.

End-of-life Product Disposal

End-of-life product disposal can also have social consequences. Improper and illicit disposal of exported waste can provoke toxic emissions and severe illnesses – not to mention the fact that such work is often carried out by children.

DEFORESTATION

Deforestation is the permanent destruction of forests in order to make the land available for other uses. An estimated 18 million acres (7.3 million hectares) of forest, which is roughly the size of the country of Panama, are lost each year, according to the United Nations' Food and Agriculture Organization (FAO).

- About half of the world's tropical forests have been cleared, according to the FAO.
- Forests currently cover about 30 percent of the world's landmass, according to National Geographic.
- The Earth loses 18.7 million acres of forests per year, which is equal to 27 soccer fields every minute, according to the World Wildlife Fund (WWF).
- It is estimated that 15 percent of all greenhouse gas emissions come from deforestation, according to the WWF.
- In 2016, global tree cover loss reached a record of 73.4 million acres (29.7 million hectares), according to the University of Maryland.

Location

Deforestation occurs around the world, though tropical rainforests are particularly targeted. If current deforestation levels proceed, the world's rainforests may completely vanish in as little as 100 years, according to National Geographic. Countries with significant deforestation in 2016 included Brazil, Indonesia, Thailand, the Democratic Republic of Congo and other parts of Africa, and parts of Eastern Europe, according to GRID-Arendal, a United Nations Environment Program collaborating center. The country with the most deforestation is Indonesia. Since the last century, Indonesia has lost at least 39 million acres (15.79 million hectares) of forest land, according to a study by the University of Maryland and the World Resource Institute.

Though deforestation has increased rapidly in the past 50 years, it has been practiced throughout history. For example, 90 percent of continental United States' indigenous forest has been removed since 1600, according to the University of Michigan. The World Resources Institute estimates that most of the world's remaining indigenous forest is located in Canada, Alaska, Russia and the Northwestern Amazon basin.

Causes

There are many causes of deforestation. The WWF& reports that half of the trees illegally removed from forests are used as fuel.

Some other common reasons are:

- To make more land available for housing and urbanization.
- To harvest timber to create commercial items such as paper, furniture and homes .

To create ingredients that are highly prized consumer items, such as the oil from palm trees:

- To create room for cattle ranching.

Common methods of deforestation are burning trees and clear cutting. These tactics leave the land completely barren and are controversial practices.

Clear cutting is when large swaths of land are cut down all at once. A forestry expert quoted by the Natural Resources Defense Council describes clear cutting as "an ecological trauma that has no precedent in nature except for a major volcanic eruption."

Burning can be done quickly, in vast swaths of land, or more slowly with the slash-and-burn technique. Slash and burn agriculture entails cutting down a patch of trees, burning them and growing crops on the land. The ash from the burned trees provides some nourishment for the plants and the land is weed-free from the burning. When the soil becomes less nourishing and weeds begin to reappear over years of use, the farmers move on to a new patch of land and begin the process again.

Deforestation and Climate Change

Deforestation is considered to be one of the contributing factors to global climate change. According to Michael Daley, an associate professor of environmental science at Lasell College in Newton, Massachusetts, the No. 1 problem caused by deforestation is the impact on the global carbon cycle. Gas molecules that absorb thermal infrared radiation are called greenhouse gases. If greenhouse gases are in large enough quantity, they can force climate change, according to Daley. While oxygen (O_2) is the second most abundant gas in our atmosphere, it does not absorb thermal infrared radiation, as greenhouse gases do. Carbon dioxide (CO_2) is the most prevalent greenhouse gas. CO_2 accounts for about 82.2 percent of all U.S. greenhouse gas, according to the Environmental Protection Agency (EPA). Trees can help, though. About 300 billion tons of carbon, 40 times the annual greenhouse gas emissions from fossil fuels, is stored in trees, according to Greenpeace.

The deforestation of trees not only lessens the amount of carbon stored, it also releases carbon dioxide into the air. This is because when trees die, they release the stored carbon. According to the 2010 Global Forest Resources Assessment, deforestation releases nearly a billion tons of carbon into the atmosphere per year, though the numbers are not as high as the ones recorded in the previous decade. Deforestation is the second largest anthropogenic (human-caused) source of carbon dioxide to the atmosphere (after fossil fuel combustion), ranging between 6 percent and 17 percent, according to a study published in 2009 in Nature.

Other effects of Deforestation

Forests are complex ecosystems that affect almost every species on the planet. When they are degraded, it can set off a devastating chain of events both locally and around the world.

1. Loss of species: Seventy percent of the world's plants and animals live in forests and are losing their habitats to deforestation, according to National Geographic. Loss of habitat can lead to species extinction. It also has negative consequences for medicinal research and local populations that rely on the animals and plants in the forests for hunting and medicine.

2. Water cycle: Trees are important to the water cycle. They absorb rain fall and produce water vapor that is released into the atmosphere. Trees also lessen the pollution in water, according to the North Carolina State University, by stopping polluted runoff. In the Amazon, more than half the water in the ecosystem is held within the plants, according to the National Geographic Society.

3. Soil erosion: Tree roots anchor the soil. Without trees, the soil is free to wash or blow away, which can lead to vegetation growth problems. The WWF states that scientists estimate that a third of the world's arable land has been lost to deforestation since 1960. After a clear cutting, cash crops like coffee, soy and palm oil are planted. Planting these types of trees can cause further soil erosion because their roots cannot hold onto the soil. "The situation in Haiti compared to the Dominican Republic is a great example of the important role forests play in the water cycle," Daley said. Both countries share the same island, but Haiti has much less forest cover than the Dominican Republic. As a result, Haiti has endured more extreme soil erosion, flooding and landslide issues.

4. Life quality: Soil erosion can also lead to silt entering the lakes, streams and other water sources. This can decrease local water quality and contribute to poor health in populations in the area.

5. The disturbance of native people: Many native tribes live in the rainforests of the world, and their destruction is the destruction of these peoples' homes and way of life. For example, the film "Under the Canopy" takes a look at the Amazon rainforest and the people who live there, including an indigenous guide named Kamanja Panashekung. "Kamanja's community is one of over 350 indigenous communities throughout Amazonia that depend on the rainforest, as we all do, for the air we breathe and the water we drink," M. Sanjayan, Conservation International's executive vice president and senior scientist, said in a statement.

Counteracting Deforestation

Many believe that to counter deforestation, people simply need to plant more trees. Though a massive replanting effort would help to alleviate the problems deforestation caused, it would not solve them all.

Reforestation would facilitate:

- Restoring the ecosystem services provided by forests including carbon storage, water cycling and wildlife habitat.
- Reducing the buildup of carbon dioxide in the atmosphere.
- Rebuilding wildlife habitats.

Reforestation won't completely fix the damage, though. For example, Daley points out that forests cannot sequester all of the carbon dioxide humans are emitting to the atmosphere through the burning of fossil fuels and a reduction in fossil fuel emissions. It is still necessary to avoid buildup in the atmosphere. Reforestation will not help with extinction due to deforestation, either. "Unfortunately, we have already diminished the population of many species to such an extreme that they might not recover, even with a massive reforestation effort," Daley told Live Science.

In addition to reforestation, some other tactics are being taken to counteract or slow deforestation. Some of them include shifting the human population to a plant-based diet. This would lower the need for land to be cleared for raising livestock.

Global Forest Watch has also initiated a project to counteract deforestation through awareness. The organization uses satellite technology, open data and crowdsourcing to detect and alert others of deforestation. Their online community is also encouraged to share their personal experiences and the negative effects of deforestation.

SOIL EROSION

Soil erosion is the displacement of the upper layer of soil, it is one form of soil degradation. This natural process is caused by the dynamic activity of erosive agents, that is, water, ice (glaciers), snow, air (wind), plants, animals, and humans. In accordance with these agents, erosion is sometimes divided into water erosion, glacial erosion, snow erosion, wind (aeolean) erosion, zoogenic erosion, and anthropogenic erosion. Soil erosion may be a slow process that continues relatively unnoticed, or it may occur at an alarming rate causing a serious loss of topsoil. The loss of soil from farmland may be reflected in reduced crop production potential, lower surface water quality and damaged drainage networks.

Human activities have increased by 10–50 times the rate at which erosion is occurring globally. Excessive (or accelerated) erosion causes both "on-site" and "off-site" problems. On-site impacts include decreases in agricultural productivity and (on natural landscapes) ecological collapse, both because of loss of the nutrient-rich upper soil layers. In some cases, the eventual end result is desertification. Off-site effects include sedimentation of waterways and eutrophication of water bodies, as well as sediment-related damage to roads and houses. Water and wind erosion are the two primary causes of land degradation; combined, they are responsible for about 84% of the global extent of degraded land, making excessive erosion one of the most significant environmental problems worldwide.

Intensive agriculture, deforestation, roads, anthropogenic climate change and urban sprawl are amongst the most significant human activities in regard to their effect on stimulating erosion. However, there are many prevention and remediation practices that can curtail or limit erosion of vulnerable soils.

Physical Processes

Rainfall and Surface Runoff

Soil and water being splashed by the impact of a single raindrop.

Rainfall, and the surface runoff which may result from rainfall, produces four main types of soil erosion: splash erosion, sheet erosion, rill erosion, and gully erosion. Splash erosion is generally seen as the first and least severe stage in the soil erosion process, which is followed by sheet erosion, then rill erosion and finally gully erosion (the most severe of the four).

In splash erosion, the impact of a falling raindrop creates a small crater in the soil, ejecting soil particles. The distance these soil particles travel can be as much as 0.6 m (two feet) vertically and 1.5 m (five feet) horizontally on level ground.

If the soil is saturated, or if the rainfall rate is greater than the rate at which water can infiltrate into the soil, surface runoff occurs. If the runoff has sufficient flow energy, it will transport loosened soil particles (sediment) down the slope. *Sheet erosion* is the transport of loosened soil particles by overland flow.

A spoil tip covered in rills and gullies due to erosion processes caused by rainfall: Rummu, Estonia.

Rill erosion refers to the development of small, ephemeral concentrated flow paths which function as both sediment source and sediment delivery systems for erosion on hillslopes. Generally, where water erosion rates on disturbed upland areas are greatest, rills are active. Flow depths in rills are typically of the order of a few centimeters (about an inch) or less and along-channel slopes may be quite steep. This means that rills exhibit hydraulic physics very different from water flowing through the deeper, wider channels of streams and rivers.

Gully erosion occurs when runoff water accumulates and rapidly flows in narrow channels during or immediately after heavy rains or melting snow, removing soil to a considerable depth.

Rivers and Streams

Dobbingstone Burn, Scotland—This photo illustrates two different types of erosion affecting the same place. Valley erosion is occurring due to the flow of the stream, and the boulders and stones (and much of the soil) that are lying on the edges are glacial till that was left behind as ice age glaciers flowed over the terrain.

Valley or stream erosion occurs with continued water flow along a linear feature. The erosion is both downward, deepening the valley, and headward, extending the valley into the hillside, creating head cuts and steep banks. In the earliest stage of stream erosion, the erosive activity is dominantly vertical, the valleys have a typical V cross-section and the stream gradient is relatively steep. When some base level is reached, the erosive activity switches to lateral erosion, which widens the valley floor and creates a narrow floodplain. The stream gradient becomes nearly flat, and lateral deposition of sediments becomes important as the stream meanders across the valley floor. In all stages of stream erosion, by far the most erosion occurs during times of flood, when more and faster-moving water is available to carry a larger sediment load. In such processes, it is not the water alone that erodes: suspended abrasive particles, pebbles and boulders can also act erosively as they traverse a surface, in a process known as *traction*.

Bank erosion is the wearing away of the banks of a stream or river. This is distinguished from changes on the bed of the watercourse, which is referred to as *scour*. Erosion and changes in the form of river banks may be measured by inserting metal rods into the bank and marking the position of the bank surface along the rods at different times.

Thermal erosion is the result of melting and weakening permafrost due to moving water. It can occur both along rivers and at the coast. Rapid river channel migration observed in the Lena River of Siberia is due to thermal erosion, as these portions of the banks are composed of permafrost-cemented non-cohesive materials. Much of this erosion occurs as the weakened banks fail in large slumps. Thermal erosion also affects the Arctic coast, where wave action and near-shore temperatures combine to undercut permafrost bluffs along the shoreline and cause them to fail. Annual erosion rates along a 100-kilometre (62-mile) segment of the Beaufort Sea shoreline averaged 5.6 metres (18 feet) per year from 1955 to 2002.

Floods

At extremely high flows, kolks, or vortices are formed by large volumes of rapidly rushing water. Kolks cause extreme local erosion, plucking bedrock and creating pothole-type geographical features called Rock-cut basins. Examples can be seen in the flood regions result from glacial Lake Missoula, which created the channeled scablands in the Columbia Basin region of eastern Washington.

Wind Erosion

Árbol de Piedra, a rock formation in the Altiplano, Bolivia sculpted by wind erosion.

Wind erosion is a major geomorphological force, especially in arid and semi-arid regions. It is also a major source of land degradation, evaporation, desertification, harmful airborne dust, and crop damage—especially after being increased far above natural rates by human activities such as deforestation, urbanization, and agriculture.

Wind erosion is of two primary varieties: *deflation*, where the wind picks up and carries away loose particles; and *abrasion*, where surfaces are worn down as they are struck by airborne particles carried by wind. Deflation is divided into three categories: (1) *surface creep*, where larger, heavier particles slide or roll along the ground; (2) *saltation*, where particles are lifted a short height into the air, and bounce and saltate across the surface of the soil; and (3) *suspension*, where very small and light particles are lifted into the air by the wind, and are often carried for long distances. Saltation is responsible for the majority (50–70%) of wind erosion, followed by suspension (30–40%), and then surface creep (5–25%). Silty soils tend to be the most affected by wind erosion; silt particles are relatively easily detached and carried away.

Wind erosion is much more severe in arid areas and during times of drought. For example, in the Great Plains, it is estimated that soil loss due to wind erosion can be as much as 6100 times greater in drought years than in wet years.

Mass Movement

Wadi in Makhtesh Ramon, Israel, showing gravity collapse erosion on its banks.

Mass movement is the downward and outward movement of rock and sediments on a sloped surface, mainly due to the force of gravity.

Mass movement is an important part of the erosional process, and is often the first stage in the breakdown and transport of weathered materials in mountainous areas. It moves material from higher elevations to lower elevations where other eroding agents such as streams and glaciers can then pick up the material and move it to even lower elevations. Mass-movement processes are always occurring continuously on all slopes; some mass-movement processes act very slowly; others occur very suddenly, often with disastrous results. Any perceptible down-slope movement of rock or sediment is often referred to in general terms as a landslide.

Slumping happens on steep hillsides, occurring along distinct fracture zones, often within materials like clay that, once released, may move quite rapidly downhill. They will often show a spoon-shaped isostatic depression, in which the material has begun to slide downhill. In some cases, the slump is caused by water beneath the slope weakening it. In many cases it is simply the result of poor engineering along highways where it is a regular occurrence.

Surface creep is the slow movement of soil and rock debris by gravity which is usually not perceptible except through extended observation. However, the term can also describe the rolling of dislodged soil particles 0.5 to 1.0 mm (0.02 to 0.04 in) in diameter by wind along the soil surface.

Factors affecting Soil Erosion

Climate

The amount and intensity of precipitation is the main climatic factor governing soil erosion by water. The relationship is particularly strong if heavy rainfall occurs at times when, or in locations where, the soil's surface is not well protected by vegetation. This might be during periods when agricultural activities leave the soil bare, or in semi-arid regions where vegetation is naturally sparse. Wind erosion requires strong winds, particularly during times of drought when vegetation is sparse and soil is dry (and so is more erodible). Other climatic factors such as average temperature and temperature range may also affect erosion, via their effects on vegetation and soil properties. In general, given similar vegetation and ecosystems, areas with more precipitation (especially high-intensity rainfall), more wind, or more storms are expected to have more erosion.

In some areas of the world (e.g. the mid-western USA), rainfall intensity is the primary determinant of erosivity, with higher intensity rainfall generally resulting in more soil erosion by water. The size and velocity of rain drops is also an important factor. Larger and higher-velocity rain drops have greater kinetic energy, and thus their impact will displace soil particles by larger distances than smaller, slower-moving rain drops.

In other regions of the world (e.g. western Europe), runoff and erosion result from relatively low intensities of stratiform rainfall falling onto previously saturated soil. In such situations, rainfall amount rather than intensity is the main factor determining the severity of soil erosion by water.

Soil Structure and Composition

Erosional gully in unconsolidated Dead Sea (Israel) sediments along the southwestern shore. This gully was excavated by floods from the Judean Mountains in less than a year.

The composition, moisture, and compaction of soil are all major factors in determining the erosivity of rainfall. Sediments containing more clay tend to be more resistant to erosion than those with sand or silt, because the clay helps bind soil particles together. Soil containing high levels of organic materials are often more resistant to erosion, because the organic materials coagulate soil colloids and create a stronger, more stable soil structure. The amount of water present in the soil before the precipitation also plays an important role, because it sets limits on the amount of water that can be absorbed by the soil (and hence prevented from flowing on the surface as erosive runoff). Wet, saturated soils will not be able to absorb as much rain water, leading to higher levels of surface runoff and thus higher erosivity for a given volume of rainfall. Soil compaction also affects the permeability of the soil to water, and hence the amount of water that flows away as runoff. More compacted soils will have a larger amount of surface runoff than less compacted soils.

Vegetative Cover

Vegetation acts as an interface between the atmosphere and the soil. It increases the permeability of the soil to rainwater, thus decreasing runoff. It shelters the soil from winds, which results in decreased wind erosion, as well as advantageous changes in microclimate. The roots of the plants bind the soil together, and interweave with other roots, forming a more solid mass that is less susceptible to both water and wind erosion. The removal of vegetation increases the rate of surface erosion.

Topography

The topography of the land determines the velocity at which surface runoff will flow, which in turn determines the erosivity of the runoff. Longer, steeper slopes (especially those without adequate vegetative cover) are more susceptible to very high rates of erosion during heavy rains than shorter, less steep slopes. Steeper terrain is also more prone to mudslides, landslides, and other forms of gravitational erosion processes.

Human Activities that Increase Soil Erosion

Agricultural Practices

Tilled farmland such as this is very susceptible to erosion from rainfall, due to the destruction of vegetative cover and the loosening of the soil during plowing.

Unsustainable agricultural practices are the single greatest contributor to the global increase in erosion rates. The tillage of agricultural lands, which breaks up soil into finer particles, is one of the primary factors. The problem has been exacerbated in modern times, due to mechanized agricultural equipment that allows for deep plowing, which severely increases the amount of soil that is available for transport by water erosion. Others include mono-cropping, farming on steep slopes, pesticide and chemical fertilizer usage (which kill organisms that bind soil together), row-cropping, and the use of surface irrigation. A complex overall situation with respect to defining nutrient losses from soils, could arise as a result of the size selective nature of soil erosion events. Loss of total phosphorus, for instance, in the finer eroded fraction is greater relative to the whole soil. Extrapolating this evidence to predict subsequent behaviour within receiving aquatic systems, the reason is that this more easily transported material may support a lower solution P concentration compared to coarser sized fractions. Tillage also increases wind erosion rates, by dehydrating the soil and breaking it up into smaller particles that can be picked up by the wind. Exacerbating this is the fact that most of the trees are generally removed from agricultural fields, allowing winds to have long, open runs to travel over at higher speeds. Heavy grazing reduces vegetative cover and causes severe soil compaction, both of which increase erosion rates.

Deforestation

In this clearcut, almost all of the vegetation has been stripped from surface of steep slopes, in an area with very heavy rains. Severe erosion occurs in cases such as this, causing stream sedimentation and the loss of nutrient rich topsoil.

In an undisturbed forest, the mineral soil is protected by a layer of *leaf litter* and an *humus* that cover the forest floor. These two layers form a protective mat over the soil that absorbs the impact of rain drops. They are porous and highly permeable to rainfall, and allow rainwater to slow percolate into the soil below, instead of flowing over the surface as runoff. The roots of the trees and plants hold together soil particles, preventing them from being washed away. The vegetative cover acts to reduce the velocity of the raindrops that strike the foliage and stems before hitting the ground, reducing their kinetic energy. However it is the forest floor, more than the canopy, that prevents surface erosion. The terminal velocity of rain drops is reached in about 8 metres (26 feet). Because forest canopies are usually higher than this, rain drops can often regain terminal velocity even after striking the canopy. However, the intact forest floor, with its layers of leaf litter and organic matter, is still able to absorb the impact of the rainfall.

Deforestation causes increased erosion rates due to exposure of mineral soil by removing the humus and litter layers from the soil surface, removing the vegetative cover that binds soil together, and causing heavy soil compaction from logging equipment. Once trees have been removed by fire or logging, infiltration rates become high and erosion low to the degree the forest floor remains intact. Severe fires can lead to significant further erosion if followed by heavy rainfall.

Globally one of the largest contributors to erosive soil loss in the year 2006 is the slash and burn treatment of tropical forests. In a number of regions of the earth, entire sectors of a country have been rendered unproductive. For example, on the Madagascar high central plateau, comprising approximately ten percent of that country's land area, virtually the entire landscape is sterile of vegetation, with gully erosive furrows typically in excess of 50 metres (160 ft) deep and 1 kilometre (0.6 miles) wide. Shifting cultivation is a farming system which sometimes incorporates the slash and burn method in some regions of the world. This degrades the soil and causes the soil to become less and less fertile.

Roads and Urbanization

Urbanization has major effects on erosion processes—first by denuding the land of vegetative cover, altering drainage patterns, and compacting the soil during construction; and next by covering the land in an impermeable layer of asphalt or concrete that increases the amount of surface runoff and increases surface wind speeds. Much of the sediment carried in runoff from urban areas (especially roads) is highly contaminated with fuel, oil, and other chemicals. This increased runoff, in addition to eroding and degrading the land that it flows over, also causes major disruption to surrounding watersheds by altering the volume and rate of water that flows through them, and filling them with chemically polluted sedimentation. The increased flow of water through local waterways also causes a large increase in the rate of bank erosion.

Climate Change

The warmer atmospheric temperatures observed over the past decades are expected to lead to a more vigorous hydrological cycle, including more extreme rainfall events. The rise in sea levels that has occurred as a result of climate change has also greatly increased coastal erosion rates.

Studies on soil erosion suggest that increased rainfall amounts and intensities will lead to greater rates of soil erosion. Thus, if rainfall amounts and intensities increase in many parts of the world as expected, erosion will also increase, unless amelioration measures are taken. Soil erosion rates are expected to change in response to changes in climate for a variety of reasons. The most direct is the change in the erosive power of rainfall. Other reasons include: a) changes in plant canopy caused by shifts in plant biomass production associated with moisture regime; b) changes in litter cover on the ground caused by changes in both plant residue decomposition rates driven by temperature and moisture dependent soil microbial activity as well as plant biomass production rates; c) changes in soil moisture due to shifting precipitation regimes and evapo-transpiration rates, which changes infiltration and runoff ratios; d) soil erodibility changes due to decrease in soil organic matter concentrations in soils that lead to a soil structure that is more susceptible to erosion and increased runoff due to increased soil surface sealing and crusting; e) a shift of winter precipitation from non-erosive snow to erosive rainfall due to increasing winter temperatures; f) melting of permafrost, which induces an erodible soil state from a previously non-erodible one; and g) shifts in land use made necessary to accommodate new climatic regimes.

Studies by Pruski and Nearing indicated that, other factors such as land use unconsidered, it is reasonable to expect approximately a 1.7% change in soil erosion for each 1% change in total precipitation under climate change. In recent studies, there are predicted increases of rainfall erosivity by 17% in the United States and by 18% in Europe.

Global Environmental Effects

During the 17th and 18th centuries, Easter Island experienced severe erosion due to deforestation and unsustainable agricultural practices. The resulting loss of topsoil ultimately led to ecological collapse, causing mass starvation and the complete disintegration of the Easter Island civilization.

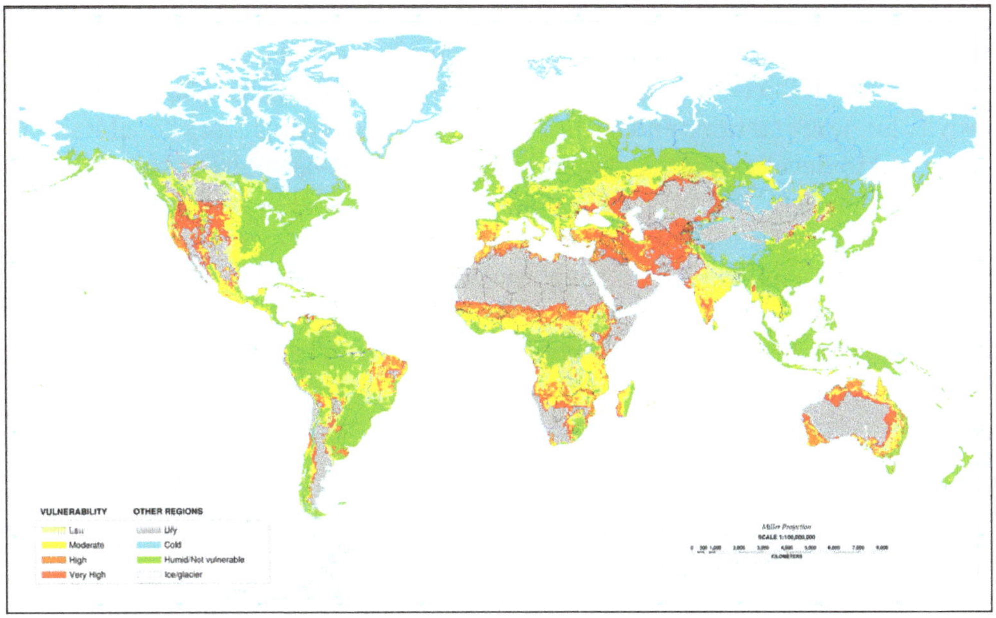

World map indicating areas that are vulnerable to high rates of water erosion.

Due to the severity of its ecological effects, and the scale on which it is occurring, erosion constitutes one of the most significant global environmental problems we face today.

Land Degradation

Water and wind erosion are now the two primary causes of land degradation; combined, they are responsible for 84% of degraded acreage.

Each year, about 75 billion tons of soil is eroded from the land—a rate that is about 13–40 times as fast as the natural rate of erosion. Approximately 40% of the world's agricultural land is seriously degraded. According to the United Nations, an area of fertile soil the size of Ukraine is lost every year because of drought, deforestation and climate change. In Africa, if current trends of soil degradation continue, the continent might be able to feed just 25% of its population by 2025, according to UNU's Ghana-based Institute for Natural Resources in Africa.

Recent modeling developments have quantified rainfall erosivity at global scale using high temporal resolution(<30 min) and high fidelity rainfall recordings. The results is an extensive global data collection effort produced the Global Rainfall Erosivity Database (GloREDa) which includes rainfall erosivity for 3,625 stations and covers 63 countries. This first ever Global Rainfall Erosivity Database was used to develop a global erosivity map at 30 arc-seconds(~1 km) based on sophisticated geostatistical process. According to a new study published in Nature Communications, almost 36 billion tons of soil is lost every year due to water, and deforestation and other changes in land use make the problem worse. The study investigates global soil erosion dynamics by means of high-resolution spatially distributed modelling (ca. 250 × 250 m cell size). The geo-statistical approach allows, for the first time, the thorough incorporation into a global soil erosion model of land use and changes in land use, the extent, types, spatial distribution of global croplands and the effects of different regional cropping systems.

The loss of soil fertility due to erosion is further problematic because the response is often to apply chemical fertilizers, which leads to further water and soil pollution, rather than to allow the land to regenerate.

Sedimentation of Aquatic Ecosystems

Soil erosion (especially from agricultural activity) is considered to be the leading global cause of diffuse water pollution, due to the effects of the excess sediments flowing into the world's waterways. The sediments themselves act as pollutants, as well as being carriers for other pollutants, such as attached pesticide molecules or heavy metals.

The effect of increased sediments loads on aquatic ecosystems can be catastrophic. Silt can smother the spawning beds of fish, by filling in the space between gravel on the stream bed. It also reduces their food supply, and causes major respiratory issues for them as sediment enters their gills. The biodiversity of aquatic plant and algal life is reduced, and invertebrates are also unable to survive and reproduce. While the sedimentation event itself might be relatively short-lived, the ecological disruption caused by the mass die off often persists long into the future.

One of the most serious and long-running water erosion problems worldwide is in the People's Republic of China, on the middle reaches of the Yellow River and the upper reaches of the Yangtze River. From the Yellow River, over 1.6 billion tons of sediment flows into the ocean each year. The sediment originates primarily from water erosion in the Loess Plateau region of the northwest.

Airborne Dust Pollution

Soil particles picked up during wind erosion of soil are a major source of air pollution, in the form of airborne particulates—"dust". These airborne soil particles are often contaminated with toxic chemicals such as pesticides or petroleum fuels, posing ecological and public health hazards when they later land, or are inhaled/ingested.

Dust from erosion acts to suppress rainfall and changes the sky color from blue to white, which leads to an increase in red sunsets. Dust events have been linked to a decline in the health of coral reefs across the Caribbean and Florida, primarily since the 1970s. Similar dust plumes originate in the Gobi desert, which combined with pollutants, spread large distances downwind, or eastward, into North America.

Monitoring, Measuring and Modeling Soil Erosion

Monitoring and modeling of erosion processes can help people better understand the causes of soil erosion, make predictions of erosion under a range of possible conditions, and plan the implementation of preventative and restorative strategies for erosion. However, the complexity of erosion processes and the number of scientific disciplines that must be considered to understand and model them (e.g. climatology, hydrology, geology, soil science, agriculture, chemistry, physics, etc.) makes accurate modelling challenging. Erosion models are also non-linear, which makes them difficult to work with numerically, and makes it difficult or impossible to scale up to making predictions about large areas from data collected by sampling smaller plots.

Terracing is an ancient technique that can significantly slow the rate of water erosion on cultivated slopes.

The most commonly used model for predicting soil loss from water erosion is the *Universal Soil Loss Equation (USLE)*. This was developed in the 1960s and 1970s. It estimates the average annual soil loss *A* on a plot-sized area as:

$$A = RKLSCP$$

where *R* is the *rainfall erosivity factor*, *K* is the *soil erodibility factor*, *L* and *S* are topographic factors representing length and slope, *C* is the cover and management factor and *P* is the support practices factor.

Despite the USLE's plot-scale spatial focus, the model has often been used to estimate soil erosion on much larger areas, such as watersheds or even whole continents. For example, RUSLE has recently been used to quantify soil erosion across the whole of Europe. One major problem is that the USLE cannot simulate gully erosion, and so erosion from gullies is ignored in any USLE-based assessment of erosion. Yet erosion from gullies can be a substantial proportion (10–80%) of total erosion on cultivated and grazed land.

During the 50 years since the introduction of the USLE, many other soil erosion models have been developed. But because of the complexity of soil erosion and its constituent processes, all erosion models can give unsatisfactory results when validated i.e. when model predictions are compared with real-world measurements of erosion. Thus new soil erosion models continue to be developed. Some of these remain USLE-based, e.g. the G2 model. Other soil erosion models have largely (e.g. the Water Erosion Prediction Project model) or wholly (e.g. the Rangeland Hydrology and Erosion Model) abandoned usage of USLE elements.

Prevention and Remediation

The most effective known method for erosion prevention is to increase vegetative cover on the land, which helps prevent both wind and water erosion. Terracing is an extremely effective means of erosion control, which has been practiced for thousands of years by people all over the world. Windbreaks (also called shelterbelts) are rows of trees and shrubs that are planted along the edges of agricultural fields, to shield the fields against winds. In addition to significantly reducing wind erosion, windbreaks provide many other benefits such as improved microclimates for crops (which are sheltered from the dehydrating and otherwise damaging effects of wind), habitat for beneficial bird species, carbon sequestration, and aesthetic improvements to the agricultural landscape. Traditional planting methods, such as mixed-cropping (instead of monocropping) and crop rotation have also been shown to significantly reduce erosion rates. Crop residues play a role in the mitigation of erosion, because they reduce the impact of raindrops breaking up the soil particles. There is a higher potential for erosion when producing potatoes than when growing cereals, or oilseed crops. Forages have a fibrous root system, which helps combat erosion by anchoring the plants to the top layer of the soil, and covering the entirety of the field, as it is a non-row crop.

A windbreak (the row of trees) planted next to an agricultural field, acting as a shield against strong winds. This reduces the effects of wind erosion, and provides many other benefits.

In tropical coastal systems, properties of mangroves have been examined as a potential means to reduce soil erosion. Their complex root structures are known to help reduce wave damage from storms and flood impacts while binding and building soils. These roots can slow down water flow, leading to the deposition of sediments and reduced erosion rates. However, in order to maintain sediment balance, adequate mangrove forest width needs to be present.

DESERTIFICATION

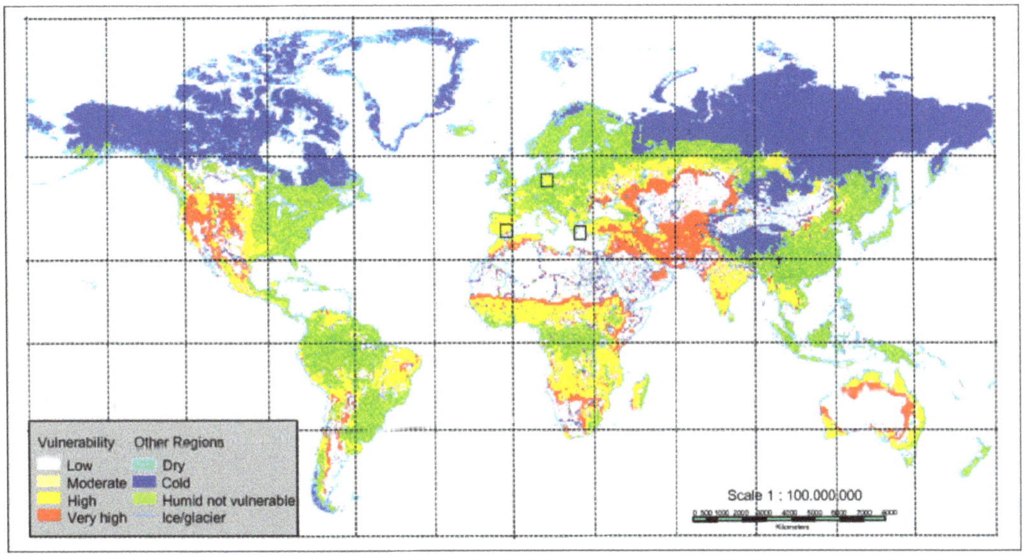

Global desertification vulnerability map.

Desertification is a type of land degradation in which a relatively dry area of land becomes a desert, typically losing its bodies of water as well as vegetation and wildlife. It is caused by a variety of factors, such as through climate change (particularly the current global warming) and through the overexploitation of soil through human activity. When deserts appear automatically over the natural course of a planet's life cycle, then it can be called a natural phenomenon; however, when deserts emerge due to the rampant and unchecked depletion of nutrients in soil that are essential for it to remain arable, then a virtual "soil death" can be spoken of, which traces its cause back to human overexploitation. Desertification is a significant global ecological and environmental problem with far reaching consequences on socio-economic and political conditions.

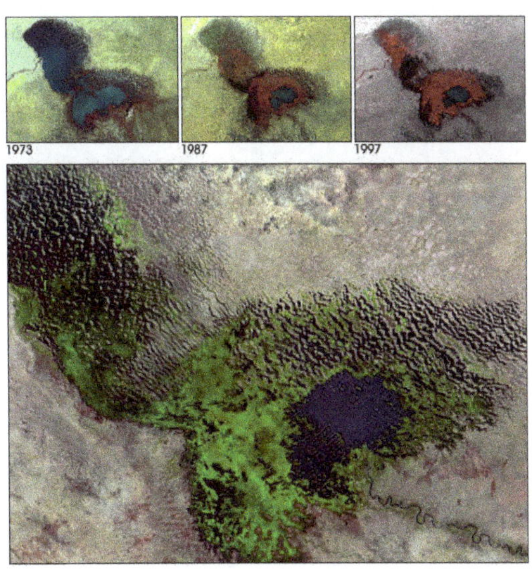

Lake Chad in a 2001 satellite image, with the actual lake in blue. The lake has shrunk by 94% since the 1960s.

Considerable controversy exists over the proper definition of the term "desertification" for which Helmut Geist has identified more than 100 formal definitions. The most widely accepted of these is that of the Princeton University Dictionary which defines it as "the process of fertile land transforming into desert typically as a result of deforestation, drought or improper/inappropriate agriculture". Desertification has been neatly defined in the text of the United Nations Convention to Combat Desertification (UNCCD) as "land degradation in arid, semi-arid and dry sub-humid regions resulting from various factors, including climatic variations and human activities."

Another major contribution to the controversy comes from the sub-grouping of types of desertification. Spanning from the very vague yet shortsighted view as the "man-made-desert" to the broader yet less focused type as the "Non-pattern-Desert".

The earliest known discussion of the topic arose soon after the French colonization of West Africa, when the Comité d'Etudes commissioned a study on *desséchement progressif* to explore the prehistoric expansion of the Sahara Desert.

The world's most noted deserts have been formed by natural processes interacting over long intervals of time. During most of these times, deserts have grown and shrunk independent of human activities. Paleodeserts are large sand seas now inactive because they are stabilized by vegetation, some extending beyond the present margins of core deserts, such as the Sahara, the largest hot desert.

Desertification has played a significant role in human history, contributing to the collapse of several large empires, such as Carthage, Greece, and the Roman Empire, as well as causing displacement of local populations. Historical evidence shows that the serious and extensive land deterioration occurring several centuries ago in arid regions had three epicenters: the Mediterranean, the Mesopotamian Valley, and the Loess Plateau of China, where population was dense.

Areas Affected

Sun, moon, and large telescopes above Chile's Atacama Desert.

Drylands occupy approximately 40–41% of Earth's land area and are home to more than 2 billion people. It has been estimated that some 10–20% of drylands are already degraded, the total area affected by desertification being between 6 and 12 million square kilometres, that about 1–6% of the inhabitants of drylands live in desertified areas, and that a billion people are under threat from further desertification.

As of 1998, the then-current degree of southward expansion of the Sahara was not well known, due to a lack of recent, measurable expansion of the desert into the Sahel at the time.

The impact of global warming and human activities are presented in the Sahel. In this area, the level of desertification is very high compared to other areas in the world. All areas situated in the eastern part of Africa (i.e. in the Sahel region) are characterized by a dry climate, hot temperatures, and low rainfall (300–750 mm rainfall per year). So, droughts are the rule in the Sahel region. Some studies have shown that Africa has lost approximately 650,000 km^2 of its productive agricultural land over the past 50 years. The propagation of desertification in this area is considerable.

Sahel region of Mali.

Some statistics have shown that since 1900 the Sahara has expanded by 250 km to the south over a stretch of land from west to east 6,000 km long. The survey, done by the research institute for development, had demonstrated that this means dryness is spreading fast in the Sahelian countries. 70% of the arid area has deteriorated and water resources have disappeared, leading to soil degradation. The loss of topsoil means that plants cannot take root firmly and can be uprooted by torrential water or strong winds.

The United Nations Convention (UNC) says that about six million Sahelian citizens would have to give up the desertified zones of sub-Saharan Africa for North Africa and Europe between 1997 and 2020.

Another major area that is being impacted by desertification is the Gobi Desert. Currently, the Gobi desert is the fastest moving desert on Earth; according to some researchers, the Gobi Desert swallows up over 1,300 square miles (3,370 km^2) of land annually. This has destroyed many villages in its path. Currently, photos show that the Gobi Desert has expanded to the point the entire nation of Croatia could fit inside its area. This is causing a major problem for the people of China. They will soon have to deal with the desert as it creeps closer. Although the Gobi Desert itself is still a distance away from Beijing, reports from field studies state there are large sand dunes forming only 70 km (43.5 mi) outside the city.

Vegetation Patterning

As the desertification takes place, the landscape may progress through different stages and continuously transform in appearance. On gradually sloped terrain, desertification can create increasingly larger empty spaces over a large strip of land, a phenomenon known as "Brousse tigrée". A mathematical model of this phenomenon proposed by C. Klausmeier attributes this patterning to dynamics in plant-water interaction. One outcome of this observation suggests an optimal planting strategy for agriculture in arid environments.

Causes by Loss

Goats inside of a pen in Norte Chico, Chile. Overgrazing of drylands by poorly managed traditional herding is one of the primary causes of desertification.

Wildebeest in Masai Mara during the Great Migration. Overgrazing is not caused by nomadic grazers in huge populations of travel herds, nor by holistic planned grazing.

The immediate cause is the loss of most vegetation. This is driven by a number of factors, alone or in combination, such as drought, climatic shifts, tillage for agriculture, overgrazing and deforestation for fuel or construction materials. Vegetation plays a major role in determining the biological composition of the soil. Studies have shown that, in many environments, the rate of erosion and runoff decreases exponentially with increased vegetation cover. Unprotected, dry soil surfaces blow away with the wind or are washed away by flash floods, leaving infertile lower soil layers that bake in the sun and become an unproductive hardpan.

Many scientists think that one of the most common causes is overgrazing, too much consumption of vegetation by cattle. Controversially, Allan Savory has claimed that the controlled movement of herds of livestock, mimicking herds of grazing wildlife, can reverse desertification.

A shepherd guiding his sheep through the high desert outside Marrakech, Morocco.

Scientists agree that the existence of a desert in the place where the Sahara desert is now located is due to a natural climate cycle; this cycle often causes a lack of water in the area from time to time. There is a suggestion that the last time that the Sahara was converted from savanna to desert it was partially due to overgrazing by the cattle of the local population.

One of the major causes of desertification in the 20th-21st centuries is probably climate change.

Poverty

At least 90% of the inhabitants of drylands live in developing countries, where they also suffer from poor economic and social conditions. This situation is exacerbated by land degradation because of the reduction in productivity, the precariousness of living conditions and the difficulty of access to resources and opportunities.

A downward spiral is created in many underdeveloped countries by overgrazing, land exhaustion and overdrafting of groundwater in many of the marginally productive world regions due to overpopulation pressures to exploit marginal drylands for farming. Decision-makers are understandably averse to invest in arid zones with low potential. This absence of investment contributes to the marginalisation of these zones. When unfavourable agro-climatic conditions are combined with an absence of infrastructure and access to markets, as well as poorly adapted production techniques and an underfed and undereducated population, most such zones are excluded from development.

Desertification often causes rural lands to become unable to support the same sized populations that previously lived there. This results in mass migrations out of rural areas and into urban areas, particularly in Africa. These migrations into the cities often cause large numbers of unemployed people, who end up living in slums.

Agriculture is a main source of income for many desert communities. The increase in desertification in theses regions has degraded the land enough where people can no longer productively farm and make a profit. This has negatively impacted the economy and increased poverty rates.

Countermeasures

Anti-sand shields in north Sahara, Tunisia.

Techniques and countermeasures exist for mitigating or reversing the effects of desertification, and some possess varying levels of difficulty. For some, there are numerous barriers to their implementation. Yet for others, the solution simply requires the exercise of human reason.

One proposed barrier is that the costs of adopting sustainable agricultural practices sometimes exceed the benefits for individual farmers, even while they are socially and environmentally beneficial. Another issue is a lack of political will, and lack of funding to support land reclamation and anti-desertification programs. Desertification is recognized as a major threat to biodiversity. Some countries have developed Biodiversity Action Plans to counter its effects, particularly in relation to the protection of endangered flora and fauna.

Reforestation gets at one of the root causes of desertification and is not just a treatment of the symptoms. Environmental organizations work in places where deforestation and desertification are contributing to extreme poverty. There they focus primarily on educating the local population about the dangers of deforestation and sometimes employ them to grow seedlings, which they transfer to severely deforested areas during the rainy season. The Food and Agriculture Organization of the United Nations launched the FAO Drylands Restoration Initiative in 2012 to draw together knowledge and experience on dryland restoration. In 2015, FAO published global guidelines for the restoration of degraded forests and landscapes in drylands, in collaboration with the Turkish Ministry of Forestry and Water Affairs and the Turkish Cooperation and Coordination Agency.

Jojoba plantations, such as those shown, have played a role in combating edge effects of desertification in the Thar Desert, India.

The *Green Wall of China* is a high-profile example of one method that has been finding success in this battle with desertification.This wall is a much larger-scale version of what American farmers did in the 1930s to stop the great Midwest dust bowl. This plan was proposed in the late 1970s, and has become a major ecological engineering project that is not predicted to end until the year 2055. According to Chinese reports, there have been nearly 66 billion trees planted in China's great green wall. Due to the success that China has been finding in stopping the spread of desertification, plans are currently be made in Africa to start a "wall" along the borders of the Sahara desert as well to be financed by the United Nations Global Environment Facility trust.

Techniques focus on two aspects: provisioning of water, and fixation and hyper-fertilizing soil. Fixating the soil is often done through the use of shelter belts, woodlots and windbreaks. Windbreaks are made from trees and bushes and are used to reduce soil erosion and evapotranspiration. They were widely encouraged by development agencies from the middle of the 1980s in the Sahel area of Africa.

Some soils (for example, clay), duc to lack of water can become consolidated rather than porous (as in the case of sandy soils). Some techniques as zaï or tillage are then used to still allow the planting of crops. Waffle gardens can also help as they can provide protection of the plants against wind/sandblasting, and increase the hours of shade falling on the plant.

Another technique that is useful is contour trenching. This involves the digging of 150 m long, 1 m deep trenches in the soil. The trenches are made parallel to the height lines of the landscape, preventing the water from flowing within the trenches and causing erosion. Stone walls are placed around the trenches to prevent the trenches from closing up again. The method was invented by Peter Westerveld.

Enriching of the soil and restoration of its fertility is often done by plants. Of these, leguminous plants which extract nitrogen from the air and fix it in the soil, and food crops/trees as grains, barley, beans and dates are the most important. Sand fences can also be used to control drifting of soil and sand erosion.

Some research centra (such as Bel-Air Research Center IRD/ISRA/UCAD) are also experimenting with the inoculation of tree species with mycorrhiza in arid zones. The mycorrhiza are basically fungi attaching themselves to the roots of the plants. They hereby create a symbiotic relation with the trees, increasing the surface area of the tree's roots greatly (allowing the tree to gather much more nutrients from the soil).

As there are many different types of deserts, there are also different types of desert reclamation methodologies. An example for this is the salt flats in the Rub' al Khali desert in Saudi Arabia. These salt flats are one of the most promising desert areas for seawater agriculture and could be revitalized without the use of freshwater or much energy.

Farmer-managed natural regeneration (FMNR) is another technique that has produced successful results for desert reclamation. Since 1980, this method to reforest degraded landscape has been applied with some success in Niger. This simple and low-cost method has enabled farmers to regenerate some 30,000 square kilometers in Niger. The process involves enabling native sprouting tree growth through selective pruning of shrub shoots. The residue from pruned trees can be used to provide mulching for fields thus increasing soil water retention and reducing evaporation. Additionally, properly spaced and pruned trees can increase crop yields. The Humbo Assisted Regeneration Project which uses FMNR techniques in Ethiopia has received money from

The World Bank's BioCarbon Fund, which supports projects that sequester or conserve carbon in forests or agricultural ecosystems.

Managed Grazing

Restoring grasslands store CO_2 from the air as plant material. Grazing livestock, usually not left to wander, would eat the grass and would minimize any grass growth while grass left alone would eventually grow to cover its own growing buds, preventing them from photosynthesizing and killing the plant. A method proposed to restore grasslands uses fences with many small paddocks and moving herds from one paddock to another after a day or two in order to mimic natural grazers and allowing the grass to grow optimally. It is estimated that increasing the carbon content of the soils in the world's 3.5 billion hectares of agricultural grassland would offset nearly 12 years of CO_2 emissions. Allan Savory, as part of holistic management, claims that while large herds are often blamed for desertification, prehistoric lands used to support large or larger herds and areas where herds were removed in the United States are still desertifying; range scientists have however not been able to experimentally confirm his claims.

SIXTH EXTINCTION

The Holocene extinction, otherwise referred to as the sixth mass extinction or Anthropocene extinction, is a current event, and is one of the most significant extinction events in the history of the Earth. This ongoing extinction of species coincides with the present Holocene epoch (approx. 11,700 years), and is a result of human activity. This large number of extinctions spans numerous families of plants and animals, including mammals, birds, amphibians, reptiles and arthropods. With widespread degradation of highly biodiverse habitats such as coral reefs and rainforests, as well as other areas, the vast majority of these extinctions are thought to be *undocumented*, as the species are undiscovered at the time of their extinction, or no one has yet discovered their extinction. The current rate of extinction of species is estimated at 100 to 1,000 times higher than natural background rates. The *Global Assessment Report on Biodiversity and Ecosystem Services* published by IPBES in 2019 posits that roughly one million species of plants and animals face extinction caused by anthropogenic impacts.

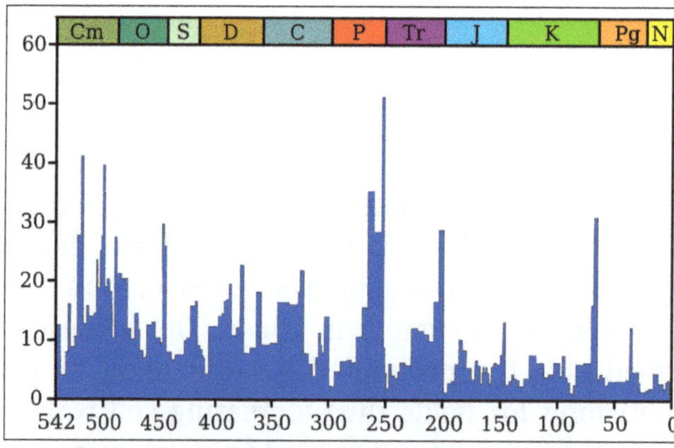

The percentage of marine animal extinction at the genus level through the five mass extinctions.

The Holocene extinction includes the disappearance of large land animals known as megafauna, starting at the end of the last Ice Age. Megafauna outside of the African continent, which did not evolve alongside humans, proved highly sensitive to the introduction of new predation, and many died out shortly after early humans began spreading and hunting across the Earth (many African species have also gone extinct in the Holocene, but —with few exceptions— megafauna of the mainland was largely unaffected until a few hundred years ago). These extinctions, occurring near the Pleistocene–Holocene boundary, are sometimes referred to as the Quaternary extinction event.

The most popular theory is that human overhunting of species added to existing stress conditions as the extinction coincides with human emergence. Although there is debate regarding how much human predation affected their decline, certain population declines have been directly correlated with human activity, such as the extinction events of New Zealand and Hawaii. Aside from humans, climate change may have been a driving factor in the megafaunal extinctions, especially at the end of the Pleistocene.

Ecologically, humanity has been noted as an unprecedented "global superpredator" that consistently preys on the adults of other apex predators, and has worldwide effects on food webs. There have been extinctions of species on every land mass and in every ocean: there are many famous examples within Africa, Asia, Europe, Australia, North and South America, and on smaller islands. Overall, the Holocene extinction can be linked to the human impact on the environment. The Holocene extinction continues into the 21st century, with meat consumption, overfishing, ocean acidification and the decline in amphibian populations being a few broader examples of an almost universal, cosmopolitan decline in biodiversity. Human overpopulation (and continued population growth) along with profligate consumption are considered to be the primary drivers of this rapid decline.

The Holocene extinction is also known as the "sixth extinction", as it is possibly the sixth mass extinct event, after the Ordovician–Silurian extinction events, the Late Devonian extinction, the Permian–Triassic extinction event, the Triassic–Jurassic extinction event, and the Cretaceous–Paleogene extinction event. Mass extinctions are characterized by the loss of at least 75% of species within a geologically short period of time. There is no general agreement on where the Holocene, or anthropogenic, extinction begins, and the Quaternary extinction event, which includes climate change resulting in the end of the last ice age, ends, or if they should be considered separate events at all. Some have suggested that anthropogenic extinctions may have begun as early as when the first modern humans spread out of Africa between 200,000 and 100,000 years ago; this is supported by rapid megafaunal extinction following recent human colonisation in Australia, New Zealand and Madagascar, as might be expected when any large, adaptable predator (invasive species) moves into a new ecosystem. In many cases, it is suggested that even minimal hunting pressure was enough to wipe out large fauna, particularly on geographically isolated islands. Only during the most recent parts of the extinction have plants also suffered large losses.

In *The Future of Life*, Edward Osborne Wilson of Harvard calculated that, if the current rate of human disruption of the biosphere continues, one-half of Earth's higher lifeforms will be extinct by 2100. A 1998 poll conducted by the American Museum of Natural History found that 70% of biologists acknowledge an ongoing anthropogenic extinction event. At present, the rate of extinction of species is estimated at 100 to 1,000 times higher than the background extinction rate, the historically typical rate of extinction (in terms of the natural evolution of the planet); also, the current rate of extinction is 10 to 100 times higher than in any of the previous mass extinctions in the history of Earth. One scientist estimates the current extinction rate may be 10,000 times the background extinction rate, although most scientists predict a much lower extinction rate than this outlying estimate. Theoretical ecologist Stuart Pimm stated that the extinction rate for plants is 100 times higher than normal.

In a pair of studies published in 2015, extrapolation from observed extinction of Hawaiian snails led to the conclusion that 7% of all species on Earth may have been lost already.

There is widespread consensus among scientists that human activity is accelerating the extinction of many animal species through the destruction of habitats, the consumption of animals as resources, and the elimination of species that humans view as threats or competitors. But some contend that this biotic destruction has yet to reach the level of the previous five mass extinctions. Stuart Pimm, for example, asserts that the sixth mass extinction "is something that hasn't happened yet – we are on the edge of it." In November 2017, a statement, titled "World Scientists' Warning to Humanity: A Second Notice", led by eight authors and signed by 15,364 scientists from 184 countries asserted that, among other things, "we have unleashed a mass extinction event, the sixth in roughly 540 million years, wherein many current life forms could be annihilated or at least committed to extinction by the end of this century."

Anthropocene

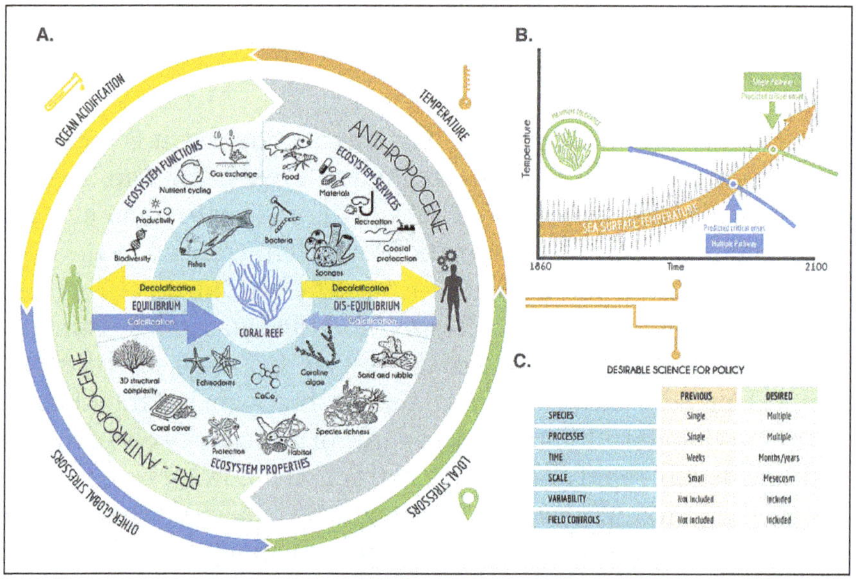

A diagram showing the ecological processes of coral reefs before and after the Anthropocene.

The abundance of species extinctions considered anthropogenic, or due to human activity, have sometimes (especially when referring to hypothesized future events) been collectively called the "Anthropocene extinction". "Anthropocene" is a term introduced in 2000. Some now postulate that a new geological epoch has begun, with the most abrupt and widespread extinction of species since the Cretaceous–Paleogene extinction event 66 million years ago.

The term "anthropocene" is being used more frequently by scientists, and some commentators may refer to the current and projected future extinctions as part of a longer Holocene extinction. The Holocene–Anthropocene boundary is contested, with some commentators asserting significant human influence on climate for much of what is normally regarded as the Holocene Epoch. Other commentators place the Holocene–Anthropocene boundary at the industrial revolution and also say that "[f]ormal adoption of this term in the near future will largely depend on its utility, particularly to earth scientists working on late Holocene successions."

It has been suggested that human activity has made the period starting from the mid-20th century different enough from the rest of the Holocene to consider it a new geological epoch, known as the Anthropocene, a term which was considered for inclusion in the timeline of Earth's history by the International Commission on Stratigraphy in 2016. In order to constitute the Holocene as an extinction event, scientists must determine exactly when anthropogenic greenhouse gas emissions began to measurably alter natural atmospheric levels on a global scale, and when these alterations caused changes to global climate. Using chemical proxies from Antarctic ice cores, researchers have estimated the fluctuations of carbon dioxide (CO_2) and methane (CH_4) gases in the Earth's atmosphere during the late Pleistocene and Holocene epochs. Estimates of the fluctuations of these two gases in the atmosphere, using chemical proxies from Antarctic ice cores, generally indicate that the peak of the Anthropocene occurred within the previous two centuries: typically beginning with the Industrial Revolution, when the highest greenhouse gas levels were recorded.

Influences

Competition by Humans

The Holocene extinction is mainly caused by human activity. Extinction of animals, plants, and other organisms caused by human actions may go as far back as the late Pleistocene, over 12,000 years ago. There is a correlation between megafaunal extinction and the arrival of humans, and human overpopulation and human population growth, along with overconsumption and consumption growth, most prominently in the past two centuries, are regarded as one of the underlying causes of extinction.

Megafauna were once found on every continent of the world and large islands such as New Zealand and Madagascar, but are now almost exclusively found on the continent of Africa, with notable comparisons on Australia and the islands previously mentioned experiencing population crashes and trophic cascades shortly after the earliest human settlers. It has been suggested that the African megafauna survived because they evolved alongside humans. The timing of South American megafaunal extinction appears to precede human arrival, although the possibility that human activity at the time impacted the global climate enough to cause such an extinction has been suggested.

It has been noted, in the face of such evidence, that humans are unique in ecology as an unprecedented 'global superpredator', regularly preying on large numbers of fully grown terrestrial and marine apex predators, and with a great deal of influence over food webs and climatic systems worldwide. Although significant debate exists as to how much human predation and indirect effects contributed to prehistoric extinctions, certain population crashes have been directly correlated with human arrival. A 2018 study published in *PNAS* found that since the dawn of human civilization, 83% of wild mammals, 80% of marine mammals, 50% of plants and 15% of fish have vanished. Currently, livestock make up 60% of the biomass of all mammals on earth, followed by humans (36%) and wild mammals (4%). As for birds, 70% are domesticated, such as poultry, whereas only 30% are wild.

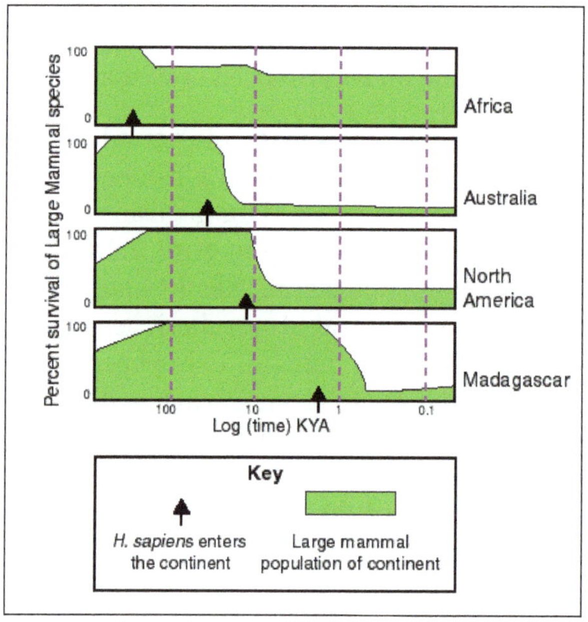

The percent of megafauna on different land masses over time, with the arrival of humans indicated.

More recently, some scholars assert that the emergence of capitalism as the dominant economic system has accelerated ecological exploitation and destruction, and has also exacerbated mass species extinction. CUNY professor David Harvey, for example, posits that the neoliberal era "happens to be the era of the fastest mass extinction of species in the Earth's recent history".

Agriculture

The dodo, a flightless bird native to Mauritius, became extinct during the mid- to late 17th century due to habitat destruction and predation by introduced mammals.

Human civilization was founded on and grew from agriculture. The more land used for farming, the greater the population a civilization could sustain, and subsequent popularization of farming led to increasing ecological disasters.

Habitat destruction by humans, including oceanic devastation, such as through overfishing and contamination; and the modification and destruction of vast tracts of land and river systems around the world to meet solely human-centered ends (with 13 percent of Earth's ice-free land surface now used as row-crop agricultural sites, 26 percent used as pastures, and 4 percent urban-industrial areas.), thus replacing the original local ecosystems. The sustained conversion of biodiversity rich forests and wetlands into poorer fields and pastures (of lesser carrying capacity for wild species), over the last 10,000 years, has considerably reduced the Earth's carrying capacity for wild birds, among other organisms, in both population size and species count.

Other, related human causes of the extinction event include deforestation, hunting, pollution, the introduction in various regions of non-native species, and the widespread transmission of infectious diseases spread through livestock and crops.

Recent investigations about hunter-gatherer landscape burning has a major implication for the current debate about the timing of the Anthropocene and the role that humans may have played in the production of greenhouse gases prior to the Industrial Revolution. Studies on early hunter-gatherers raises questions about the current use of population size or density as a proxy for the amount of land clearance and anthropogenic burning that took place in pre-industrial times. Scientists have questioned the correlation between population size and early territorial alterations. Ruddiman and Ellis' research paper in 2009 makes the case that early farmers involved in systems of agriculture used more land per capita than growers later in the Holocene, who intensified their labor to produce more food per unit of area (thus, per laborer); arguing that agricultural involvement in rice production implemented thousands of years ago by relatively small populations have created significant environmental impacts through large-scale means of deforestation.

While a number of human-derived factors are recognized as contributing to rising atmospheric concentrations of CH_4 (methane) and CO_2 (carbon dioxide), deforestation and territorial clearance practices associated with agricultural development may be contributing most to these concentrations globally. Scientists that are employing a variance of archaeological and paleoecological data argue that the processes contributing to substantial human modification of the environment spanned many thousands of years ago on a global scale and thus, not originating as early as the Industrial Revolution. Gaining popularity on his uncommon hypothesis, palaeoclimatologist William Ruddiman in 2003, stipulated that in the early Holocene 11,000 years ago, atmospheric carbon dioxide and methane levels fluctuated in a pattern which was different from the Pleistocene epoch before it. He argued that the patterns of the significant decline of CO_2 levels during the last ice age of the Pleistocene inversely correlates to the Holocene where there have been dramatic increases of CO_2 around 8000 years ago and CH_4 levels 3000 years after that. The correlation between the decrease of CO_2 in the Pleistocene and the increase of it during the Holocene implies that the causation of this spark of greenhouse gases into the atmosphere was the growth of human agriculture during the Holocene such as the anthropogenic expansion of (human) land use and irrigation.

Islands

Genyornis newtoni, a 2-metre (7 ft) tall flightless bird. Evidence of egg cooking in this species is the first evidence of megafaunal hunting by humans on Australia.

Human arrival in the Caribbean around 6,000 years ago is correlated with the extinction of many species. Examples include many different genera of ground and arboreal sloths across all islands. These sloths were generally smaller than those found on the South American continent. *Megalocnus* were the largest genus at up to 90 kilograms (200 lb), *Acratocnus* were medium-sized relatives of modern two-toed sloths endemic to Cuba, *Imagocnus* also of Cuba, *Neocnus* and many others.

Recent research, based on archaeological and paleontological digs on 70 different Pacific islands has shown that numerous species became extinct as people moved across the Pacific, starting 30,000 years ago in the Bismarck Archipelago and Solomon Islands. It is currently estimated that among the bird species of the Pacific, some 2000 species have gone extinct since the arrival of humans, representing a 20% drop in the biodiversity of birds worldwide.

The first settlers are thought to have arrived in the islands between 300 and 800 CE, with European arrival in the 16th century. Hawaii is notable for its endemism of plants, birds, insects, mollusks and fish; 30% of its organisms are endemic. Many of its species are endangered or have gone extinct, primarily due to accidentally introduced species and livestock grazing. Over 40% of its bird species have gone extinct, and it is the location of 75% of extinctions in the United States. Extinction has increased in Hawaii over the last 200 years and is relatively well documented, with extinctions among native snails used as estimates for global extinction rates.

Australia

Australia was once home to a large assemblage of megafauna, with many parallels to those found on the African continent today. Australia's fauna is characterised by primarily marsupial mammals, and many reptiles and birds, all existing as giant forms until recently. Humans arrived on the continent very early, about 50,000 years ago. The extent human arrival contributed is controversial; climatic drying of Australia 40,000–60,000 years ago was an unlikely cause, as it was less severe in speed or magnitude than previous regional climate change which failed to kill off megafauna. Extinctions in Australia continued from original settlement until today in both plants and animals, whilst many more animals and plants have declined or are endangered.

Due to the older timeframe and the soil chemistry on the continent, very little subfossil preservation evidence exists relative to elsewhere. However, continent-wide extinction of all genera weighing over 100 kilograms, and six of seven genera weighing between 45 and 100 kilograms occurred around 46,400 years ago (4,000 years after human arrival) and the fact that megafauna survived until a later date on the island of Tasmania following the establishment of a land bridge suggest direct hunting or anthropogenic ecosystem disruption such as fire-stick farming as likely causes. The first evidence of direct human predation leading to extinction in Australia was published in 2016.

Madagascar

Within 500 years of the arrival of humans between 2,500–2,000 years ago, nearly all of Madagascar's distinct, endemic and geographically isolated megafauna became extinct. The largest animals, of more than 150 kilograms (330 lb), were extinct very shortly after the first human arrival, with large and medium-sized species dying out after prolonged hunting pressure from an expanding human population moving into more remote regions of the island around 1000 years ago. Smaller fauna experienced initial increases due to decreased competition, and then subsequent declines over the last 500 years. All fauna weighing over 10 kilograms (22 lb) died out. The primary reasons for this are human hunting and habitat loss from early aridification, both of which persist and threaten Madagascar's remaining taxa today.

The eight or more species of elephant birds, giant flightless ratites in the genera *Aepyornis*, *Vorombe*, and *Mullerornis*, are extinct from over-hunting, as well as 17 species of lemur, known as giant, subfossil lemurs. Some of these lemurs typically weighed over 150 kilograms (330 lb), and fossils have provided evidence of human butchery on many species.

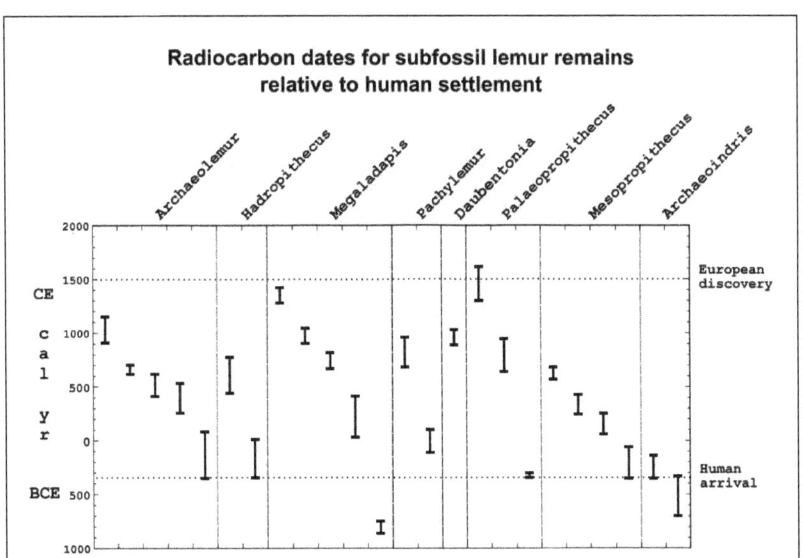

Radiocarbon dating of multiple subfossil specimens shows that now extinct giant lemurs were present in Madagascar until after human arrival.

New Zealand

New Zealand is characterised by its geographic isolation and island biogeography, and had been isolated from mainland Australia for 80 million years. It was the last large land mass to be colonised by humans. The arrival of Polynesian settlers circa 12th century resulted in the extinction of all of the islands' megafaunal birds within several hundred years. The last moa, large flightless ratites, became extinct within 200 years of the arrival of human settlers. The Polynesians also introduced the Polynesian rat. This may have put some pressure on other birds but at the time of early European contact (18th Century) and colonisation (19th Century) the bird life was prolific. With them, the Europeans brought ship rats, possums, cats and mustelids which decimated native bird life, some of which had adapted flightlessness and ground nesting habits and others had no defensive behavior as a result of having no extant endemic mammalian predators. The kakapo, the world's biggest parrot, which is flightless, now only exists in managed breeding sanctuaries. New Zealand's national emblem, the kiwi, is on the endangered bird list.

Americas

There has been a debate as to the extent to which the disappearance of megafauna at the end of the last glacial period can be attributed to human activities by hunting, or even by slaughter of prey populations. Discoveries at Monte Verde in South America and at Meadowcroft Rock Shelter in Pennsylvania have caused a controversy regarding the Clovis culture. There likely would have been human settlements prior to the Clovis Culture, and the history of humans in the Americas may extend back many thousands of years before the Clovis culture. The amount of correlation between human arrival and megafauna extinction is still being debated: for example, in Wrangel Island in Siberia the extinction of dwarf woolly mammoths (approximately 2000 BCE) did not coincide with the arrival of humans, nor did megafaunal mass extinction on the South American continent, although it has been suggested climate changes induced by anthropogenic effects elsewhere in the world may have contributed.

Reconstructed woolly mammoth bone hut, based on finds in Mezhyrich.

Comparisons are sometimes made between recent extinctions (approximately since the industrial revolution) and the Pleistocene extinction near the end of the last glacial period. The latter is exemplified by the extinction of large herbivores such as the woolly mammoth and the carnivores that preyed on them. Humans of this era actively hunted the mammoth and the mastodon, but it is not known if this hunting was the cause of the subsequent massive ecological changes, widespread extinctions and climate changes.

The passenger pigeon was a species of pigeon endemic to North America. It experienced a rapid decline in the late 1800s due to habitat destruction and intense hunting after the arrival of Europeans. The last wild bird is thought to have been shot in 1901.

The ecosystems encountered by the first Americans had not been exposed to human interaction, and may have been far less resilient to human made changes than the ecosystems encountered by industrial era humans. Therefore, the actions of the Clovis people, despite seeming insignificant by today's standards could indeed have had a profound effect on the ecosystems and wild life which was entirely unused to human influence.

Afroeurasia

Africa experienced the smallest decline in megafauna compared to the other continents. This is presumably due to the idea that Afroeurasian megafauna evolved alongside humans, and thus developed a healthy fear of them, unlike the comparatively tame animals of other continents. Unlike other continents, the megafauna of Eurasia went extinct over a relatively long period of time, possibly due to climate fluctuations fragmenting and decreasing populations, leaving them vulnerable to over-exploitation, as with the steppe bison (*Bison priscus*). The warming of the arctic region caused the rapid decline of grasslands, which had a negative effect on the grazing megafauna of Eurasia. Most of what once was mammoth steppe has been converted to mire, rendering the environment incapable of supporting them, notably the woolly mammoth.

Climate Change

One of the main theories to the extinction is climate change. The climate change theory has suggested that a change in climate near the end of the late Pleistocene stressed the megafauna to the point of extinction. Some scientists favor abrupt climate change as the catalyst for the extinction of the mega-fauna at the end of the Pleistocene, but there are many who believe increased hunting from early modern humans also played a part, with others even suggesting that the two interacted. However, the annual mean temperature of the current interglacial period for the last 10,000 years is no higher than that of previous interglacial periods, yet some of the same megafauna survived similar temperature increases. In the Americas, a controversial explanation for the shift in climate is presented under the Younger Dryas impact hypothesis, which states that the impact of comets cooled global temperatures.

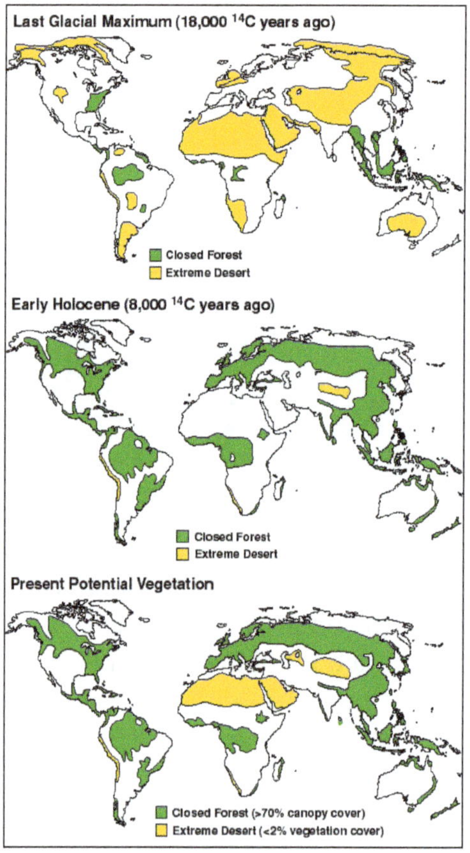

Top: Arid ice age climate Middle: Atlantic Period, warm and wet
Bottom: Potential vegetation in climate now if not for human effects like agriculture.

Bramble Cay melomys were declared extinct in June 2016. This is likely the first mammalian extinction due to anthropogenic climate change.

Megafaunal Extinction

Megafauna play a significant role in the lateral transport of mineral nutrients in an ecosystem, tending to translocate them from areas of high to those of lower abundance. They do so by their movement between the time they consume the nutrient and the time they release it through elimination (or, to a much lesser extent, through decomposition after death). In South America's Amazon Basin, it is estimated that such lateral diffusion was reduced over 98% following the megafaunal extinctions that occurred roughly 12,500 years ago. Given that phosphorus availability is thought to limit productivity in much of the region, the decrease in its transport from the western part of the basin and from floodplains (both of which derive their supply from the uplift of the

Andes) to other areas is thought to have significantly impacted the region's ecology, and the effects may not yet have reached their limits. The extinction of the mammoths allowed grasslands they had maintained through grazing habits to become birch forests. The new forest and the resulting forest fires may have induced climate change. Such disappearances might be the result of the proliferation of modern humans; some recent studies favor this theory.

Large populations of megaherbivores have the potential to contribute greatly to the atmospheric concentration of methane, which is an important greenhouse gas. Modern ruminant herbivores produce methane as a byproduct of foregut fermentation in digestion, and release it through belching or flatulence. Today, around 20% of annual methane emissions come from livestock methane release. In the Mesozoic, it has been estimated that sauropods could have emitted 520 million tons of methane to the atmosphere annually, contributing to the warmer climate of the time (up to 10 °C warmer than at present). This large emission follows from the enormous estimated biomass of sauropods, and because methane production of individual herbivores is believed to be almost proportional to their mass.

Recent studies have indicated that the extinction of megafaunal herbivores may have caused a reduction in atmospheric methane. This hypothesis is relatively new. One study examined the methane emissions from the bison that occupied the Great Plains of North America before contact with European settlers. The study estimated that the removal of the bison caused a decrease of as much as 2.2 million tons per year. Another study examined the change in the methane concentration in the atmosphere at the end of the Pleistocene epoch after the extinction of megafauna in the Americas. After early humans migrated to the Americas about 13,000 BP, their hunting and other associated ecological impacts led to the extinction of many megafaunal species there. Calculations suggest that this extinction decreased methane production by about 9.6 million tons per year. This suggests that the absence of megafaunal methane emissions may have contributed to the abrupt climatic cooling at the onset of the Younger Dryas. The decrease in atmospheric methane that occurred at that time, as recorded in ice cores, was 2–4 times more rapid than any other decrease in the last half million years, suggesting that an unusual mechanism was at work.

Disease

The hyperdisease hypothesis, proposed by Ross MacPhee in 1997, states that the megafaunal die-off was due to an indirect transmission of diseases by newly arriving aboriginal humans. According to MacPhee, aboriginals or animals travelling with them, such as domestic dogs or livestock, introduced one or more highly virulent diseases into new environments whose native population had no immunity to them, eventually leading to their extinction. K-selection animals, such as the now-extinct megafauna, are especially vulnerable to diseases, as opposed to r-selection animals who have a shorter gestation period and a higher population size. Humans are thought to be the sole cause as other earlier migrations of animals into North America from Eurasia did not cause extinctions.

There are many problems with this theory, as this disease would have to meet several criteria: it has to be able to sustain itself in an environment with no hosts; it has to have a high infection rate; and be extremely lethal, with a mortality rate of 50–75%. Disease has to be very virulent to kill off all the individuals in a genus or species, and even such a virulent disease as West Nile Virus is unlikely to have caused extinction.

However, diseases have been the cause for some extinctions. The introduction of avian malaria and avipoxvirus, for example, have had a negative impact on the endemic birds of Hawaii.

Defaunation

Recent Extinction

Recent extinctions are more directly attributable to human influences, whereas prehistoric extinctions can be attributed to other factors, such as global climate change. The International Union for Conservation of Nature (IUCN) characterises 'recent' extinction as those that have occurred past the cut-off point of 1500, and at least 875 species have gone extinct since that time and 2012. Some species, such as the Père David's deer and the Hawaiian crow, are extinct in the wild, and survive solely in captive populations. Other species, such as the Florida panther, are ecologically extinct, surviving in such low numbers that they essentially have no impact on the ecosystem. Other populations are only locally extinct (extirpated), still existence elsewhere, but reduced in distribution, as with the extinction of gray whales in the Atlantic, and of the leatherback sea turtle in Malaysia.

Most recently, insect populations have experienced rapid surprising declines. Insects have declined at an annual rate of 2.5% over the last 25–30 years. The most severe effects may include Puerto Rico, where insect ground fall has declined by 98% in the previous 35 years. Butterflies and moths are experiencing some of the most severe effect. Butterfly species have declined by 58% on farmland in England. In the last ten years, 40% of insect species and 22% of mammal species have disappeared. Germany is experiencing a 75% decline. Climate change and agriculture are believed to be the most significant contributors to the change.

The Nature Communications found that rapid biodiversity loss is impacting larger mammals and birds to a much greater extent than smaller ones, with the body mass of such animals expected to shrink by 25% over the next century. Over the past 125,000 years, the average body size of wildlife has fallen by 14% as human actions eradicated megafauna on all continents with the exception of Africa.

Habitat Destruction

Satellite image of rainforest converted to oil palm plantations.

Global warming is widely accepted as being a contributor to extinction worldwide, in a similar way that previous extinction events have generally included a rapid change in global climate and meteorology. It is also expected to disrupt sex ratios in many reptiles which have temperature-dependent sex determination.

The removal of land to clear way for palm oil plantations releases carbon emissions held in the peatlands of Indonesia. Palm oil mainly serves as a cheap cooking oil, and also as a (controversial) biofuel. However, damage to peatland contributes to 4% of global greenhouse gas emissions, and 8% of those caused by burning fossil fuels. Palm oil cultivation has also been criticized for other impacts to the environment, including deforestation, which has threatened critically endangered species such as the orangutan and the tree-kangaroo. The IUCN stated in 2016 that the species could go extinct within a decade if measures are not taken to preserve the rainforests in which they live.

Some scientists and academics assert that industrial agriculture and the growing demand for meat is contributing to significant global biodiversity loss as this is a significant driver of deforestation and habitat destruction; species-rich habitats, such as significant portions of the Amazon region, are being converted to agriculture for meat production. A 2017 study by the World Wildlife Fund (WWF) found that 60% of biodiversity loss can be attributed to the vast scale of feed crop cultivation required to rear tens of billions of farm animals. Moreover, a 2006 report by the Food and Agriculture Organization (FAO) of the United Nations, *Livestock's Long Shadow*, also found that the livestock sector is a "leading player" in biodiversity loss. More recently, in 2019, the IPBES *Global Assessment Report on Biodiversity and Ecosystem Services* attributed much of this ecological destruction to agriculture and fishing, with the meat industry having a very significant impact. Since the 1970s food production has soared in order to feed a growing human population and bolster economic growth, but at a huge price to the environment and other species. The report says some 25% of the earth's ice-free land is used for cattle grazing.

Rising levels of carbon dioxide are resulting in influx of this gas into the ocean, increasing its acidity. Marine organisms which possess calcium carbonate shells or exoskeletons experience physiological pressure as the carbonate reacts with acid. For example, this is already resulting in coral bleaching on various coral reefs worldwide, which provide valuable habitat and maintain a high biodiversity. Marine gastropods, bivalves and other invertebrates are also affected, as are the organisms that feed on them.According to a 2018 study published in *Science*, global Orca populations are poised to collapse due to toxic chemical and PCB pollution. PCBs are still leaking into the sea in spite of being banned for decades.

Some researchers suggest that by 2050 there could be more plastic than fish in the oceans by weight, with about 8,800,000 metric tons (9,700,000 short tons) of plastic being discharged into the oceans annually. Single-use plastics, such as plastic shopping bags, make up the bulk of this, and can often be ingested by marine life, such as with sea turtles. These plastics can degrade into microplastics, smaller particles that can affect a larger array of species. Microplastics make up the bulk of the Great Pacific Garbage Patch, and their smaller size is detrimental to cleanup efforts.

In March 2019, *Nature Climate Change* published a study by ecologists from Yale University, who found that over the next half century, human land use will reduce the habitats of 1,700 species by up to 50%, pushing them closer to extinction. That same month *PLOS Biology* published a similar study drawing on work at the University of Queensland, which found that "more than 1,200 species globally face threats to their survival in more than 90% of their habitat and will almost certainly face extinction without conservation intervention".

Overexploitation

The vaquita, the world's most endangered marine mammal, has been reduced to only 30 individuals as of February 2017. They are often killed by commercial fishing nets. As of March 2019, only 10 remain, according to The International Committee for the Recovery of the Vaquita.

Overhunting can reduce the local population of game animals by more than half, as well as reducing population density, and may lead to extinction for some species. Populations located nearer to villages are significantly more at risk of depletion. Several conservationist organizations, among them IFAW and HSUS, assert that trophy hunters, particularly from the United States, are playing a significant role in the decline of giraffes, which they refer to as a "silent extinction".

The surge in the mass killings by poachers involved in the illegal ivory trade along with habitat loss is threatening African elephant populations. In 1979, their populations stood at 1.7 million; at present there are fewer than 400,000 remaining. Prior to European colonization, scientists believe Africa was home to roughly 20 million elephants. According to the Great Elephant Census, 30% of African elephants (or 144,000 individuals) disappeared over a seven-year period, 2007 to 2014. African elephants could become extinct by 2035 if poaching rates continue.

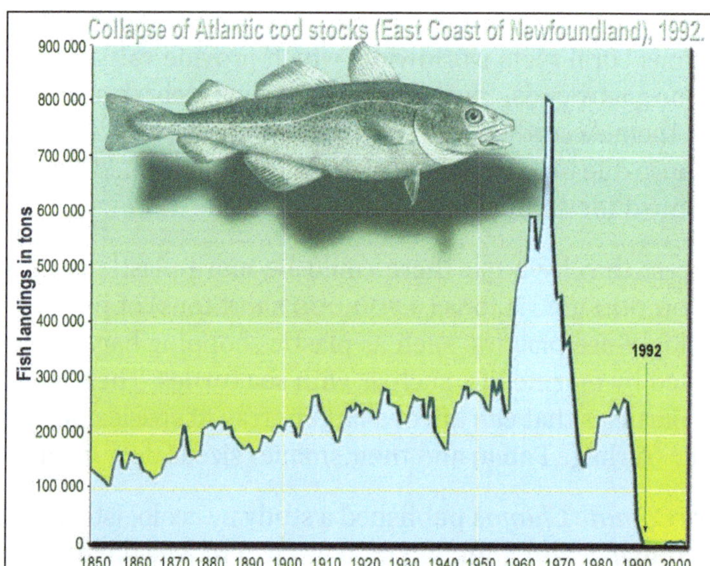

The collapse of Atlantic cod off the coast of Newfoundland in 1992 as a result of overfishing.

Fishing has had a devastating effect on marine organism populations for several centuries even before the explosion of destructive and highly effective fishing practices like trawling. Humans are unique among predators in that they regularly prey on other adult apex predators, particularly in marine environments; bluefin tuna, blue whales, North Atlantic right whales and over fifty species of sharks and rays are vulnerable to predation pressure from human fishing, in particular commercial fishing. A 2016 study published in *Science* concludes that humans tend to hunt larger species, and this could disrupt ocean ecosystems for millions of years.

Disease

The golden toad of Costa Rica, extinct since around 1989. Its disappearance has been attributed to a confluence of several factors, including El Niño warming, fungus, habitat loss and the introduction of invasive species.

The decline of amphibian populations has also been identified as an indicator of environmental degradation. As well as habitat loss, introduced predators and pollution, Chytridiomycosis, a fungal infection accidentally spread by human travel, globalization and the wildlife trade, has caused severe population drops of over 500 amphibian species, and perhaps 90 extinctions, including (among many others) the extinction of the golden toad in Costa Rica and the Gastric-brooding frog in Australia. Many other amphibian species now face extinction, including the reduction of Rabb's fringe-limbed treefrog to an endling, and the extinction of the Panamanian golden frog in the wild. Chytrid fungus has spread across Australia, New Zealand, Central America and Africa, including countries with high amphibian diversity such as cloud forests in Honduras and Madagascar. *Batrachochytrium salamandrivorans* is a similar infection currently threatening salamanders. Amphibians are now the most endangered vertebrate group, having existed for more than 300 million years through three other mass extinctions.

Toughie, the last Rabbs' fringe-limbed treefrog, died in September 2016. The species was killed off from the chytrid fungus Batrachochytrium dendrobatidis.

Millions of bats in the US have been dying off since 2012 due to a fungal infection spread from European bats, which appear to be immune. Population drops have been as great as 90% within five years, and extinction of at least one bat species is predicted. There is currently no form of treatment, and such declines have been described as "unprecedented" in bat evolutionary history by Alan Hicks of the New York State Department of Environmental Conservation.

Between 2007 and 2013, over ten million beehives were abandoned due to colony collapse disorder, which causes worker bees to abandon the queen. This disorder has been attributed to – amongst other things – neonicotinoids consumed by worker bees from the extensive use of pesticides in human farming methods.

Mitigation

Some leading scientists have advocated for the global community to designate as protected areas 30 percent of the planet by 2030, and 50 percent by 2050, in order to mitigate the contemporary extinction crisis as the human population is projected to grow to 10 billion by the middle of the century. Human consumption of food and water resources is also projected to double by this time.

In November 2018, the UN's biodiversity chief Cristiana Paşca Palmer urged people around the world to put pressure on governments to implement significant protections for wildlife by 2020, as rampant biodiversity loss is a "silent killer" as dangerous as global warming, but has received little attention by comparison. She says that "It's different from climate change, where people feel the impact in everyday life. With biodiversity, it is not so clear but by the time you feel what is happening, it may be too late.

GREENHOUSES GASES

A greenhouse gas is a gas that absorbs and emits radiant energy within the thermal infrared range. Greenhouse gases cause the greenhouse effect. The primary greenhouse gases in Earth's atmosphere are water vapor, carbon dioxide, methane, nitrous oxide and ozone. Without greenhouse gases, the average temperature of Earth's surface would be about −18 °C (0 °F), rather than the present average of 15 °C (59 °F). The atmospheres of Venus, Mars and Titan also contain greenhouse gases.

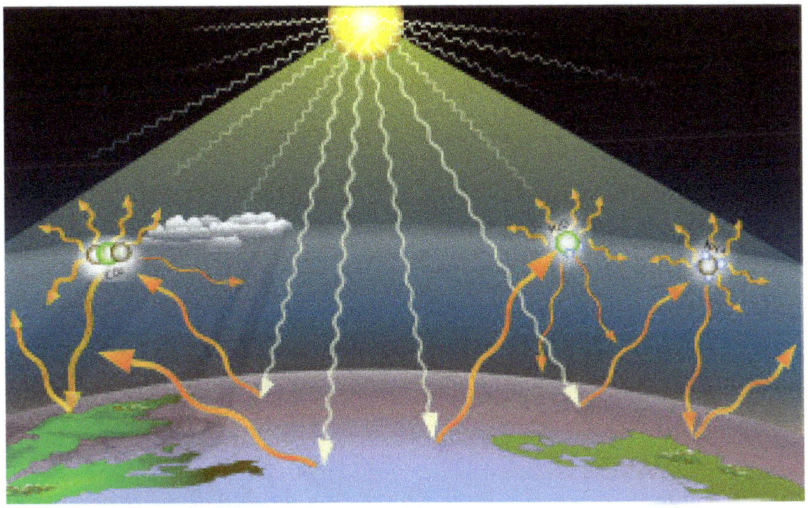

The greenhouse effect of solar radiation on the Earth's surface caused by greenhouse gases.

Human activities since the beginning of the Industrial Revolution (around 1750) have produced a 45% increase in the atmospheric concentration of carbon dioxide (CO_2), from 280 ppm in 1750 to 406 ppm in early 2017. This increase has occurred despite the uptake of more than half of the emissions by various natural "sinks" involved in the carbon cycle. The vast majority of anthropogenic carbon dioxide emissions (i.e., emissions produced by human activities) come from combustion of fossil fuels, principally coal, oil, and natural gas, with additional contributions coming from deforestation, changes in land use, soil erosion and agriculture (including livestock).

Should greenhouse gas emissions continue at their rate in 2017, global warming could cause Earth's surface temperature to exceed historical values as early as 2047, with potentially harmful effects on ecosystems, biodiversity and human livelihoods. At current emission rates temperatures could increase by 2 °C, which the United Nations' IPCC designated as the upper limit to avoid "dangerous" levels, by 2036.

Gases in Earth's Atmosphere

The most common gases in Earth's atmosphere are nitrogen (78%), oxygen (21%), and argon (0.9%). The next most common gases are carbon dioxide, nitrous oxides, methane, and ozone. They are trace gases that account for almost one tenth of 1% of Earth's atmosphere.

Greenhouse gases are those that absorb and emit infrared radiation in the wavelength range emitted by Earth. In order, the most abundant greenhouse gases in Earth's atmosphere are:

- Water vapor (H_2O),
- Carbon dioxide (CO_2),
- Methane (CH_4),
- Nitrous oxide (N_2O),

- Ozone (O_3),
- Chlorofluorocarbons (CFCs),
- Hydrofluorocarbons (includes HCFCs and HFCs).

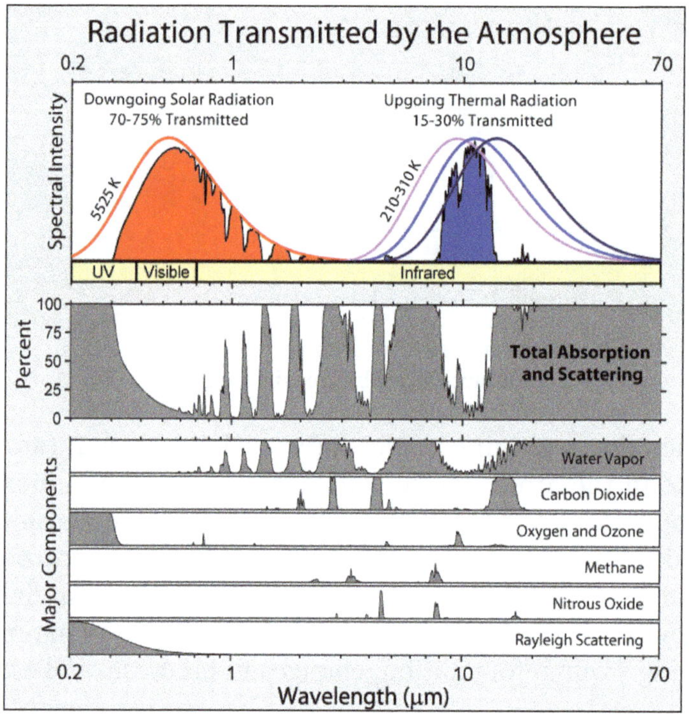

Atmospheric absorption and scattering at different wavelengths of electromagnetic waves. The largest absorption band of carbon dioxide is not far from the maximum in the thermal emission from ground, and it partly closes the window of transparency of water; hence its major effect.

Atmospheric concentrations are determined by the balance between sources (emissions of the gas from human activities and natural systems) and sinks (the removal of the gas from the atmosphere by conversion to a different chemical compound or absorption by bodies of water). The proportion of an emission remaining in the atmosphere after a specified time is the "airborne fraction" (AF). The *annual airborne fraction* is the ratio of the atmospheric increase in a given year to that year's total emissions. As of 2006 the annual airborne fraction for CO2 was about 0.45. The annual airborne fraction increased at a rate of 0.25 ± 0.21% per year over the period 1959–2006.

Non-greenhouse Gases

The major atmospheric constituents, nitrogen (N_2), oxygen (O_2), and argon (Ar), are not greenhouse gases because molecules containing two atoms of the same element such as N_2 and O_2 have no net change in the distribution of their electrical charges when they vibrate, and monatomic gases such as Ar do not have vibrational modes. Hence they are almost totally unaffected by infrared radiation. Some molecules containing just two atoms of different elements, such as carbon monoxide (CO) and hydrogen chloride (HCl), do absorb infrared radiation, but these molecules are short-lived in the atmosphere owing to their reactivity and solubility. Therefore, they do not contribute significantly to the greenhouse effect and often are omitted when discussing greenhouse gases.

Indirect Radiative Effects

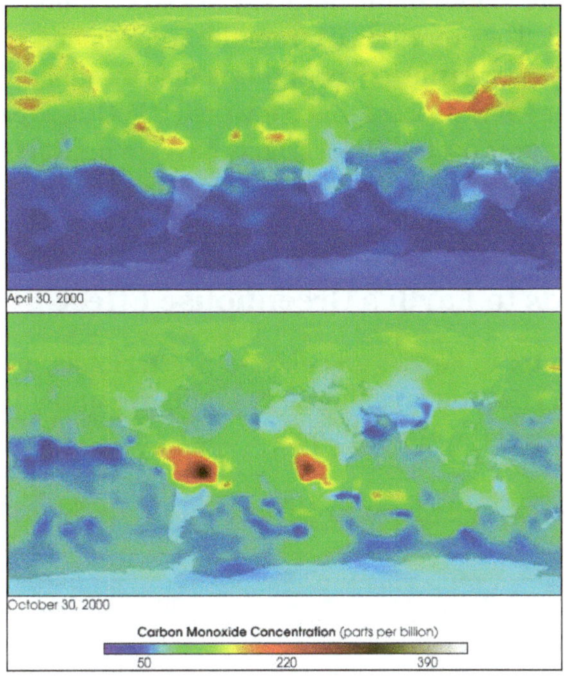

The false colors in this image represent concentrations of carbon monoxide in the lower atmosphere, ranging from about 390 parts per billion (dark brown pixels), to 220 parts per billion (red pixels), to 50 parts per billion (blue pixels).

Some gases have indirect radiative effects (whether or not they are greenhouse gases themselves). This happens in two main ways. One way is that when they break down in the atmosphere they produce another greenhouse gas. For example, methane and carbon monoxide (CO) are oxidized to give carbon dioxide (and methane oxidation also produces water vapor). Oxidation of CO to CO_2 directly produces an unambiguous increase in radiative forcing although the reason is subtle. The peak of the thermal IR emission from Earth's surface is very close to a strong vibrational absorption band of CO_2 (wavelength 15 microns, or wavenumber 667 cm^{-1}). On the other hand, the single CO vibrational band only absorbs IR at much shorter wavelengths (4.7 microns, or 2145 cm^{-1}), where the emission of radiant energy from Earth's surface is at least a factor of ten lower. Oxidation of methane to CO_2, which requires reactions with the OH radical, produces an instantaneous reduction in radiative absorption and emission since CO_2 is a weaker greenhouse gas than methane. However, the oxidations of CO and CH_4 are entwined since both consume OH radicals. In any case, the calculation of the total radiative effect includes both direct and indirect forcing.

A second type of indirect effect happens when chemical reactions in the atmosphere involving these gases change the concentrations of greenhouse gases. For example, the destruction of non-methane volatile organic compounds (NMVOCs) in the atmosphere can produce ozone. The size of the indirect effect can depend strongly on where and when the gas is emitted.

Methane has indirect effects in addition to forming CO_2. The main chemical that reacts with methane in the atmosphere is the hydroxyl radical (OH), thus more methane means that the concentration of OH goes down. Effectively, methane increases its own atmospheric lifetime and therefore its overall radiative effect. The oxidation of methane can produce both ozone and water; and is a major source of water vapor in the normally dry stratosphere. CO and NMVOCs produce CO_2 when they are oxidized. They remove OH from the atmosphere, and this leads to higher concentrations of methane. The surprising effect of this is that the global warming potential of CO is three times that of CO_2. The same process that converts NMVOCs to carbon dioxide can also lead to the formation of tropospheric ozone. Halocarbons have an indirect effect because they destroy stratospheric ozone. Finally, hydrogen can lead to ozone production and CH_4 increases as well as producing stratospheric water vapor.

Contribution of Clouds to Earth's Greenhouse Effect

The major non-gas contributor to Earth's greenhouse effect, clouds, also absorb and emit infrared radiation and thus have an effect on greenhouse gas radiative properties. Clouds are water droplets or ice crystals suspended in the atmosphere.

Impacts on the Overall Greenhouse Effect

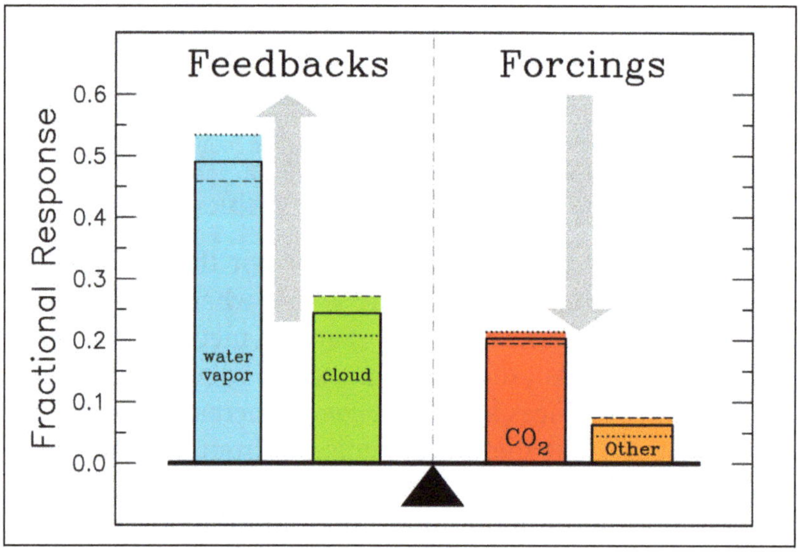

Schmidt et al. analysed how individual components of the atmosphere contribute to the total greenhouse effect. They estimated that water vapor accounts for about 50% of Earth's greenhouse effect, with clouds contributing 25%, carbon dioxide 20%, and the minor greenhouse gases and aerosols accounting for the remaining 5%. In the study, the reference model atmosphere is for 1980 conditions.

The contribution of each gas to the greenhouse effect is determined by the characteristics of that gas, its abundance, and any indirect effects it may cause. For example, the direct radiative effect of a mass of methane is about 84 times stronger than the same mass of carbon dioxide over a 20-year time frame but it is present in much smaller concentrations so that its total direct radiative effect is smaller, in part due to its shorter atmospheric lifetime. On the other hand, in addition to its direct radiative impact, methane has a large, indirect radiative effect because it contributes to ozone formation. Shindell *et al.* argue that the contribution to climate change from methane is at least double previous estimates as a result of this effect.

When ranked by their direct contribution to the greenhouse effect, the most important are:

Compound	Formula	Concentration in atmosphere (ppm)	Contribution (%)
Water vapor and clouds	H_2O	10–50,000	36–72%
Carbon dioxide	CO_2	~400	9–26%
Methane	CH_4	~1.8	4–9%
Ozone	O_3	2–8	3–7%

In addition to the main greenhouse gases listed above, other greenhouse gases include sulfur hexafluoride, hydrofluorocarbons and perfluorocarbons. Some greenhouse gases are not often listed. For example, nitrogen trifluoride has a high global warming potential (GWP) but is only present in very small quantities.

Proportion of Direct effects at a Given Moment

It is not possible to state that a certain gas causes an exact percentage of the greenhouse effect. This is because some of the gases absorb and emit radiation at the same frequencies as others, so that the total greenhouse effect is not simply the sum of the influence of each gas. The higher ends of the ranges quoted are for each gas alone; the lower ends account for overlaps with the other gases. In addition, some gases, such as methane, are known to have large indirect effects that are still being quantified.

Atmospheric Lifetime

Aside from water vapor, which has a residence time of about nine days, major greenhouse gases are well mixed and take many years to leave the atmosphere. Although it is not easy to know with precision how long it takes greenhouse gases to leave the atmosphere, there are estimates for the principal greenhouse gases. Jacob defines the lifetime τ of an atmospheric species X in a one-box model as the average time that a molecule of X remains in the box. Mathematically τ can be defined as the ratio of the mass m (in kg) of X in the box to its removal rate, which is the sum of the flow of X out of the box F_{out} chemical loss of $X(L)$ and deposition of $X(D)$ (all in kg/s): $\tau = \frac{m}{F_{out} + L + D}$. If output of this gas into the box ceased, then after time τ its concentration would decrease by about 63%.

The atmospheric lifetime of a species therefore measures the time required to restore equilibrium following a sudden increase or decrease in its concentration in the atmosphere. Individual atoms or molecules may be lost or deposited to sinks such as the soil, the oceans and other waters, or vegetation and other biological systems, reducing the excess to background concentrations. The average time taken to achieve this is the mean lifetime.

Carbon dioxide has a variable atmospheric lifetime, and cannot be specified precisely. The atmospheric lifetime of CO_2 is estimated of the order of 30–95 years. This figure accounts for CO_2 molecules being removed from the atmosphere by mixing into the ocean, photosynthesis, and other processes. However, this excludes the balancing fluxes of CO_2 into the atmosphere from the geological reservoirs, which have slower characteristic rates. Although more than half of the CO_2 emitted is removed from the atmosphere within a century, some fraction (about 20%) of emitted CO_2 remains in the atmosphere for many thousands of years. Similar issues apply to other greenhouse gases, many of which have longer mean lifetimes than CO_2, e.g. N_2O has a mean atmospheric lifetime of 121 years.

Radiative Forcing

Earth absorbs some of the radiant energy received from the sun, reflects some of it as light and reflects or radiates the rest back to space as heat. Earth's surface temperature depends on this balance between incoming and outgoing energy. If this energy balance is shifted, Earth's surface becomes warmer or cooler, leading to a variety of changes in global climate.

A number of natural and man-made mechanisms can affect the global energy balance and force changes in Earth's climate. Greenhouse gases are one such mechanism. Greenhouse gases absorb and emit some of the outgoing energy radiated from Earth's surface, causing that heat to be retained in the lower atmosphere. As explained above, some greenhouse gases remain in the atmosphere for decades or even centuries, and therefore can affect Earth's energy balance over a long period. Radiative forcing quantifies the effect of factors that influence Earth's energy balance, including changes in the concentrations of greenhouse gases. Positive radiative forcing leads to warming by increasing the net incoming energy, whereas negative radiative forcing leads to cooling.

Global Warming Potential

The global warming potential (GWP) depends on both the efficiency of the molecule as a greenhouse gas and its atmospheric lifetime. GWP is measured relative to the same mass of CO_2 and evaluated for a specific timescale. Thus, if a gas has a high (positive) radiative forcing but also a short lifetime, it will have a large GWP on a 20-year scale but a small one on a 100-year scale. Conversely, if a molecule has a longer atmospheric lifetime than CO2 its GWP will increase when the timescale is considered. Carbon dioxide is defined to have a GWP of 1 over all time periods.

Methane has an atmospheric lifetime of 12 ± 3 years. The 2007 IPCC report lists the GWP as 72 over a time scale of 20 years, 25 over 100 years and 7.6 over 500 years. A 2014 analysis, however, states that although methane's initial impact is about 100 times greater than that of CO_2, because of the shorter atmospheric lifetime, after six or seven decades, the impact of the two gases is about equal, and from then on methane's relative role continues to decline. The decrease in GWP at longer times is because methane is degraded to water and CO_2 through chemical reactions in the atmosphere.

Examples of the atmospheric lifetime and GWP relative to CO_2 for several greenhouse gases are given in the following table:

Table: Atmospheric lifetime and GWP relative to CO_2 at different time horizon for various greenhouse gases.

Gas name	Chemical formula	Lifetime (years)	Global warming potential (GWP) for given time horizon		
			20-yr	100-yr	500-yr
Carbon dioxide	CO_2	30–95	1	1	1
Methane	CH_4	12	84	28	7.6
Nitrous oxide	N_2O	121	264	265	153
CFC-12	CCl_2F_2	100	10 800	10 200	5 200
HCFC-22	$CHClF_2$	12	5 280	1 760	549
Tetrafluoromethane	CF_4	50 000	4 880	6 630	11 200
Hexafluoroethane	C_2F_6	10 000	8 210	11 100	18 200
Sulfur hexafluoride	SF_6	3 200	17 500	23 500	32 600
Nitrogen trifluoride	NF_3	500	12 800	16 100	20 700

The use of CFC-12 (except some essential uses) has been phased out due to its ozone depleting properties. The phasing-out of less active HCFC-compounds will be completed in 2030.

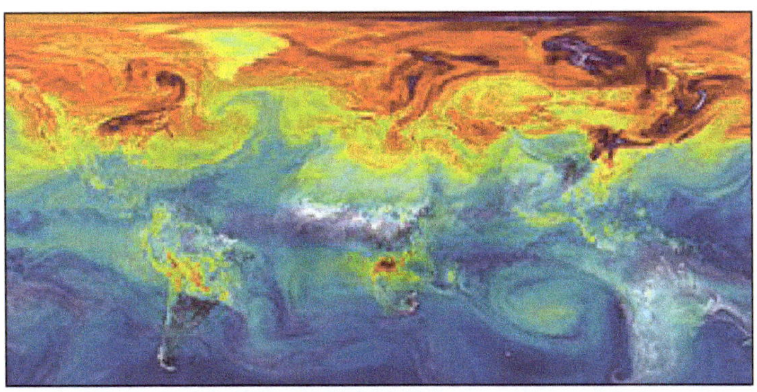

Carbon dioxide in Earth's atmosphere if half of global-warming emissions are not absorbed.

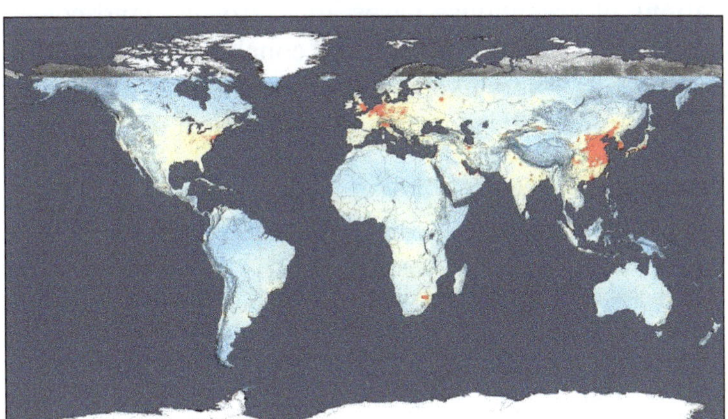

Nitrogen dioxide 2014 – global air quality levels.

Natural and Anthropogenic Sources

This diagram shows a simplified representation of the contemporary global carbon cycle. Changes are measured in gigatons of carbon per year (GtC/y). Canadell *et al.* estimated the growth rate of global average atmospheric CO_2 for 2000–2006 as 1.93 parts-per-million per year (4.1 petagrams of carbon per year).

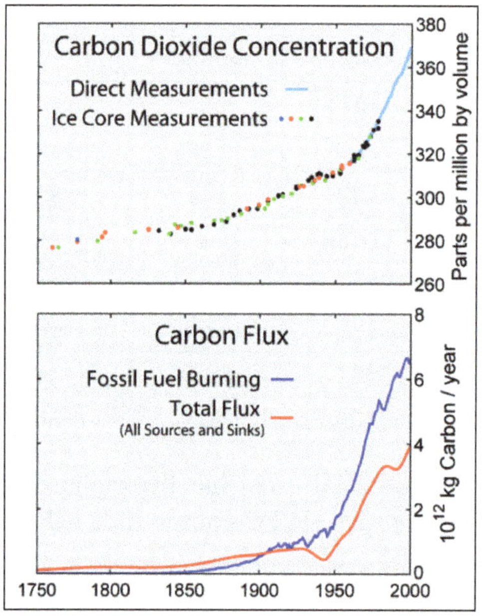

Top: Increasing atmospheric carbon dioxide levels as measured in the atmosphere and reflected in ice cores. Bottom: The amount of net carbon increase in the atmosphere, compared to carbon emissions from burning fossil fuel.

Aside from purely human-produced synthetic halocarbons, most greenhouse gases have both natural and human-caused sources. During the pre-industrial Holocene, concentrations of existing gases were roughly constant, because the large natural sources and sinks roughly balanced. In the industrial era, human activities have added greenhouse gases to the atmosphere, mainly through the burning of fossil fuels and clearing of forests.

The 2007 Fourth Assessment Report compiled by the IPCC (AR4) noted that "changes in atmospheric concentrations of greenhouse gases and aerosols, land cover and solar radiation alter the energy balance of the climate system", and concluded that "increases in anthropogenic greenhouse gas concentrations is very likely to have caused most of the increases in global average temperatures since the mid-20th century". In AR4, "most of" is defined as more than 50%.

Table: Current greenhouse gas concentrations.

Gas	Pre-1750 tropospheric concentration	Recent tropospheric concentration	Absolute increase since 1750	Percentage increase since 1750	Increased radiative forcing (W/m^2)
Carbon dioxide (CO_2)	280 ppm	395.4 ppm	115.4 ppm	41.2%	1.88
Methane (CH_4)	700 ppb	1893 ppb/ 1762 ppb	1193 ppb / 1062 ppb	170.4% /151.7%	0.49
Nitrous oxide (N_2O)	270 ppb	326 ppb / 324 ppb	56 ppb / 54 ppb	20.7% / 20.0%	0.17
Tropospheric ozone (O_3)	237 ppb	337 ppb	100 ppb	42%	0.4

Table: Relevant to radiative forcing and/or ozone depletion; all of the following have no natural sources and hence zero amounts pre-industrial.

Gas	Recenttroposphericconcentration	Increasedradiative forcing(W/ m^2)
CFC-11(trichlorofluoromethane) (CCl_3F)	236 ppt /234 ppt	0.061
CFC-12 (CC_2F_2)	527 ppt /527 ppt	0.169
CFC-113 (Cl_2FC-$CClF_2$)	74 ppt /74 ppt	0.022
HCFC-22 ($CHClF_2$)	231 ppt /210 ppt	0.046
HCFC-141b (CH_3CCl_2F)	24 ppt /21 ppt	0.0036
HCFC-142b(CH_3CClF_2)	23ppt /21 ppt	0.0042
Halon 1211 ($CBrClF_2$)	4.1 ppt /4.0 ppt	0.0012
Halon 1301 ($CBrClF_3$)	3.3 ppt /3.3 ppt	0.001
HFC-134a (CH_2FCF_3)	75 ppt /64 ppt	0.0108
Carbon tetrachloride (CCl_4)	85 ppt /83 ppt	0.0143
Sulfur hexafluoride (SF_6)	7.79 ppt /7.39 ppt	0.0043
Other halocarbons	Varies bysubstance	collectivelyo.02
Halocarbons in total		0.3574

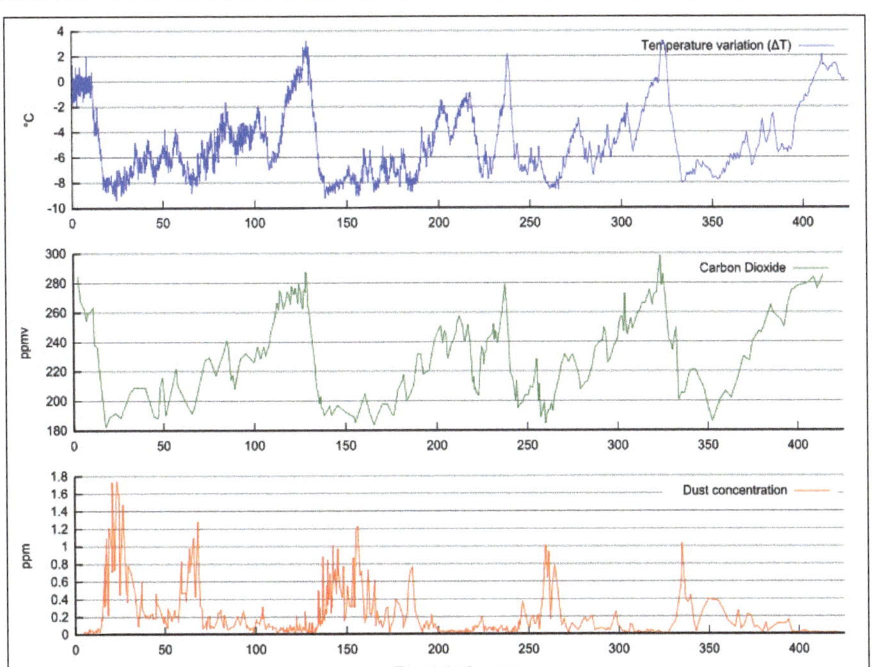

400,000 years of ice core data.

Ice cores provide evidence for greenhouse gas concentration variations over the past 800,000 years. Both CO_2 and CH_4 vary between glacial and interglacial phases, and concentrations of these gases correlate strongly with temperature. Direct data does not exist for periods earlier than those represented in the ice core record, a record that indicates CO_2 mole fractions stayed within a range of 180 ppm to 280 ppm throughout the last 800,000 years, until the increase of the last 250 years. However, various proxies and modeling suggests larger variations in past epochs; 500 million years ago CO_2 levels were likely 10 times higher than now. Indeed, higher CO_2 concentrations are thought to have prevailed throughout most of the Phanerozoic eon, with concentrations four to six times current concentrations during the Mesozoic era, and ten to fifteen times current concentrations during the early Palaeozoic era until the middle of the Devonian period, about 400 Ma.

The spread of land plants is thought to have reduced CO_2 concentrations during the late Devonian, and plant activities as both sources and sinks of CO_2 have since been important in providing stabilising feedbacks. Earlier still, a 200-million year period of intermittent, widespread glaciation extending close to the equator (Snowball Earth) appears to have been ended suddenly, about 550 Ma, by a colossal volcanic outgassing that raised the CO_2 concentration of the atmosphere abruptly to 12%, about 350 times modern levels, causing extreme greenhouse conditions and carbonate deposition as limestone at the rate of about 1 mm per day. This episode marked the close of the Precambrian eon, and was succeeded by the generally warmer conditions of the Phanerozoic, during which multicellular animal and plant life evolved. No volcanic carbon dioxide emission of comparable scale has occurred since. In the modern era, emissions to the atmosphere from volcanoes are approximately 0.645 billion tons of CO_2 per year, whereas humans contribute 29 billion tons of CO_2 each year.

Ice Cores

Measurements from Antarctic ice cores show that before industrial emissions started atmospheric CO_2 mole fractions were about 280 parts per million (ppm), and stayed between 260 and 280 during the preceding ten thousand years. Carbon dioxide mole fractions in the atmosphere have gone up by approximately 35 percent since the 1900s, rising from 280 parts per million by volume to 387 parts per million in 2009. One study using evidence from stomata of fossilized leaves suggests greater variability, with carbon dioxide mole fractions above 300 ppm during the period seven to ten thousand years ago, though others have argued that these findings more likely reflect calibration or contamination problems rather than actual CO_2 variability. Because of the way air is trapped in ice (pores in the ice close off slowly to form bubbles deep within the firn) and the time period represented in each ice sample analyzed, these figures represent averages of atmospheric concentrations of up to a few centuries rather than annual or decadal levels.

Changes Since the Industrial Revolution

Since the beginning of the Industrial Revolution, the concentrations of most of the greenhouse gases have increased. For example, the mole fraction of carbon dioxide has increased from 280 ppm to 400 ppm, or 120 ppm over modern pre-industrial levels. The first 30 ppm increase took place in about 200 years, from the start of the Industrial Revolution to 1958; however the next 90 ppm increase took place within 56 years, from 1958 to 2014.

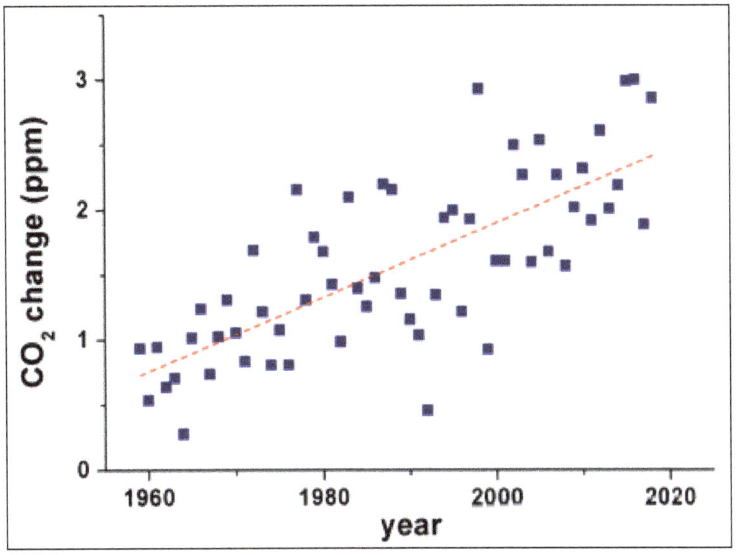

Recent year-to-year increase of atmospheric CO_2.

Recent data also shows that the concentration is increasing at a higher rate. In the 1960s, the average annual increase was only 37% of what it was in 2000 through 2007.

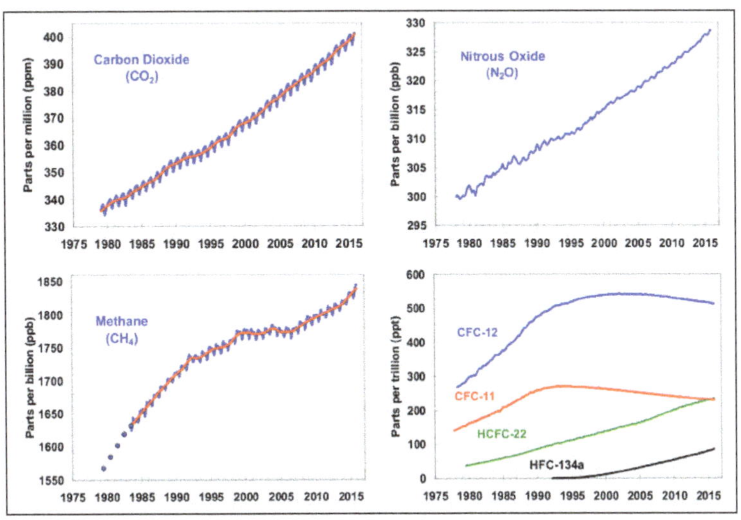

Major greenhouse gas trends.

Total cumulative emissions from 1870 to 2017 were 425±20 GtC (1539 $GtCO_2$) from fossil fuels and industry, and 180±60 GtC (660 $GtCO_2$) from land use change. Land-use change, such as deforestation, caused about 31% of cumulative emissions over 1870–2017, coal 32%, oil 25%, and gas 10%.

Today, the stock of carbon in the atmosphere increases by more than 3 million tonnes per annum (0.04%) compared with the existing stock. This increase is the result of human activities by burning fossil fuels, deforestation and forest degradation in tropical and boreal regions.

The other greenhouse gases produced from human activity show similar increases in both amount and rate of increase. Many observations are available online in a variety of Atmospheric Chemistry Observational Databases.

Anthropogenic Greenhouse Gases

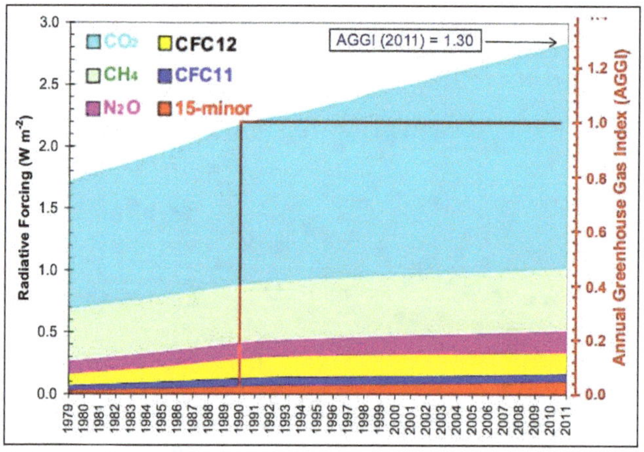

This graph shows changes in the annual greenhouse gas index (AGGI) between 1979 and 2011. The AGGI measures the levels of greenhouse gases in the atmosphere based on their ability to cause changes in Earth's climate.

Since about 1750 human activity has increased the concentration of carbon dioxide and other greenhouse gases. Measured atmospheric concentrations of carbon dioxide are currently 100 ppm higher than pre-industrial levels. Natural sources of carbon dioxide are more than 20 times greater than sources due to human activity, but over periods longer than a few years natural sources are closely balanced by natural sinks, mainly photosynthesis of carbon compounds by plants and marine plankton. As a result of this balance, the atmospheric mole fraction of carbon dioxide remained between 260 and 280 parts per million for the 10,000 years between the end of the last glacial maximum and the start of the industrial era.

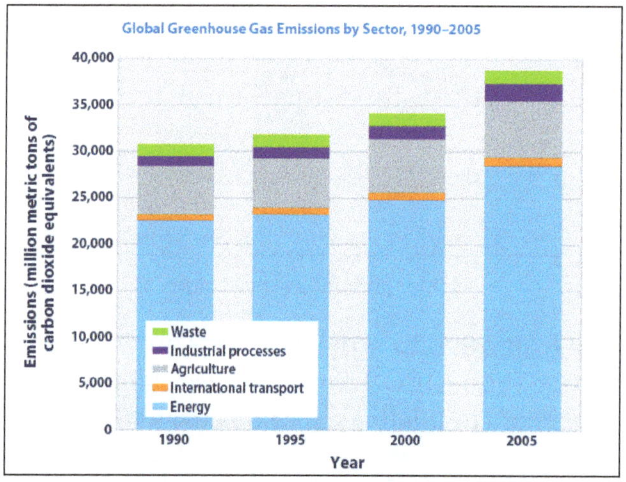

This bar graph shows global greenhouse gas emissions by sector from 1990 to 2005, measured in carbon dioxide equivalents.

It is likely that anthropogenic (i.e., human-induced) warming, such as that due to elevated greenhouse gas levels, has had a discernible influence on many physical and biological systems. Future warming is projected to have a range of impacts, including sea level rise, increased frequencies and severities of some extreme weather events, loss of biodiversity, and regional changes in agricultural productivity.

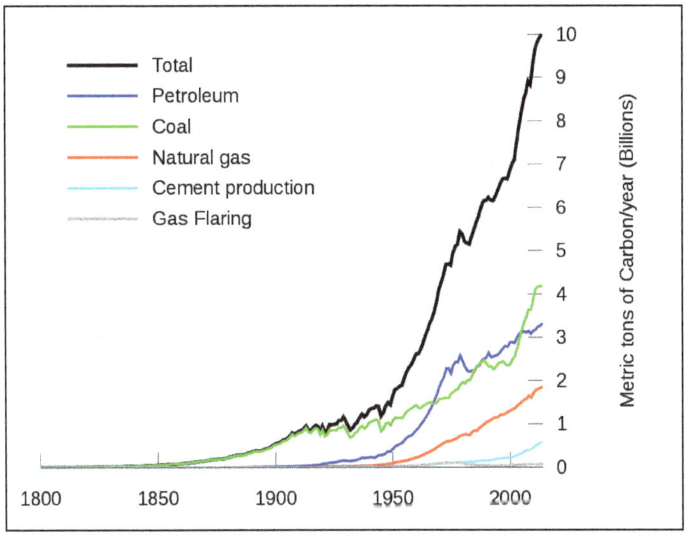

Modern global CO_2 emissions from the burning of fossil fuels.

The main sources of greenhouse gases due to human activity are:

- Burning of fossil fuels and deforestation leading to higher carbon dioxide concentrations in the air. Land use change (mainly deforestation in the tropics) account for up to one third of total anthropogenic CO_2 emissions.
- Livestock enteric fermentation and manure management, paddy rice farming, land use and wetland changes, man-made lakes, pipeline losses, and covered vented landfill emissions leading to higher methane atmospheric concentrations. Many of the newer style fully vented septic systems that enhance and target the fermentation process also are sources of atmospheric methane.
- Use of chlorofluorocarbons (CFCs) in refrigeration systems, and use of CFCs and halons in fire suppression systems and manufacturing processes.
- Agricultural activities, including the use of fertilizers, that lead to higher nitrous oxide (N_2O) concentrations.

Table: The seven sources of CO_2 from fossil fuel combustion are (with percentage contributions for 2000–2004).

Seven main fossil fuel combustion sources	Contribution (%)
Liquid fuels (e.g., gasoline, fuel oil)	36%
Solid fuels (e.g., coal)	35%
Gaseous fuels (e.g., natural gas)	20%
Cement production	3 %
Flaring gas industrially and at wells	< 1%
Non-fuel hydrocarbons	< 1%
"International bunker fuels" of transport not included in national inventories	4 %

Carbon dioxide, methane, nitrous oxide (N_2O) and three groups of fluorinated gases (sulfur hexafluoride (SF_6), hydrofluorocarbons (HFCs), and perfluorocarbons (PFCs)) are the major anthropogenic greenhouse gases, and are regulated under the Kyoto Protocol international treaty, which came into force in 2005. Emissions limitations specified in the Kyoto Protocol expired in 2012. The Cancún agreement, agreed on in 2010, includes voluntary pledges made by 76 countries to control emissions. At the time of the agreement, these 76 countries were collectively responsible for 85% of annual global emissions.

Although CFCs are greenhouse gases, they are regulated by the Montreal Protocol, which was motivated by CFCs' contribution to ozone depletion rather than by their contribution to global warming. Note that ozone depletion has only a minor role in greenhouse warming, though the two processes often are confused in the media. On 15 October 2016, negotiators from over 170 nations meeting at the summit of the United Nations Environment Programme reached a legally binding accord to phase out hydrofluorocarbons (HFCs) in an amendment to the Montreal Protocol.

Greenhouse Gases Emissions Per Sector

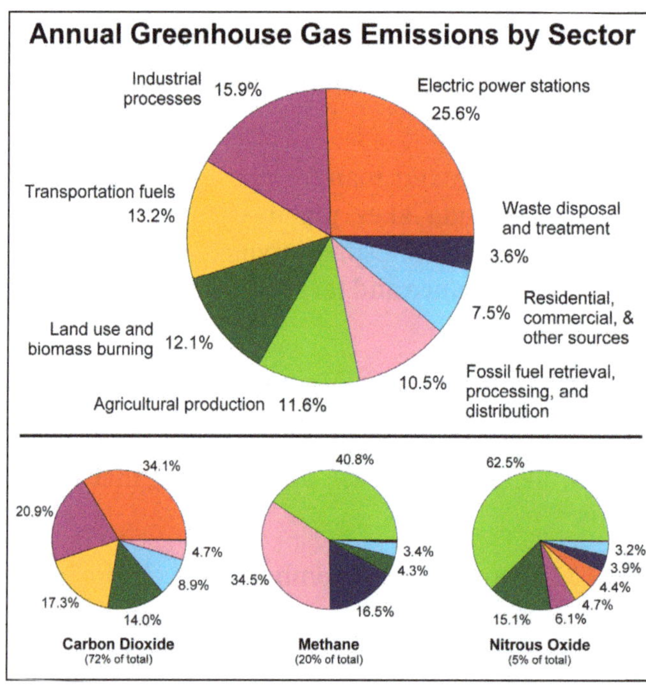

This figure shows the relative fraction of anthropogenic greenhouse gases coming from each of eight categories of sources, as estimated by the Emission Database for Global Atmospheric Research version 4.2, fast track 2010 project. These values are intended to provide a snapshot of global annual greenhouse gas emissions in the year 2010. The top panel shows the sum over all anthropogenic greenhouse gases, weighted by their global warming potential over the next 100 years. This consists of 72% carbon dioxide, 20% methane, 5% nitrous oxide and 3% other gases. Lower panels show the comparable information for each of these three primary greenhouse gases, with the same coloring of sectors as used in the top chart. Segments with less than 1% fraction are not labeled.

Tourism

According to UNEP global tourism is closely linked to climate change. Tourism is a significant contributor to the increasing concentrations of greenhouse gases in the atmosphere. Tourism accounts for about 50% of traffic movements. Rapidly expanding air traffic contributes about 2.5% of the production of CO_2. The number of international travelers is expected to increase from 594 million in 1996 to 1.6 billion by 2020, adding greatly to the problem unless steps are taken to reduce emissions.

Trucking and Haulage

The trucking and haulage industry plays a part in production of CO_2, contributing around 20% of the UK's total carbon emissions a year, with only the energy industry having a larger impact at around 39%. Average carbon emissions within the haulage industry are falling—in the thirty year period from 1977 to 2007, the carbon emissions associated with a 200-mile journey fell by 21 percent; NOx emissions are also down 87 percent, whereas journey times have fallen by around a third. Due to their size, HGVs often receive criticism regarding their CO_2 emissions; however, rapid development in engine technology and fuel management is having a largely positive effect.

Plastic

Plastic is produced mainly from Fossil fuels. Plastic manufacturing is estimated to use 8 percent of yearly global oil production. The EPA estimates as many as five ounces of carbon dioxide are emitted for each ounce of polyethylene terephthalate (PET) produced—the type of plastic most commonly used for beverage bottles, the transportation produce greenhouse gases also. Plastic waste emits carbon dioxide when it degrades. In 2018 research claimed that some of the most common plastics in the environment release the greenhouse gases methane and ethylene when exposed to sunlight in an amount that can affect the earth climate.

From the other side, if it is placed in a landfill, it becomes a carbon sink although biodegradable plastics have caused methane emissions. Due to the lightness of plastic versus glass or metal, plastic may reduce energy consumption. For example, packaging beverages in PET plastic rather than glass or metal is estimated to save 52% in transportation energy, if the glass or metal package is single use, of course.

In 2019 a new report "Plastic and Climate" was published. According to the report plastic will contribute greenhouse gases in the equivalent of 850 million tons of carbon dioxide (CO_2) to the atmosphere in 2019. In current trend, annual emissions will grow to 1.34 billion tons by 2030. By 2050 plastic could emit 56 billion tons of Greenhouse gas emissions, as much as 14 percent of the Earth's remaining carbon budget. The report says that only solutions which involve a reduction in consumption can solve the problem, while others like biodegradable plastic, ocean cleanup, using renewable energy in plastic industry can do little, and in some cases may even worsen it.

Role of Water Vapor

Water vapor accounts for the largest percentage of the greenhouse effect, between 36% and 66% for clear sky conditions and between 66% and 85% when including clouds. Water vapor concentrations fluctuate regionally, but human activity does not directly affect water vapor concentrations except at local scales, such as near irrigated fields. Indirectly, human activity that increases global temperatures will increase water vapor concentrations, a process known as water vapor feedback. The atmospheric concentration of vapor is highly variable and depends largely on temperature, from less than 0.01% in extremely cold regions up to 3% by mass in saturated air at about 32 °C.

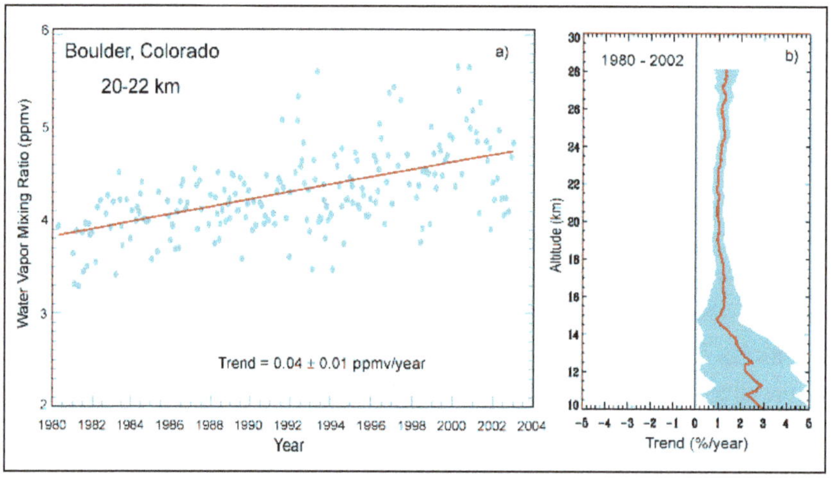

Increasing water vapor in the stratosphere at Boulder, Colorado.

The average residence time of a water molecule in the atmosphere is only about nine days, compared to years or centuries for other greenhouse gases such as CH_4 and CO_2. Thus, water vapor responds to and amplifies effects of the other greenhouse gases. The Clausius–Clapeyron relation establishes that more water vapor will be present per unit volume at elevated temperatures. This and other basic principles indicate that warming associated with increased concentrations of the other greenhouse gases also will increase the concentration of water vapor (assuming that the relative humidity remains approximately constant; modeling and observational studies find that this is indeed so). Because water vapor is a greenhouse gas, this results in further warming and so is a "positive feedback" that amplifies the original warming. Eventually other earth processes offset these positive feedbacks, stabilizing the global temperature at a new equilibrium and preventing the loss of Earth's water through a Venus-like runaway greenhouse effect.

Direct Greenhouse Gas Emissions

Between the period 1970 to 2004, greenhouse gas emissions (measured in CO_2-equivalent) increased at an average rate of 1.6% per year, with CO_2 emissions from the use of fossil fuels growing at a rate of 1.9% per year. Total anthropogenic emissions at the end of 2009 were estimated at 49.5 gigatonnes CO_2-equivalent. These emissions include CO_2 from fossil fuel use and from land use, as well as emissions of methane, nitrous oxide and other greenhouse gases covered by the Kyoto Protocol.

At present, the primary source of CO_2 emissions is the burning of coal, natural gas, and petroleum for electricity and heat.

Regional and National Attribution of Emissions

According to the Environmental Protection Agency (EPA), GHG emissions in the United States can be traced from different sectors.

There are several different ways of measuring greenhouse gas emissions, for example. Some variables that have been reported include:

- Definition of measurement boundaries: Emissions can be attributed geographically, to the area where they were emitted (the territory principle) or by the activity principle to the territory produced the emissions. These two principles result in different totals when measuring, for example, electricity importation from one country to another, or emissions at an international airport.
- Time horizon of different gases: Contribution of a given greenhouse gas is reported as a CO_2 equivalent. The calculation to determine this takes into account how long that gas remains in the atmosphere. This is not always known accurately and calculations must be regularly updated to reflect new information.
- What sectors are included in the calculation (e.g., energy industries, industrial processes, agriculture etc.): There is often a conflict between transparency and availability of data.
- The measurement protocol itself: This may be via direct measurement or estimation. The four main methods are the emission factor-based method, mass balance method, predictive emissions monitoring systems, and continuous emissions monitoring systems. These methods differ in accuracy, cost, and usability.

These different measures are sometimes used by different countries to assert various policy/ethical positions on climate change. The use of different measures leads to a lack of comparability, which is problematic when monitoring progress towards targets. There are arguments for the adoption of a common measurement tool, or at least the development of communication between different tools.

Emissions may be measured over long time periods. This measurement type is called historical or cumulative emissions. Cumulative emissions give some indication of who is responsible for the build-up in the atmospheric concentration of greenhouse gases.

The national accounts balance would be positively related to carbon emissions. The national accounts balance shows the difference between exports and imports. For many richer nations, such as the United States, the accounts balance is negative because more goods are imported than they are exported. This is mostly due to the fact that it is cheaper to produce goods outside of developed countries, leading the economies of developed countries to become increasingly dependent on services and not goods. We believed that a positive accounts balance would means that more production was occurring in a country, so more factories working would increase carbon emission levels.

Emissions may also be measured across shorter time periods. Emissions changes may, for example, be measured against a base year of 1990. 1990 was used in the United Nations Framework Convention on Climate Change (UNFCCC) as the base year for emissions, and is also used in the Kyoto Protocol (some gases are also measured from the year 1995). A country's emissions may also be reported as a proportion of global emissions for a particular year.

Another measurement is of per capita emissions. This divides a country's total annual emissions by its mid-year population.Per capita emissions may be based on historical or annual emissions.

While cities are sometimes considered to be disproportionate contributors to emissions, per-capita emissions tend to be lower for cities than the averages in their countries.

From Land-use Change

Land-use change, e.g., the clearing of forests for agricultural use, can affect the concentration of greenhouse gases in the atmosphere by altering how much carbon flows out of the atmosphere into carbon sinks. Accounting for land-use change can be understood as an attempt to measure "net" emissions, i.e., gross emissions from all sources minus the removal of emissions from the atmosphere by carbon sinks.

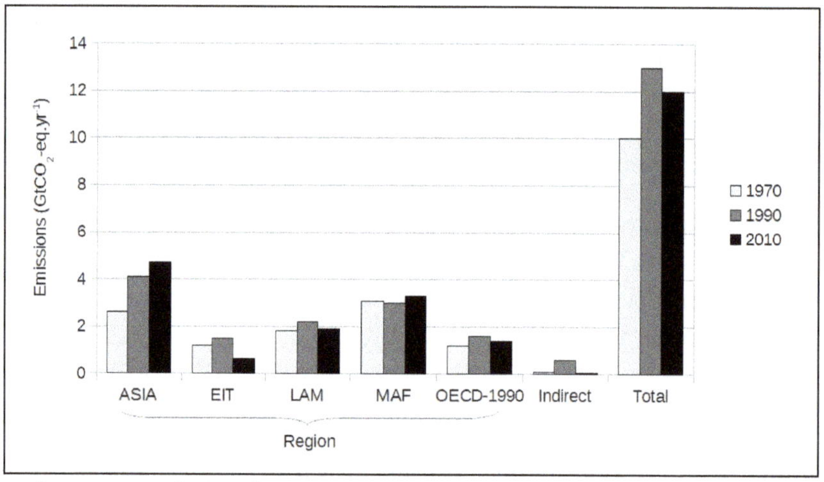

Greenhouse gas emissions from agriculture, forestry and other land use, 1970–2010.

There are substantial uncertainties in the measurement of net carbon emissions. Additionally, there is controversy over how carbon sinks should be allocated between different regions and over time. For instance, concentrating on more recent changes in carbon sinks is likely to favour those regions that have deforested earlier, e.g., Europe.

Greenhouse Gas Intensity

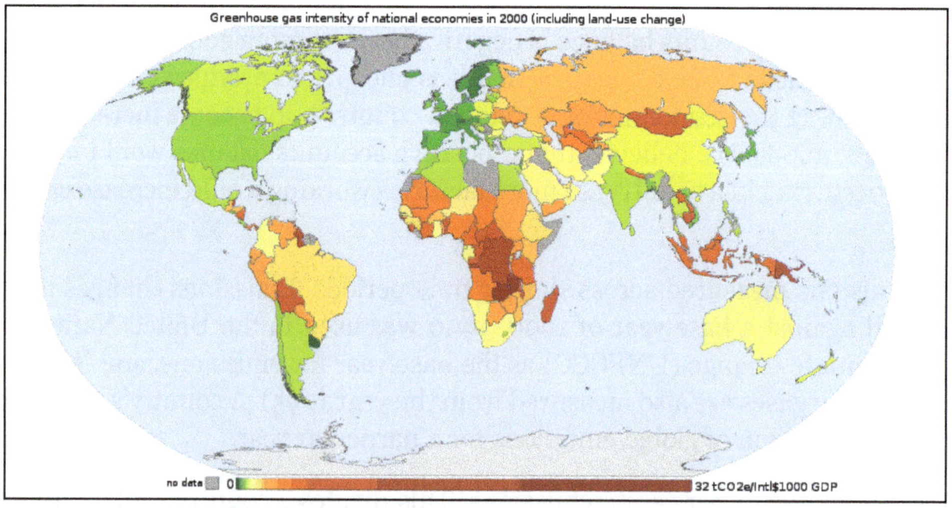

Greenhouse gas intensity in the year 2000, including land-use change.

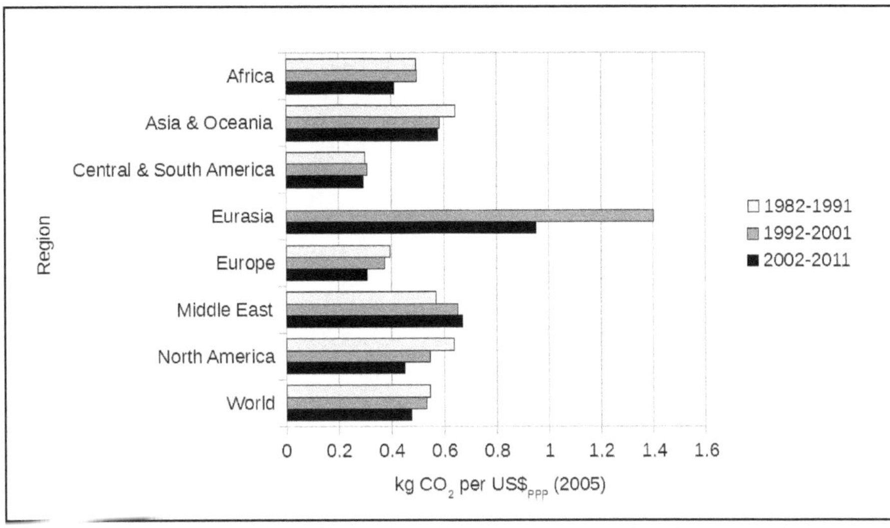

Carbon intensity of GDP (using PPP) for different regions, 1982–2011.

Greenhouse gas intensity is a ratio between greenhouse gas emissions and another metric, e.g., gross domestic product (GDP) or energy use. The terms "carbon intensity" and "emissions intensity" are also sometimes used. Emission intensities may be calculated using market exchange rates (MER) or purchasing power parity (PPP). Calculations based on MER show large differences in intensities between developed and developing countries, whereas calculations based on PPP show smaller differences.

Cumulative and Historical Emissions

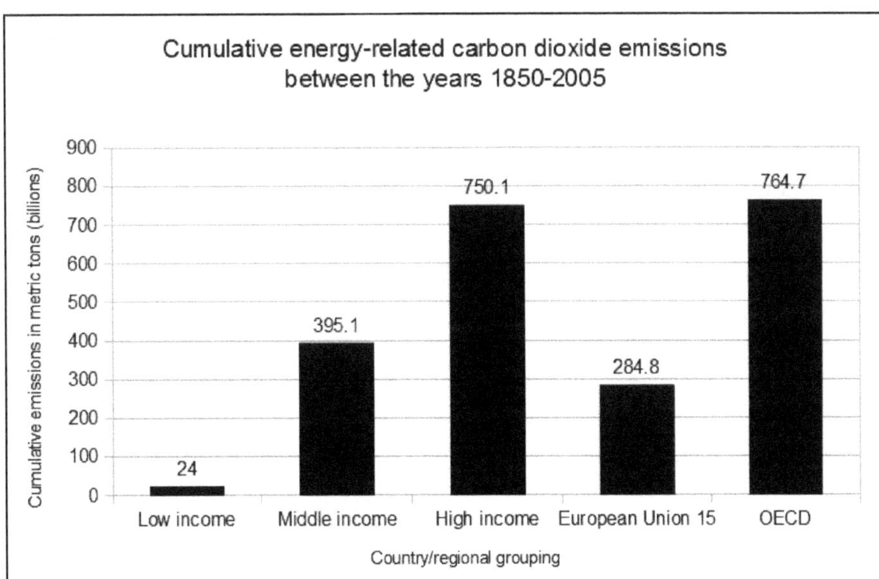

Cumulative energy-related CO_2 emissions between the years 1850–2005 grouped into low-income, middle-income, high-income, the EU-15, and the OECD countries.

Cumulative anthropogenic (i.e., human-emitted) emissions of CO_2 from fossil fuel use are a major cause of global warming, and give some indication of which countries have contributed most to human-induced climate change.

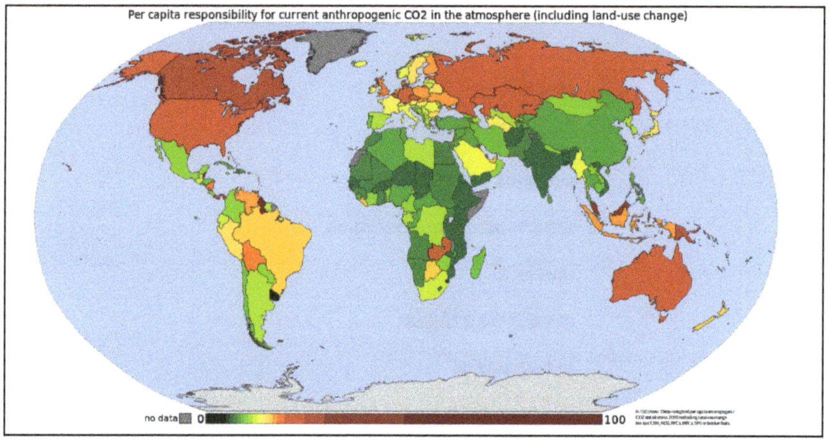

Map of cumulative per capita anthropogenic atmospheric CO2 emissions by country. Cumulative emissions include land use change, and are measured between the years 1950 and 2000.

Top-5 historic CO_2 contributors by region over the years 1800 to 1988 (in %)		
Region	Industrial CO_2	Total CO_2
OECD North America	33.2	29.7
OECD Europe	26.1	16.6
Former USSR	14.1	12.5
China	5.5	6.0
Eastern Europe	5.5	4.8

The table is based on Banuri *et al.* Overall, developed countries accounted for 83.8% of industrial CO_2 emissions over this time period, and 67.8% of total CO_2 emissions. Developing countries accounted for industrial CO_2 emissions of 16.2% over this time period, and 32.2% of total CO_2 emissions. The estimate of total CO_2 emissions includes biotic carbon emissions, mainly from deforestation. Banuri *et al.* calculated per capita cumulative emissions based on then-current population. The ratio in per capita emissions between industrialized countries and developing countries was estimated at more than 10 to 1.

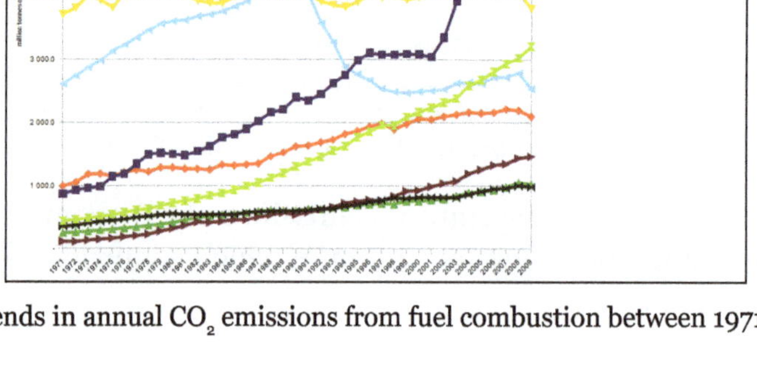

Regional trends in annual CO_2 emissions from fuel combustion between 1971 and 2009.

Including biotic emissions brings about the same controversy mentioned earlier regarding carbon sinks and land-use change. The actual calculation of net emissions is very complex, and is affected by how carbon sinks are allocated between regions and the dynamics of the climate system.

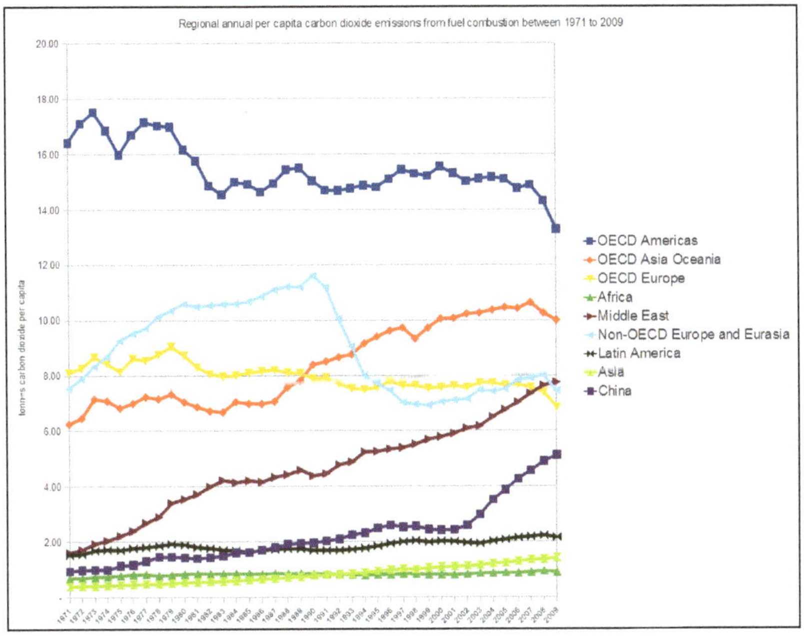

Regional trends in annual per capita CO_2 emissions from fuel combustion between 1971 and 2009.

Non-OECD countries accounted for 42% of cumulative energy-related CO_2 emissions between 1890 and 2007. Over this time period, the US accounted for 28% of emissions; the EU, 23%; Russia, 11%; China, 9%; other OECD countries, 5%; Japan, 4%; India, 3%; and the rest of the world, 18%.

Changes Since a Particular Base Year

Between 1970 and 2004, global growth in annual CO_2 emissions was driven by North America, Asia, and the Middle East. The sharp acceleration in CO_2 emissions since 2000 to more than a 3% increase per year (more than 2 ppm per year) from 1.1% per year during the 1990s is attributable to the lapse of formerly declining trends in carbon intensity of both developing and developed nations. China was responsible for most of global growth in emissions during this period. Localised plummeting emissions associated with the collapse of the Soviet Union have been followed by slow emissions growth in this region due to more efficient energy use, made necessary by the increasing proportion of it that is exported. In comparison, methane has not increased appreciably, and N_2O by 0.25% y^{-1}.

Using different base years for measuring emissions has an effect on estimates of national contributions to global warming. This can be calculated by dividing a country's highest contribution to global warming starting from a particular base year, by that country's minimum contribution to global warming starting from a particular base year. Choosing between different base years of 1750, 1900, 1950, and 1990 has a significant effect for most countries. Within the G8 group of countries, it is most significant for the UK, France and Germany. These countries have a long history of CO_2 emissions.

Annual Emissions

Annual per capita emissions in the industrialized countries are typically as much as ten times the average in developing countries. Due to China's fast economic development, its annual per capita emissions are quickly approaching the levels of those in the Annex I group of the Kyoto Protocol (i.e., the developed countries excluding the US). Other countries with fast growing emissions are South Korea, Iran, and Australia (which apart from the oil rich Persian Gulf states, now has the highest percapita emission rate in the world). On the other hand, annual per capita emissions of the EU-15 and the US are gradually decreasing over time. Emissions in Russia and Ukraine have decreased fastest since 1990 due to economic restructuring in these countries.

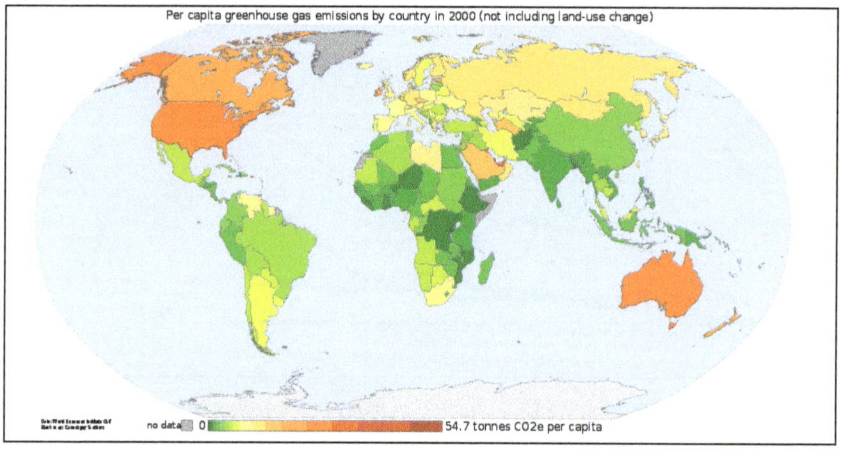

Per capita anthropogenic greenhouse gas emissions by country for the year 2000 including land-use change.

Energy statistics for fast growing economies are less accurate than those for the industrialized countries. For China's annual emissions in 2008, the Netherlands Environmental Assessment Agency estimated an uncertainty range of about 10%. The greenhouse gas footprint refers to the emissions resulting from the creation of products or services. It is more comprehensive than the commonly used carbon footprint, which measures only carbon dioxide, one of many greenhouse gases and 2015 was the first year to see both total global economic growth and a reduction of carbon emissions.

Top Emitter Countries

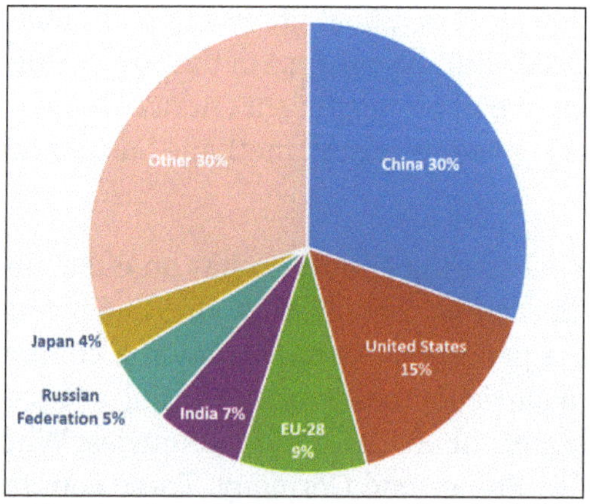

Global carbon dioxide emissions by country.

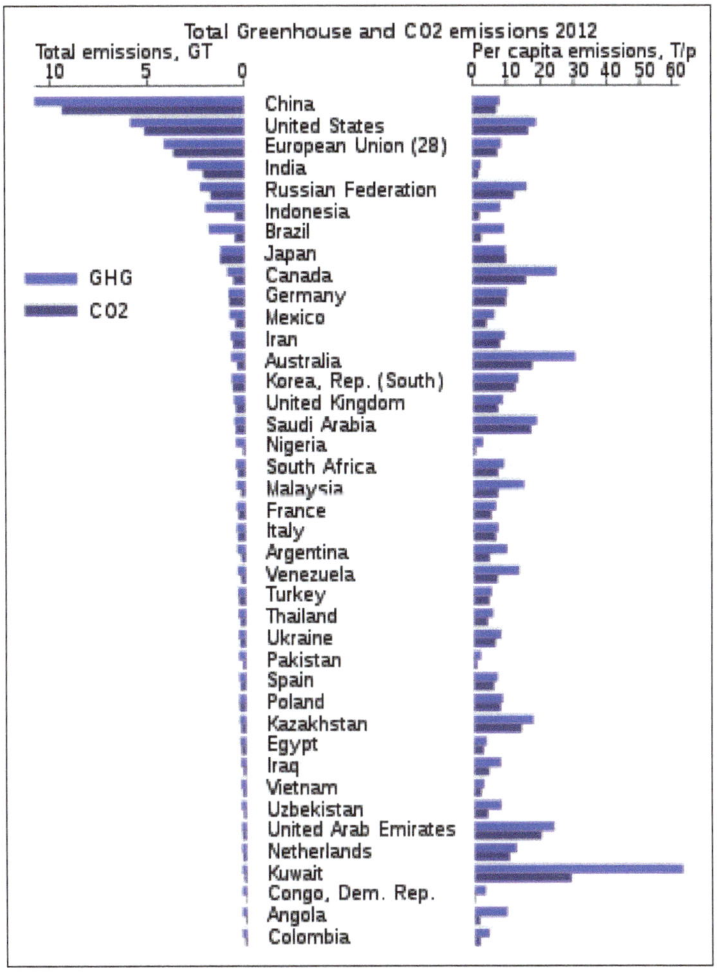

The top 40 countries emitting all greenhouse gases, showing both that derived from all sources including land clearance and forestry and also the CO_2 component excluding those sources. Per capita figures are included.

Annual

In 2009, the annual top ten emitting countries accounted for about two-thirds of the world's annual energy-related CO_2 emissions.

Top-10 annual energy-related CO_2 emitters for the year 2009		
Country	% of global total annual emissions	Tonnes of GHG per capita
China	23.6	5.1
United States	17.9	16.9
India	5.5	1.4
Russia	5.3	10.8
Japan	3.8	8.6
Germany	2.6	9.2
Iran	1.8	7.3

Canada	1.8	15.4
South Korea	1.8	10.6
United Kingdom	1.6	7.5

Cumulative

Table: Top-10 cumulative energy-related CO_2 emitters between 1850 and 2008.

Country	% of world total	Metric tonnes CO_2 per person
United States	28.5	1,132.7
China	9.36	85.4
Russia	7.95	677.2
Germany	6.78	998.9
United Kingdom	5.73	1,127.8
Japan	3.88	367
France	2.73	514.9
India	2.52	26.7
Canada	2.17	789.2
Ukraine	2.13	556.4

Embedded Emissions

One way of attributing greenhouse gas (GHG) emissions is to measure the embedded emissions (also referred to as "embodied emissions") of goods that are being consumed. Emissions are usually measured according to production, rather than consumption. For example, in the main international treaty on climate change (the UNFCCC), countries report on emissions produced within their borders, e.g., the emissions produced from burning fossil fuels. Under a production-based accounting of emissions, embedded emissions on imported goods are attributed to the exporting, rather than the importing, country. Under a consumption-based accounting of emissions, embedded emissions on imported goods are attributed to the importing country, rather than the exporting, country.

Davis and Caldeira found that a substantial proportion of CO_2 emissions are traded internationally. The net effect of trade was to export emissions from China and other emerging markets to consumers in the US, Japan, and Western Europe. Based on annual emissions data from the year 2004, and on a per-capita consumption basis, the top-5 emitting countries were found to be (in CO_2 per person, per year): Luxembourg (34.7), the US (22.0), Singapore (20.2), Australia (16.7), and Canada (16.6). Carbon Trust research revealed that approximately 25% of all CO_2 emissions from human activities 'flow' (i.e., are imported or exported) from one country to another. Major developed economies were found to be typically net importers of embodied carbon emissions—with UK consumption emissions 34% higher than production emissions, and Germany (29%), Japan (19%) and the US (13%) also significant net importers of embodied emissions.

Effect of Policy

Governments have taken action to reduce greenhouse gas emissions (climate change mitigation). Assessments of policy effectiveness have included work by the Intergovernmental Panel on Climate Change, International Energy Agency, and United Nations Environment Programme. Policies implemented by governments have included national and regional targets to reduce emissions, promoting energy efficiency, and support for renewable energy such as Solar energy as an effective use of renewable energy because solar uses energy from the sun and does not release pollutants into the air.

Countries and regions listed in Annex I of the United Nations Framework Convention on Climate Change (UNFCCC) (i.e., the OECD and former planned economies of the Soviet Union) are required to submit periodic assessments to the UNFCCC of actions they are taking to address climate change. Analysis by the UNFCCC suggested that policies and measures undertaken by Annex I Parties may have produced emission savings of 1.5 thousand Tg CO_2-eq in the year 2010, with most savings made in the energy sector. The projected emissions saving of 1.5 thousand Tg CO_2-eq is measured against a hypothetical "baseline" of Annex I emissions, i.e., projected Annex I emissions in the absence of policies and measures. The total projected Annex I saving of 1.5 thousand CO_2-eq does not include emissions savings in seven of the Annex I Parties.

Projections

A wide range of projections of future emissions have been produced. Rogner *et al.* assessed the scientific literature on greenhouse gas projections. Rogner *et al.* concluded that unless energy policies changed substantially, the world would continue to depend on fossil fuels until 2025–2030. Projections suggest that more than 80% of the world's energy will come from fossil fuels. This conclusion was based on "much evidence" and "high agreement" in the literature. Projected annual energy-related CO_2 emissions in 2030 were 40–110% higher than in 2000, with two-thirds of the increase originating in developing countries. Projected annual per capita emissions in developed country regions remained substantially lower (2.8–5.1 tonnes CO_2) than those in developed country regions (9.6–15.1 tonnes CO_2). Projections consistently showed increase in annual world emissions of "Kyoto" gases, measured in CO_2-equivalent) of 25–90% by 2030, compared to 2000.

Relative CO_2 Emission from Various Fuels

One liter of gasoline, when used as a fuel, produces 2.32 kg (about 1300 liters or 1.3 cubic meters) of carbon dioxide, a greenhouse gas. One US gallon produces 19.4 lb (1,291.5 gallons or 172.65 cubic feet).

Table: Mass of carbon dioxide emitted per quantity of energy for various fuels.

Fuel name	CO_2 emitted (lbs/10^6 Btu)	CO_2 emitted (g/MJ)	CO_2 emitted (g/kWh)
Natural gas	117	50.30	181.08
Liquefied petroleum gas	139	59.76	215.14
Propane	139	59.76	215.14
Aviation gasoline	153	65.78	236.81
Automobile gasoline	156	67.07	241.45

Fuel name	CO_2 emitted (lbs/10^6 Btu)	CO_2 emitted (g/MJ)	CO_2 emitted (g/kWh)
Kerosene	159	68.36	246.10
Fuel oil	161	69.22	249.19
Tires/tire derived fuel	189	81.26	292.54
Wood and wood waste	195	83.83	301.79
Coal (bituminous)	205	88.13	317.27
Coal (sub-bituminous)	213	91.57	329.65
Coal (lignite)	215	92.43	332.75
Petroleum coke	225	96.73	348.23
Tar-sand Bitumen			
Coal (anthracite)	227	97.59	351.32

Life-cycle Greenhouse-gas Emissions of Energy Sources

A 2011 IPCC report included a literature review of numerous energy sources' total life cycle CO_2 emissions. Below are the CO_2 emission values that fell at the 50th percentile of all studies surveyed.

Table: Lifecycle greenhouse gas emissions by electricity source.

Technology	Description	50th percentile (g CO_2/kWh$_e$)
Hydroelectric	Reservoir	4
Ocean Energy	Wave and tidal	8
Wind	Onshore	12
Nuclear	Various generation II reactor types	16
Biomass	Various	18
Solar thermal	Parabolic trough	22
Geothermal	Hot dry rock	45
Solar PV	Polycrystalline silicon	46
Natural gas	Various combined cycle turbines without scrubbing	469
Coal	Various generator types without scrubbing	1001

Removal from the Atmosphere

Natural Processes

Greenhouse gases can be removed from the atmosphere by various processes, as a consequence of:

- A physical change (condensation and precipitation remove water vapor from the atmosphere).
- A chemical reaction within the atmosphere. For example, methane is oxidized by reaction with naturally occurring hydroxyl radical, OH· and degraded to CO_2 and water vapor (CO_2 from the oxidation of methane is not included in the methane Global warming potential).

Other chemical reactions include solution and solid phase chemistry occurring in atmospheric aerosols.

- A physical exchange between the atmosphere and the other compartments of the planet. An example is the mixing of atmospheric gases into the oceans.
- A chemical change at the interface between the atmosphere and the other compartments of the planet. This is the case for CO_2, which is reduced by photosynthesis of plants, and which, after dissolving in the oceans, reacts to form carbonic acid and bicarbonate and carbonate ions.
- A photochemical change. Halocarbons are dissociated by UV light releasing Cl· and F· as free radicals in the stratosphere with harmful effects on ozone (halocarbons are generally too stable to disappear by chemical reaction in the atmosphere).

Negative Emissions

A number of technologies remove greenhouse gases emissions from the atmosphere. Most widely analysed are those that remove carbon dioxide from the atmosphere, either to geologic formations such as bio-energy with carbon capture and storage and carbon dioxide air capture, or to the soil as in the case with biochar. The IPCC has pointed out that many long-term climate scenario models require large-scale manmade negative emissions to avoid serious climate change.

Scientific Research

In the late 19th century scientists experimentally discovered that N_2 and O_2 do not absorb infrared radiation (called, at that time, "dark radiation"), while water (both as true vapor and condensed in the form of microscopic droplets suspended in clouds) and CO_2 and other poly-atomic gaseous molecules do absorb infrared radiation. In the early 20th century researchers realized that greenhouse gases in the atmosphere made Earth's overall temperature higher than it would be without them. During the late 20th century, a scientific consensus evolved that increasing concentrations of greenhouse gases in the atmosphere cause a substantial rise in global temperatures and changes to other parts of the climate system, with consequences for the environment and for human health.

FORCED MIGRATION

Forced displacement or forced immigration is the coerced movement of a person or people away from their home or home region and it often connotes violent coercion. Someone who has experienced forced displacement is a "forced immigrant", a "displaced person" (DP), rarely also a "displacee", or if it is within the same country, an internally displaced person (IDP). In some cases the forced immigrant can also become a refugee, as that term has a specific legal definition. A specific form of forced displacement is population transfer, which is a coherent policy to move unwanted groups, for example, as an attempt at ethnic cleansing. Another form is deportation.

Deportees to Siberia by Kazimierz Alchimowicz, National Museum in Warsaw, illustrating the torment of Polish Siberian deportees, patriots from the Russian zone of partitioned Poland in the period following the collapse of the January Uprising.

General deportation currents of the dekulakization 1930–1931.

Forced displacement has accompanied persecution, as well as war, throughout human history but has only become a topic of serious study and discussion relatively recently. This increased attention is the result of greater ease of travel, allowing displaced people to flee to nations far removed from their homes, the creation of an international legal structure of human rights, and the realizations that the destabilizing effects of forced immigration, especially in parts of Africa, the Middle East, south and central Asia, ripple out well beyond the immediate region.

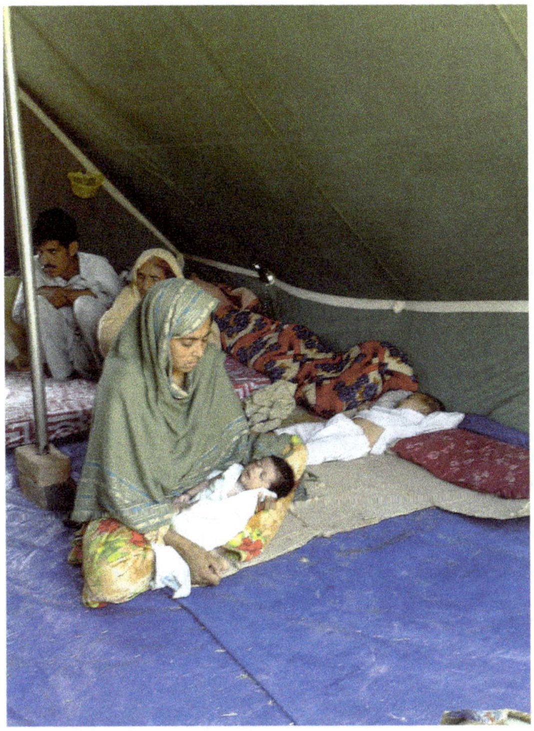

The Amam refugee camp is named after its first native is born in 2009.
Its name, Amam, means peace

The concept of forced displacement envelopes demographic movements like flight, evacuation, displacement, and resettlement. The International Organization for Migration defines a forced migrant as any person who migrates to "escape persecution, conflict, repression, natural and human-made disasters, ecological degradation, or other situations that endanger their lives, freedom or livelihood".

The International Association for the Study of Forced Migration (IASFM) defines it as "the movements of refugees and internally displaced people (those displaced by conflicts) as well as people displaced by natural or environmental disasters, chemical or nuclear disasters, famine, or development projects."

According to Alden Speare, "in the strictest sense migration can be considered to be involuntary only when a person is physically transported from a country and has no opportunity to escape from those transporting him." Movement under threat, even the immediate threat to life, contains a voluntary element, as long as there is an option to escape to another part of the country, go into hiding or to remain and hope to avoid persecution." However this thought has been questioned, especially by Marxians, who argue that in most cases migrants have little or no choice.

Causes

Causes for forced displacement can include:

- Natural disaster: Occurrence of a disaster – such as floods, tsunamis, landslides, earthquakes or volcanoes – leads to temporary or permanent displacement of population from that area. In such a scenario, migration becomes more of a survival strategy, as natural disasters often cause the loss of money, homes, and jobs. For example, Hurricane Katrina resulted in displacement of almost the entire population of New Orleans, leaving the community and government with several economic and social challenges.

- Environmental problems: The term environmental refugee has been in use recently representing people who are forced to leave their traditional habitat because of environmental factors which negatively impact their livelihood, or even environmental disruption i.e. biological, physical or chemical change in ecosystem. Migration can also occur as a result of slow-onset climate change, such as desertification or sea-level rise, of deforestation or land degradation.
- Man-made disasters: Examples are industrial accidents and especially accidents that involve chemicals or radioactivity, such as in Chernobyl, Bhopal or Fukushima.
- War, civil war, political repression or religious conflicts: Some migrants are impelled to cross national borders by war or persecution, due to political, social, ethnic, religious reasons. These immigrants may be considered refugees if they apply for asylum in the receiving country.
- Development-induced displacement: Such displacement or population transfer is the forcing of communities and individuals out of their homes, often also their homelands, for the purposes of economic development. It has been historically associated with the construction of dams for hydroelectric power and irrigation purposes but also appears due to many other activities, such as mining and transport (roads, ports, airports). The best-known recent example of such development-induced displacement may be that resulting from the construction of the Three Gorges Dam in China. This type of forced migration disproportionately affects low income earners and ethnic minorities. According to estimates, between 90 and 100 million people were forced to leave their homes due to development projects in the 1990s.
- Human trafficking and human smuggling: Migrants displaced through deception or coercion with purpose of their exploitation fall under this category. The data on such forced migration are limited since the activities involved are clandestine in nature. While migration of this nature is well covered for male migrants (working in agriculture, construction etc.), same cannot be said for their female counterparts as the market situation for them might be unscrupulous (sex work or domestic service). The International Labour Organization considers trafficking an offence against labor protection and denies them the opportunity of utilizing their resources for their country. ILO's Multilateral Framework includes principle no. 11 that recommends, "Governments should formulate and implement, in consultation with the social partners, measures to prevent abusive practices, migrant smuggling and people trafficking; they should also work towards preventing irregular labor migration.
- Slavery: History's greatest forced migration was the Middle Passage of the Atlantic slave trade during the 15th through the 19th centuries. Of the 20 million Africans captured for the trade, half died in their forced march to the African coast, and another ten to twenty percent died on slave ships carrying them from Africa to the Americas.

- Ethnic cleansing: The systematic forced removal of ethnic or religious groups from a given territory by a more powerful ethnic group, with the intent of making it ethnically homogeneous. For example, during counter-Reformation the Catholics removed of Protestants during the 16th through 19th centuries in Europe (e.g. Salzburg Protestants).

Conditions

In the majority of cases forced migration across borders takes place without the required documentation. It may even involve human smugglers and traffickers. Displaced persons are often forced to place their lives at risk, are obliged to travel in inhumane conditions and may be exposed to exploitation and abuse. The states where they seek protection may regard them as a threat to their security. Displaced persons face risks of becoming poorer than before displacement, of being financially vulnerable, and socially disintegrated. The impacts of forced displacement vary according to the displaced person's ability to recover from the shock of displacement. Individuals are displaced by conflict and then depleted of their assets upon arrival to a new country where they can also face cultural, social, and economic discontinuity.

Responses to Forced Displacement

Responses for forcibly displaced persons vary across multiple levels. Response at the global stage is done by participating international agencies (e.g. the UNHCR) and by members of international conventions. The rights and protections of the different categories of forcibly displaced persons have been addressed by, e.g., the 1951 Refugee Convention, the 1967 Protocol, the Kampala Convention, or the 1998 Guiding Principles. These protections, however, are not always respected or met.

World organizations such as the United Nations and the World Bank, as well as individual countries have also directly responded to the challenges faced by displaced people by providing humanitarian assistance or forcibly intervening in the country of conflict. The absence of neutrality and limited resources has affected the capabilities of international humanitarian action to mitigate the forces causing mass displacement. These broad forms of assistance can also not fully address the multidimensional needs of displaced persons.

Sources of action can occur at more local levels such as the individual's place of relocation. Lived in experiences of displaced persons will vary according to the state and local policies of their country of relocation. Policies reflecting national exclusion of displaced persons may be undone by inclusive urban policies. Sanctuary cities are an example of spaces that regulate their cooperation or participation with immigration law enforcement. The practice of urban membership upon residence allows displaced persons to have access to city services and benefits, regardless of their legal status. Sanctuary cities have been able to provide migrants with greater mobility and participation in activities limiting the collection of personal information, issuing identification cards to all residents, and providing access to crucial services such as health care. Access to these services can ease the hardships of displaced people by allowing them to healthily adjust to life after displacement.

Distinctions between the Terms

- The term 'Refugee Studies' denotes an academic discipline or field of study which covers the study of refugees, often their experiences in seeking refuge. There are several categories of individuals who are included in this study, with labels that include: 'Refugee'; 'expellees'; 'exile'; 'displaced person'; 'internally displaced person (IDP)'; 'economic refugees'; 'humanitarian refugee'; 'stateless person'; 'tsunami refugee'; 'development refugee'; 'environmental refugee'; 'government assisted refugee (GAR)' etc.

- The term displaced person (DP) was first widely used during World War II and the resulting refugee outflows from Eastern Europe, when it was used to specifically refer to one removed from their native country as a refugee, prisoner or a slave laborer. Most of the victims of war, political refugees and DPs of the immediate post-Second World War period were Ukrainians, Poles, other Slavs, as well as citizens of the Baltic states – Lithuanians, Latvians, and Estonians, who refused to return to Soviet-dominated eastern Europe. A.J. Jaffe claimed that the term was originally coined by Eugene M. Kulischer. The meaning has significantly broadened in the past half-century.
- If the displaced person has crossed an international border and falls under one of the relevant international legal instruments, they may become a refugee. The term "refugee" is also commonly used as a synonym for displaced person, causing confusion between the general descriptive class of anyone who has left their home and the subgroup of legally defined refugees who enjoy specified international legal protection. However, forced migrants may not apply for asylum in the country they fled to, so they may not be classed as asylum seekers or – if application would be successful – refugees. The terms refugee and asylum seeker always have a legal framework or system as context. If forced migrants do not access this legal system or it does not exist in the country they have fled to, they cannot be categorised as such.
- Forced migrants are always either IDPs or displaced people, as both of these terms do not require a legal framework and the fact that they left their homes is sufficient. The distinction between the terms displaced person and forced migrant is minor, however, the term displaced person has an important historic context (e.g. World War II).
- A displaced person who crosses an international border without permission from the country they are entering, and without applying for asylum, may be considered an illegal immigrant.
- A displaced person who left their home because of political persecution or violence, but did not cross an international border, is commonly considered to be the less well-defined category of internally displaced person (IDP), and is subject to more tenuous international protection. In 1998, the UN Commission of Human Rights published the Guiding Principles which defined internally displaced people as "persons or groups of persons who have been forced or obliged to flee or leave their homes or places of habitual residence in particular as a result of or in order to avoid the effects of armed conflict, situations of generalized violence, violations of human rights, or natural or human-made disasters and who have not crossed an internationally recognized State border." Bogumil Terminski distinguishes two general categories of internal displacement: displacement of risk (mostly conflict-induced displacement, deportations and disaster-induced displacement) and displacement of adaptation (associated with voluntary resettlement, development-induced displacement and environmentally-induced displacement).

- If the displaced person was forced out their home because of economically driven projects like that of the Three Gorges Dam in China and various Indian dams, it is called development-induced displacement. People are also often displaced due to natural or man-made disasters. Displacement can also occur as a result of slow-onset climate change, such as desertification or sea-level rise. A person who is displaced due to environmental factors which negatively impact their livelihood is generally known as an environmental migrant. Such displacement can be cross-border in nature but is frequently internal. No specific international legal instrument applies to such individuals. Foreign nations often offer disaster relief to mitigate the effects of such disaster displacement.
- Displaced person generally refers to one who is forced to migrate for reasons other than economic conditions, such as war or persecution. A migrant who fled because of economic hardship is an economic migrant.

NATURAL DISASTER

A natural disaster is a major adverse event resulting from natural processes of the Earth; examples are floods, hurricanes, tornadoes, volcanic eruptions, earthquakes, tsunamis, and other geologic processes. A natural disaster can cause loss of life or damage property, and typically leaves some economic damage in its wake, the severity of which depends on the affected population's resilience, or ability to recover and also on the infrastructure available.

Ablizzard in Maryland in 2009.

An adverse event will not rise to the level of a disaster if it occurs in an area without vulnerable population. In a vulnerable area, however, such as Nepal during the 2015 earthquake, an earthquake can have disastrous consequences and leave lasting damage, which can require years to repair.

A rope tornado in its dissipating stage, Tecumseh, Oklahoma.

A daytime wildfire in California.

Geological Disasters

Avalanches and Landslides

A landslide is described as an outward and downward slope movement of an abundance of slope-forming materials including rock, soil, artificial, or even a combination of these things.

A landslide in San Clemente, California in 1966.

During World War I, an estimated 40,000 to 80,000 soldiers died as a result of avalanches during the mountain campaign in the Alps at the Austrian-Italian front. Many of the avalanches were caused by artillery fire.

Earthquakes

An earthquake is the result of a sudden release of energy in the Earth's crust that creates seismic waves. At the Earth's surface, earthquakes manifest themselves by vibration, shaking, and sometimes displacement of the ground. Earthquakes are caused by slippage within geological faults. The underground point of origin of the earthquake is called the *seismic focus*. The point directly above the focus on the surface is called the *epicenter*. Earthquakes by themselves rarely kill people or wildlife. It is usually the secondary events that they trigger such as building collapse, fires, tsunamis (seismic sea waves) and volcanoes. Many of these could possibly be avoided by better construction, safety systems, early warning and planning.

Sinkholes

The Red Lake in Croatia.

When natural erosion, human mining or underground excavation makes the ground too weak to support the structures built on it, the ground can collapse and produce a sinkhole. For example, the 2010 Guatemala City sinkhole which killed fifteen people was caused when heavy rain from Tropical Storm Agatha, diverted by leaking pipes into a pumice bedrock, led to the sudden collapse of the ground beneath a factory building.

Volcanic Eruptions

Artist's impression of the volcanic eruptions that formed the Deccan Traps in India.

Volcanoes can cause widespread destruction and consequent disaster in several ways. The effects include the volcanic eruption itself that may cause harm following the explosion of the volcano or falling rocks. Secondly, lava may be produced during the eruption of a volcano, and so as it leaves the volcano the lava destroys many buildings, plants and animals due to its extreme heat. Thirdly, volcanic ash, generally meaning the cooled ash, may form a cloud, and settle thickly in nearby locations. When mixed with water this forms a concrete-like material. In sufficient quantities, ash may cause roofs to collapse under its weight but even small quantities will harm humans if inhaled. Since the ash has the consistency of ground glass, it causes abrasion damage to moving parts such as engines. The main killer of humans in the immediate surroundings of a volcanic eruption is the pyroclastic flows, which consist of a cloud of hot volcanic ash which builds up in the air above the volcano and rushes down the slopes when the eruption no longer supports the lifting of the gases. It is believed that Pompeii was destroyed by a pyroclastic flow. A lahar is a volcanic mudflow or landslide. The 1953 Tangiwai disaster was caused by a lahar, as was the 1985 Armero tragedy in which the town of Armero was buried and an estimated 23,000 people were killed.

Volcanoes rated at 8 (the highest level) on the Volcanic Explosivity Index are known as supervolcanoes. According to the Toba catastrophe theory, 75,000 to 80,000 years ago a supervolcanic eruption at what is now Lake Toba in Sumatra reduced the human population to 10,000 or even 1,000 breeding pairs, creating a bottleneck in human evolution, and killed three-quarters of all plant life in the northern hemisphere. However, there is considerable debate regarding the veracity of this theory. The main danger from a supervolcano is the immense cloud of ash, which has a disastrous global effect on climate and temperature for many years.

Hydrological Disasters

A violent, sudden and destructive change either in the quality of Earth's water or in the distribution or movement of water on land below the surface or in the atmosphere.

The Limpopo River during the 2000 Mozambique flood.

Floods

A flood is an overflow of water that 'submerges' land. The EU Floods Directive defines a flood as a temporary covering the land with water which is usually not covered by water. In the sense of 'flowing water', the word may also be applied to the inflow of the tides. Flooding may result from the volume of water within a body of water, such as a river or lake, which overflows, causing some of the water to escape its usual boundaries. While the size of a lake or other body of water will vary with seasonal changes in precipitation and snow melt, it is not a significant flood unless the water covers land used by man, like a village, city or other inhabited area, roads, expanses of farmland, etc.

Tsunami

A tsunami also known as a seismic sea wave or as a tidal wave, is a series of waves in a water body caused by the displacement of a large volume of water, generally in an ocean or a large lake. Tsunamis can be caused by undersea earthquakes such as the 2004 Boxing Day tsunami, or by landslides such as the one in 1958 at Lituya Bay, Alaska, or by volcanic eruptions such as the ancient eruption of Santorini. On March 11, 2011, a tsunami occurred near Fukushima, Japan and spread through the Pacific Ocean.

Limnic Eruptions

A limnic eruption occurs when a gas, usually CO_2, suddenly erupts from deep lake water, posing the threat of suffocating wildlife, livestock and humans. Such an eruption may also cause tsunamis in the lake as the rising gas displaces water. Scientists believe landslides, volcanic activity, or explosions can trigger such an eruption. To date, only two limnic eruptions have been observed and recorded. In 1984, in Cameroon, a limnic eruption in Lake Monoun caused the deaths of 37 nearby residents, and at near-by Lake Nyos in 1986 a much larger eruption killed between 1,700 and 1,800 people by asphyxiation.

Meteorological Disasters

Cyclone, tropical cyclone, hurricane, and typhoon are different names for the same phenomenon, which is a cyclonic storm system that forms over the oceans. The determining factor on which term is used is based on where they originate. In the Atlantic and Northeast Pacific, the term "hurricane" is used; in the Northwest Pacific it is referred to as a "typhoon" and "cyclones" occur in the South Pacific and Indian Ocean.

Cyclonic storms.

The deadliest hurricane ever was the 1970 Bhola cyclone; the deadliest Atlantic hurricane was the Great Hurricane of 1780 which devastated Martinique, St. Eustatius and Barbados. Another notable hurricane is Hurricane Katrina, which devastated the Gulf Coast of the United States in 2005.

Blizzards

Blizzards are severe winter storms characterized by heavy snow and strong winds. When high winds stir up snow that has already fallen, it is known as a ground blizzard. Blizzards can impact local economic activities, especially in regions where snowfall is rare. The Great Blizzard of 1888 affected the United States, when many tons of wheat crops were destroyed, and in Asia, 2008 Afghanistan blizzard and the 1972 Iran blizzard were also significant events. The 1993 Superstorm originated in the Gulf of Mexico and traveled north, causing damage in 26 states as well as Canada and leading to more than 300 deaths.

Hailstorms

Hailstorms are precipitation in the form of ice, with the ice not melting before it hits the ground. Hailstones usually measure between 0.2-inch (5 millimetres) and 6 inches (15 centimetres) in diameter. A particularly damaging hailstorm hit Munich, Germany, on July 12, 1984, causing about $2 billion in insurance claims.

Ice Storms

An ice storm is a type of winter storm characterized by freezing rain. The U.S. National Weather Service defines an ice storm as a storm which results in the accumulation of at least 0.25-inch (6.4 mm) of ice on exposed surfaces.

Cold Waves

A cold wave (known in some regions as a cold snap or cold spell) is a weather phenomenon that is distinguished by a cooling of the air. Specifically, as used by the U.S. National Weather Service, a cold wave is a rapid fall in temperature within a 24-hour period requiring substantially increased protection to agriculture, industry, commerce, and social activities. The precise criterion for a cold wave is determined by the rate at which the temperature falls, and the minimum to which it falls. This minimum temperature is dependent on the geographical region and time of year.

Heat Waves

A heat wave is a period of unusually and excessively hot weather. The worst heat wave in recent history was the European Heat Wave of 2003. A summer heat wave in Victoria, Australia, created conditions which fuelled the massive bushfires in 2009. Melbourne experienced three days in a row of temperatures exceeding 40 °C (104 °F) with some regional areas sweltering through much higher temperatures. The bushfires, collectively known as "Black Saturday", were partly the act of arsonists. The 2010 Northern Hemisphere summer resulted in severe heat waves, which killed over 2,000 people. It resulted in hundreds of wildfires which caused widespread air pollution, and burned thousands of square miles of forest.

A classic anvil-shaped, and clearly-developed Cumulonimbus incus.

Droughts

Drought is the unusual dryness of soil caused by levels of rainfall significantly below average over a prolonged period. Hot dry winds, shortage of water, high temperatures and consequent evaporation of moisture from the ground can also contribute to conditions of drought. Droughts result in crop failure and shortages of water.

Well-known historical droughts include the 1997–2009 Millennium Drought in Australia led to a water supply crisis across much of the country. As a result, many desalination plants were built for the first time. In 2011, the State of Texas lived under a drought emergency declaration for the entire calendar year and severe economic losses. The drought caused the Bastrop fires.

Thunderstorms

Severe storms, dust clouds, and volcanic eruptions can generate lightning. Apart from the damage typically associated with storms, such as winds, hail, and flooding, the lightning itself can damage buildings, ignite fires and kill by direct contact. Especially deadly lightning incidents include a 2007 strike in Ushari Dara, a remote mountain village in northwestern Pakistan, that killed 30 people, the crash of LANSA Flight 508 which killed 91 people, and a fuel explosion in Dronka, Egypt caused by lightning in 1994 which killed 469. Most lightning deaths occur in the poor countries of America and Asia, where lightning is common and adobe mud brick housing provides little protection.

A large hailstone, about 6 cm (2.4 in) in diameter.

Tornadoes

A tornado is a violent and dangerous rotating column of air that is in contact with both the surface of the Earth and a cumulonimbus cloud, or the base of a cumulus cloud in rare cases. It is also referred to as a *twister* or a *cyclone*, although the word cyclone is used in meteorology in a wider sense, to refer to any closed low pressure circulation. Tornadoes come in many shapes and sizes, but are typically in the form of a visible condensation funnel, whose narrow end touches the Earth and is often encircled by a cloud of debris and dust. Most tornadoes have wind speeds less than 110 miles per hour (177 km/h), are approximately 250 feet (80 m) across, and travel a few miles (several kilometers) before dissipating. The most extreme tornadoes can attain wind speeds of more than 300 mph (480 km/h), stretch more than two miles (3 km) across, and stay on the ground for dozens of miles (perhaps more than 100 km).

Wildfires

Wildfires are large fires which often start in wildland areas. Common causes include lightning and drought but wildfires may also be started by human negligence or arson. They can spread to populated areas and can thus be a threat to humans and property, as well as wildlife. Notable cases of wildfires were the 1871 Peshtigo Fire in the United States, which killed at least 1700 people, and the 2009 Victorian bushfires in Australia.

Space Disasters

Fallen trees caused by the Tunguska meteoroid of the Tunguska event in June 1908.

Impact Events and Airburst

Asteroids that impact the Earth have led to several major extinction events, including one which created the Chicxulub crater 64.9 million years ago and which is associated with the demise of the dinosaurs. Scientists estimate that the likelihood of death for a living human from a global impact event is comparable to the probability of death from an airliner crash.

No human death has been definitively attributed to an impact event, but the 1490 Ch'ing-yang event in which over 10,000 people may have died has been linked to a meteor shower. Even asteroids and comets that burn up in the atmosphere can cause significant destruction on the ground due to the air burst explosion: notable air bursts include the Tunguska event in June 1908, which devastated large areas of Siberian countryside, and the Chelyabinsk meteor on 15 February 2013, which caused widespread property damage in the city of Chelyabinsk and injured 1,491.

Solar Flare

A solar flare is a phenomenon where the Sun suddenly releases a great amount of solar radiation, much more than normal. Solar flares are unlikely to cause any direct injury, but can destroy electrical equipment. The potential of solar storms to cause disaster was seen during the 1859 Carrington event, which disrupted the telegraph network, and the March 1989 geomagnetic storm which blacked out Quebec. Some major known solar flares include the X20 event on August 16, 1989, and a similar flare on April 2, 2001. The most powerful flare ever recorded occurred on November 4, 2003 (estimated at between X40 and X45).

Protection by International Law

International law, for example Geneva Conventions defines International Red Cross and Red Crescent Movement the Convention on the Rights of Persons with Disabilities, requires that "States shall take, in accordance with their obligations under international law, including international humanitarian law and international human rights law, all necessary measures to ensure the protection and safety of persons with disabilities in situations of risk, including the occurrence of natural disaster." And further United Nations Office for the Coordination of Humanitarian Affairs is formed by General Assembly Resolution 44/182. People displaced due to natural disasters are currently protected under international law (Guiding Principles of International Displacement, Campala Convention of 2009).

Location

According to the UN, Asia-Pacific is the world's most disaster prone region. According to ReliefWeb, a person in Asia-Pacific is five times more likely to be hit by a natural disaster than someone living in other regions.

Disproportionate Impact on Women

Direct Impact

Due to the social, political and cultural context of many places throughout the world, women are often disproportionately affected by disaster. In settings where women and children are likely to remain at home, natural disasters, such as earthquakes, can result in greater morbidity and mortality among women. For example, during the 1993 earthquake in Maharastra, India, more women died than men as they were more likely to be in the home, due to their role as caregivers. In the 2004 Indian Ocean tsunami, more women died than men, partly due to the fact that fewer women knew how to swim.

Gender-based and Sexual Violence

During and after a natural disaster, women are at increased risk of being affected by gender based violence and are increasingly vulnerable to sexual violence. Disrupted police enforcement, lax regulations, and displacement all contribute to increased risk of gender based violence and sexual assault. As food, water, and shelter becomes scarce, women may be forced into sexual relations as a bargain for providing essential resources. Furthermore, health care during times of disaster often focuses on life saving & critical care. However, as a result, many health care workers are not adequately trained to respond to sexual violence, screen for appropriate complications and treating non-life/limb threatening emergencies. As a result, women who have been affected by sexual violence are at a significantly increased risk of sexually transmitted infections, unique physical injuries and long term psychological consequences. All of these long-term health outcomes can prevent successful reintegration into society after the disaster recovery period.

Reproductive and Sexual Health

During and after natural disasters, routine health behaviors become interrupted. Women who were taking contraceptives may forget or may no longer have access to these medications. In addition, health care systems may have broken down as a result of the disaster, further reducing access to contraceptives. Unprotected intercourse during this time can lead to increased rates of childbirth, unintended pregnancies and sexually transmitted infections (STIs). Methods used to prevent STIs (such as condom use) are often forgotten or not accessible during times surrounding a disaster. Lack of health care infrastructure and medical shortages hinder the ability to treat individuals once they acquire an STI. In addition, health efforts to prevent, monitor or treat HIV/AIDS are often disrupted, leading to increased rates of HIV complications and increased transmission of the virus through the population.

Maternal Health

Pregnant women are one of the groups disproportionately affected by natural disasters. Inadequate nutrition, little access to clean water, lack of health-care services and psychological stress in the aftermath of the disaster can lead to a significant increase in maternal morbidity and mortality. Furthermore, shortage of healthcare resources during this time can convert even routine obstetric complications into emergencies.

During and after a disaster, women's prenatal, peri-natal and postpartum care can become disrupted. After disasters, there is often a significant increase in the number of women who receive late or no prenatal care. Among women affected by natural disaster, there are significantly higher rates of low birth weight infants, preterm infants and infants with low head circumference. Separation of mothers and babies as a result of poor infrastructure and displacement practices can interfere with breastfeeding and cause significant emotional stress for mom and baby. It can also lead to negative long-term health outcome mother and especially babies. In addition, it can be particularly difficult to find clean water for sterilizing bottles for breast milk or pre-made formula. These factors can further hinder breastfeeding practices and adequate infant nutrition, resulting in long term health consequences for the baby.

Political Consequences

Natural disasters can also affect political relations with countries and vice versa. Violent conflicts within states can exacerbate the impact of natural disasters by weakening the ability of states, communities and individuals to provide disaster relief. Natural disasters can also worsen ongoing conflicts within states by weakening the capacity of states to fight rebels. In developed countries like the US, studies find that incumbents lose votes when the electorate perceives them as responsible for a poor disaster response. In Chinese and Japanese history, it has been routine for era names or capital cities and palaces of emperors to be changed after a major natural disaster, chiefly for political reasons such as association with hardships by the populace and fear of upheaveal. (i.e. in East asian government chronicles, such fears were recorded in a low profile way as an unlucky name or place requiring change.) Disasters and responses can dictate political careers; the once popular President Benigno Aquino III of Philippines, following a weak and confused response to Typhoon Yolanda which killed over 6,000 people and survivors were largely left to fend for themselves, this widely accepted sentiment carried over and the President never recovered his popularity, his hand picked successor Mar Roxas lost the subsequent election to a rival party in a landslide vote. Post-disaster mishandling can spread despair as bad news travels fast and far, and contribute to the appeal of electing a strongman out of sheer desperation.

References

- The-exploitation-of-natural-environment-philosophy-essay, essays, philosophy: ukessays.com, Retrieved 8 March, 2019
- Bray, John (2003). "Attracting Reputable Companies to Risky Environments: Petroleum and Mining Companies". Natural Resources and Conflict: Options and Actions. World Bank Publications. Pp. 287–347. Retrieved 2012-03-12
- Resource-use-its-consequences, waste-resources: umweltbundesamt.de, Retrieved 9 April, 2019
- Pedro, Antonio M.A. (2004). Mainstreaming Mineral Wealth in Growth and Poverty Reduction Strategies. Economic Commission for Africa. Pp. 5–6. ISBN 9789211250978. Retrieved 20 March 2012
- Deforestation-27692: livescience.com, Retrieved 10 May, 2019
- Montgomery, D. R. (8 August 2007). "Soil erosion and agricultural sustainability". Proceedings of the National Academy of Sciences. 104 (33): 13268–13272. Bibcode:2007PNAS..10413268M. Doi:10.1073/pnas.0611508104. PMC 1948917. PMID 17686990
- "Thermal Erosion". NSIDC Glossary. National Snow and Ice Data Center. Archived from the original on 2010-12-18. Retrieved 21 December 2009
- Veltmeyer, Henry; Petras, James (2014). The New Extractivism: A Post-Neoliberal Development Model or Imperialism of the Twenty-First Century. London: Zen books. Pp. 9–10. ISBN 9781780329925

Depletion of Natural Resources

CHAPTER 4

The consumption of a resource faster than it can be replenished can lead to resource depletion. Some of the natural resources which are being depleted are oil, gas, groundwater, freshwater and ozone. The chapter closely examines the key aspects related to the depletion of these natural resources to provide an extensive understanding of the subject.

Depletion of natural resources occurs when resources are consumed at a faster rate than that of replacement. Natural resources are those resources that are in existence without human's actions and they can either be renewable or non-renewable. And when it gets down to the discussion of natural resource depletion, it a terminology used in reference to water usage, farming, fossil fuel consumption, fishing, and mining. And above all, natural resource depletion is defined on the premise that the value of a resource is measured in terms of its availability in nature.

A resource that is rare on earth due to depletion has a higher value than a natural resource which is in abundance. Due to the increasing global population, the levels of natural resource degradation is also increasing. Consequently, the world's eco-footprint is estimated to be one and a half times the ability of the earth to sustainably provide each individual with enough resources that meet their consumption levels.

Causes of Depletion of Natural Resources

Overpopulation

The total global population is more than seven billion people. Still, there is a consistent increase in the overall earth populace and this has been a critical factor in accelerating the depletion of natural resources. An increase in populace expands the need for resources and conditions necessary to sustain it.

In addition, it contributes to increased ecological contamination. Research further indicates that developing countries are using more and more resources to industrialize and support their ever-increasing population. Hence, the depletion of natural resources will continue as long as the world population increases.

Poor Farming Practices

Humans are causing a lot of stress to land resources due to the over-reliance on food production for daily nutritional requirements. Poor irrigation practices, for example, is a key contributing factor to salinization and alkalization of the soil that sustains plants growth. Poor soil management practices and the use of heavy machinery and farming equipment also destroy the soil structure making it unsuitable for plant growth.

Some farming practices such as excessive use of pesticides, fungicides, and herbicides equally kill important soil micro-organisms that are essential in replenishing nutrients in the soil.

Logging

The World Bank reported that the net loss of global forest between 1990 and 2016 was 1.3 million square kilometers. On the same note, tropical deforestation is estimated to occur at a rate of one percent annually, especially in Latin America regions. People are clearing forests primarily for agricultural reasons due to the increase in the population pressure.

Humans are also cutting down trees to make space for residential complexes and multiplexes. Through deforestation, the planet not only loses tress but also thousands of animals and great plant biodiversity due to the destruction of their natural habitats. Moreover, increased logging activities lead to soil erosion that degrades natural soil minerals.

Over Consumption of Natural Resources

The 1760 industrial revolution saw large-scale mineral and oil exploration and the practice has been gradually growing, leading to more and more natural oil and mineral depletion. And together with the advancements in technology, development and research in the contemporary era; exploitation of minerals has become easier and humans are digging deeper to access different ore. The increased exploitation of different minerals has led to some of them entering into a production decline.

For example, minerals such as Gasoline, Copper, and Zinc production are estimated to decline in the next 20 years. Plus, oil mining continue to rise due to the upsurge in the number of engines that use petroleum thereby magnifying its depletion. The peak oil theory supports this fact by putting forward that it will come a time when the globe will experience uncertainties on alternative means of fuels owing to the over-harvesting of petroleum.

Pollution

An increase in population and modern anthropogenic activities is a major contributor to the disposal of pollutants into the natural environment and as such, the value of natural environments are gradually exposed to degradation. The soil, air, lakes, and seas are being contaminated with sewage, radioactive, materials, and toxic chemicals among other pollutants.

Uncontrolled release of carbon monoxide, nitrous oxide, sulfur oxide, and carbon dioxide, for example, have resulted in the degradation of the ozone layer and global warming – environmental changes with their resultant depletive impacts on different natural habitats. Millions of different animal and plant species have thus lost their natural habitats and are on the verge of extinction.

Industrial and Technological Development

The present-day world is incessantly becoming industrialized as more and more countries make major technological breakthroughs. But as technological advancements continue, there is similarly a considerable growth in industries that release toxins and chemical by-products which are eventually deposited in lakes, soils, and lands. As a result, the by-products and toxic materials alter natural habits such as aquatic systems and wildlife.

Examples of the impacts include acidic lakes, dead zones, and the death of wildlife as well as aquatic life. Industrial and technological advancements have also driven the demand for virgin materials for research, development, and production. More resources are hence being used to satisfy the industrial demands, increasing the rate of natural resource depletion.

Effects of Depletion of Natural Resources

Water Shortages

Poor farming practices, deforestation, and pollution are major causes of water resource depletion due to contamination, wastage, and the destruction of natural water catchment areas. As of today, approximately one billion people lack access to clean water because of the effects of deforestation and contamination of water sources and groundwater. Water shortage further contribute to famine and food insecurity.

Oil Depletion

Oil is a non-renewable resource that accounts for approximately 40 percent of the total energy used globally. Research by EIA's International Energy Outlook in the year 2013 had shown that due to the high rate of oil exploitation, the amount of oil remaining would last for only 25 years.

Oil is an essential commodity in manufacturing, planting, mining, and transportation among many activities, and its depletion would be devastating. The adverse effects of oil depletion include fall of business, high cost of living in developing countries, and uncertainty in the transport sector.

Loss of Forest Cover

Approximately 18 million acres of forest cover is destroyed annually. This means that half of the world's natural forest cover has already been cleared. Furthermore, studies indicate an increase in deforestation in the past three decades has resulted in 12% to 17% rise of greenhouse gases globally.

Other devastating effects of deforestation include soil erosion, an increase in the greenhouse gases leading to global warming, loss of biodiversity, increased flooding, and drought.

Depletion of Minerals

There has been an increase in the exploitation of minerals such as phosphorus, gasoline, copper, and zinc among others to sustain the seven billion people on earth. Studies by Global Phosphorus Research Institute, for example, shows that the earth could run out of phosphorus – an essential element for plant growth, in the next 50 to 100 years.

Studies by the United States Geological Survey also indicate that there is an increase in non-renewable resources consumption of natural minerals and construction materials such as copper, sand, gravel, and stone.

Extinction of Species

Due to the changes in the living conditions of animals as a result of resource overexploitation and habitat degradation, some species may go extinct. Forested regions are known to be a habitat for thousands of animals but deforestation is progressively destroying forest habitats. Practices such as overfishing and pollution have similarly led to a drastic reduction in the number of marine species such as the tuna fish.

Solutions of Depletion of Natural Resources

Controlling Deforestation

Programs aimed at checking against deforestation such as REDD (Reducing Emissions from Deforestation and Forest Degradation) created by the World Bank, the New York Declaration on Forests, and the United Nations are initiatives that could help reduce the depletion of natural resources.

The initiatives may also act as incentives for encouraging the general public to conserve forests as these are the habitat and protectors of some of the world's unique plant/animal species and water sources respectively. Sustainability programs that aim to educate people about the importance of conserving natural resources should also be enacted as a way of focusing on the long-term risks associated with environmental degradation.

Reducing Oil, Mineral and Material Consumption

Oil-rich countries together with the World Bank, states, and consumables' regulatory bodies should join hands towards a common international objective of discussing how oil and mineral consumption as well as exploitation can be reduced. Manufactures can, for instance, be trained on lean manufacturing (recycling, re-use, and reducing wastage) while consumers sensitized on how to adopt re-use, reducing wastage, and recycling techniques.

More Exploration and use of Renewable Sources of Energy

Renewables such as solar and wind power can be explored more and utilized to reduce the dependency on fossil fuel, which is a major cause of environmental pollution, climate change, global warming, and destruction of natural habitats.

Protecting Wetlands and Coastal Ecosystems

Wetlands are regions saturated with groundwater that serve a significant role in sustaining vegetation cover. The coastal and wetland ecosystems are thus vital in sustaining the food chain as they replenish water sources and avail minerals and nutrients for primary producers (green and flowering plants), essential for maintaining plant and animal biodiversity. Also when coastal ecosystems are protected, they aid in controlling marine overfishing and protect coral reefs.

Sensitization and Awareness Creation

People need to be educated on how their daily practices put a strain on the scarce natural resources and their individual contributions to the depletion of natural resources. The main purpose of creating awareness would be to encourage people to preserve and restore the natural environment by getting involved in conservation efforts.

FOSSIL FUEL DEPLETION

Fossil fuel depletion is the extraction of natural gas, oil and coal reserves at a rate higher than nature replenishes them.

These carbonaceous fuels supply the energy that keeps power plants, trains, household furnaces and automobiles running. They provide feedstock in the manufacturing of plastics, detergents and agricultural pesticides and fertilizers. They make up the key ingredient in asphalt that paves our roads and seals our roofs. They make possible life-saving pharmaceuticals.

But these underground stores of nonrenewable energy are being depleted. Of the three fossil fuels, oil is in most critical supply. Today, the world consumes 85.2 million barrels of oil a day. By 2020 this amount is expected to increase by 60 percent.

Americans currently account for 25 percent of the world's total oil consumption even though they make up only four percent of the world's population. Of the 21 million barrels used in the

U.S. each day, nearly 70 percent is devoted to transportation. The majority of this oil fills the gas tanks of automobiles whose fuel efficiency is among the lowest in the world. According to a 2007 survey by BP, the British oil giant, Americans consume twice the annual total of India and China combined.

By contrast, coal is a more abundant and widely distributed fossil fuel. Like oil, the burning of coal also is on the rise. Since 1950, the amount of coal consumption has more than doubled. In countries such as China, double-digit growth in the economy has fast-tracked the construction of new coal-fired power plants which provide the country with 70 percent of its energy. Between 2008 and 2018, China is expected to build 500 new coal-fired power plants, an average of one facility per week. At current rates of consumption, coal supplies are expected to last 200 years or more.

For Example:

The burning of fossil fuels, especially oil and coal, is the main contributor to global warming. China's heavy reliance on coal is one reason that the country has pulled ahead of the U.S. as the world's leading producer of carbon dioxide, a greenhouse gas. The burning of coal pumps 25 percent more carbon dioxide into the atmosphere per pound than oil.

Some energy experts say that natural gas will be the key to making the transition to a more sustainable energy future. Natural gas emits fewer greenhouse gases—some 80 percent less CO_2, for example, than coal. And natural gas can be easily compressed and readily transported.

Design Mitigation Strategies

Designers can address the depletion of fossil fuels in two primary ways. The first is investigating the full range of technological solutions that can reduce the quantity of fossil fuel consumed to deliver a given amount of resulting material or energy. The second way is to employ alternative energy technologies that do not rely on fossil fuels (including solar thermal, solar electric, wind electric, tidal power, nuclear power and so forth). Although there are many potential environmental consequences from any energy source, it is possible to model alternatives and determine which directions cause the least harm to the environment.

OIL DEPLETION

Oil depletion is the decline in oil production of a well, oil field, or geographic area. The Hubbert peak theory makes predictions of production rates based on prior discovery rates and anticipated production rates. Hubbert curves predict that the production curves of non-renewing resources approximate a bell curve. Thus, according to this theory, when the peak of production is passed, production rates enter an irreversible decline.

The United States Energy Information Administration predicted in 2006 that world consumption of oil will increase to 98.3 million barrels per day (15,630,000 m^3/d) (mbd) in 2015 and 118 million barrels per day in 2030. With 2009 world oil consumption at 84.4 mbd, reaching the projected 2015 level of consumption would represent an average annual increase between 2009 and 2015 of 2.7% per year.

Resource Availability

The World's natural oil supply is fixed because petroleum is naturally formed far too slowly to be replaced at the rate at which it is being extracted. Over many millions of years, plankton, bacteria, and other plant and animal matter became buried in sediments on the ocean floor. When conditions were right – a lack of oxygen for decomposition, and sufficient depth and temperature of burial – these organic remains were converted into petroleum compounds, while the sediment accompanying them was converted into sandstone, siltstone, and other porous sedimentary rock. When capped by impermeable rocks such as shale, salt, or igneous intrusions, they formed the petroleum reservoirs which are exploited today.

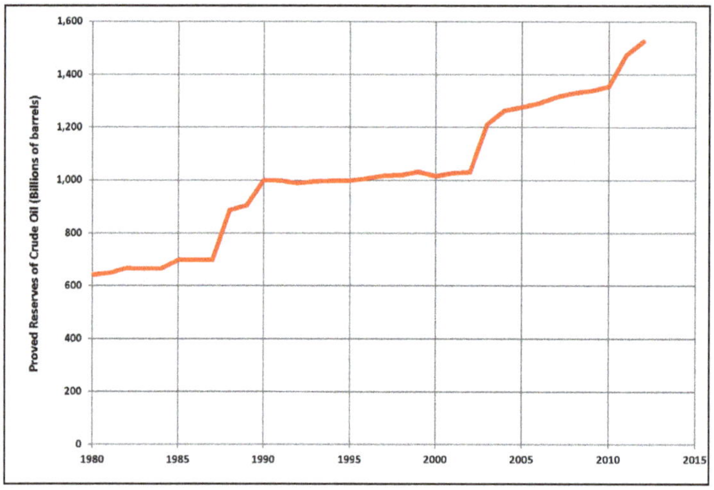

World proved reserves of crude oil, 1980-2012.

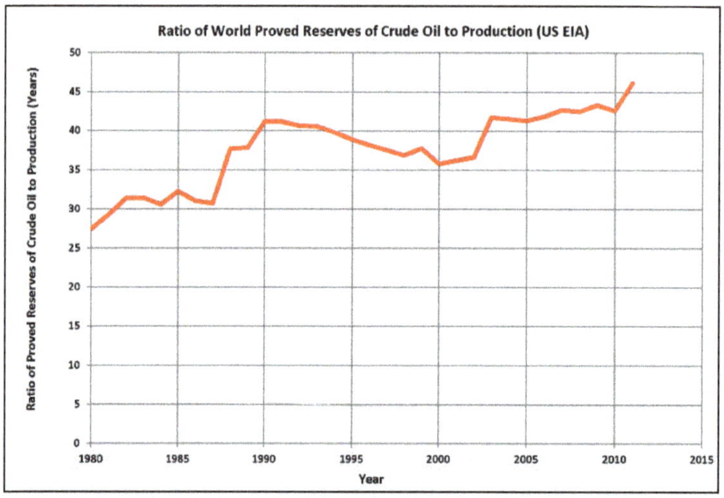

Ratio of world proved oil reserves to production, 1980-2011.

Production Decline Models

For the short and medium-term, oil production decline occurs in a predictable manner based on geological circumstances, governmental policies, and engineering practices. The shape of the decline curve varies depending upon whether one considers a well, a field, or a set of fields. In the longer term, technological developments have defied some of the predictions.

Oil Well Production Decline

An individual oil well usually produces at its maximum rate at the start of its life; the production rate eventually declines to a point at which it no longer produces profitable amounts. The shape of the decline curve depends on the oil reservoir and the reservoir drive mechanism. Wells in water-drive and gas-cap drive reservoirs often produce at a near constant rate until the encroaching water or expanding gas cap reaches the well, causing a sudden decline in oil production. Wells in gas solution drive and oil expansion drive reservoirs have exponential or hyperbolic declines: rapid declines at first, then leveling off.

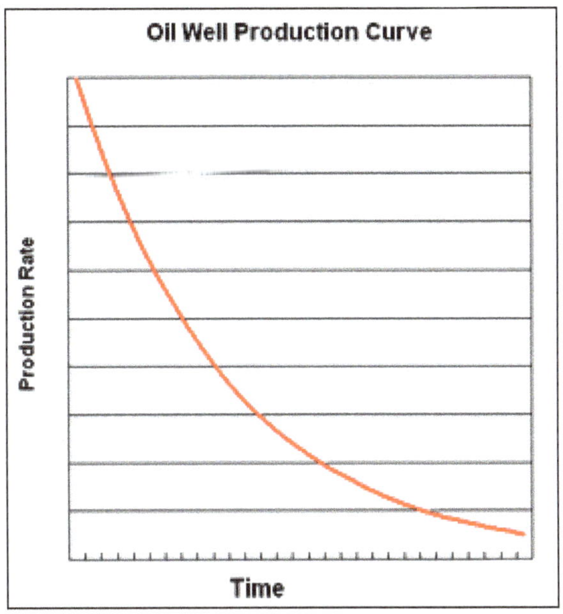

Theoretical oil production curve for a well with exponential decline.

The shape of production curve of an oil well can also be affected by a number of nongeologic factors:

- Well may be restricted by choice by lack of market demand or government regulation. This decreases the rate of decline, but will not change the well's total production significantly.
- Hydraulic fracturing (fracking) or acidizing may be used to cause a sharp spike in production, and may increase the recoverable reserves of a given well.
- The field may undergo a secondary or tertiary recovery project.

Oil Field Production Decline

Individual oil wells are typically within multi-well oil fields. As with individual wells, the production curves for oil fields vary depending on geology and how they are developed and produced. Some fields have symmetric bell-shaped production profiles, but it is more common that the period of inclining production is briefer and steeper than the subsequent decline. More than half the production usually occurs after a field has reached a peak or plateau. Production profiles of many fields show distinct peaks, but for giant oil fields, it is more common for production to reach and maintain a plateau before declining. Once a field declines, it usually follows an exponential decline.

As this decline levels off, production can continue at relatively low rates. A number of oil fields in the U.S. have been producing for over 100 years.

Oil field production curves can be modified by a number of factors:

- Production may be restricted by market conditions or government regulation.
- A secondary recovery project, such as water or gas injection, can repressurize the field and increase the total recovery.
- the field may undergo an enhanced oil recovery project, such as drilling of wells for injection of solvents, carbon dioxide, or steam. This allows more oil to be coaxed out of the rock, increasing the ultimate production of the field.

Multi-field Production Decline

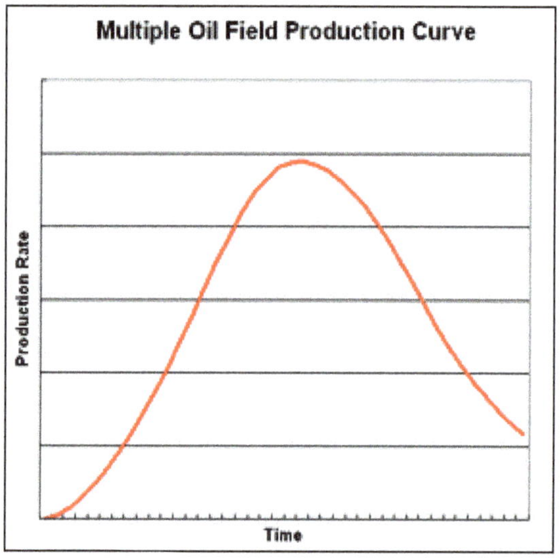

Hubbert-theory graph of multiple oil field production.

Most oil is found in a small number of very large oil fields. According to Hubbert peak theory, production starts off slowly, rises faster and faster, then slows down and flattens until it reaches a peak, after which production declines. In the late stage, production often enters a period of exponential decline in which the decline becomes less and less steep. Oil production may never actually reach zero, but eventually becomes very low. Factors which can modify this curve include:

- Inadequate demand for oil, which reduces steepness of the curve and pushes its peak into the future.
- Sharp price increases when the production peak is reached, as production fails to meet demand. If price increases cause a sharp drop in demand, a dip in the top of the curve may occur.
- Development of new drilling technology or marketing of unconventional oil can reduce the steepness of the decline as more oil is produced than initially anticipated.

United States Production

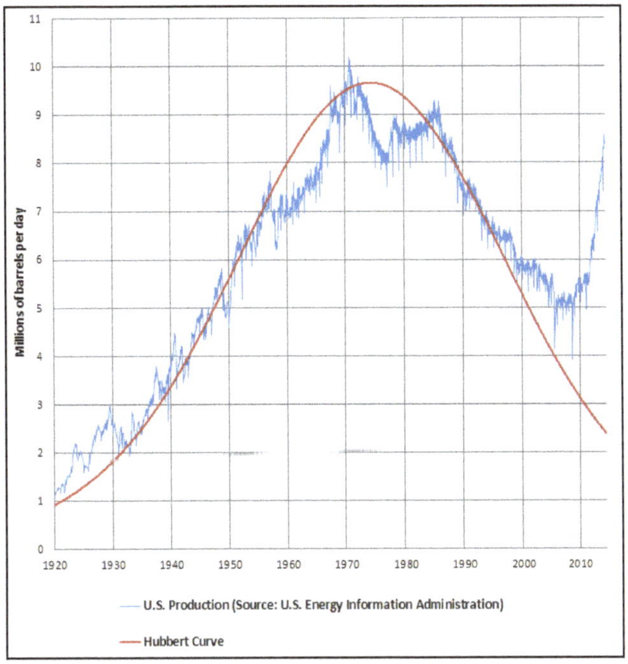

Historical US crude oil production showing initial similarity to a Hubbert curve.

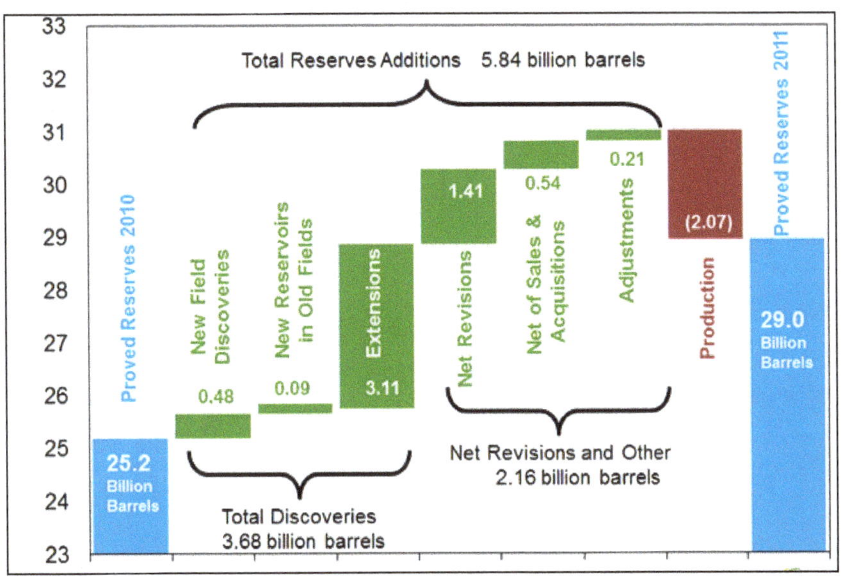

Although US proved oil reserves grew by 3.8 billion barrels in 2011, even after deducting 2.07 billion barrels of production, only 8 percent of the 5.84 billion barrels of the newly booked oil was due to new field discoveries (US EIA).

Oil production in the United States, provided one excludes Alaska, began by following the theoretical Hubbert curve for a few decades but is now deviating strongly from it. U.S. oil production reached a peak in 1970 and by the mid-2000s it had fallen to 1940s levels. In 1950, the United States produced over half the world's oil, but by 2005 that proportion had dropped to about 8%. In 2005, U.S. crude oil imports peaked at a rate twice as high as domestic production; since then, U.S. oil production has increased, and imports have fallen 41%.

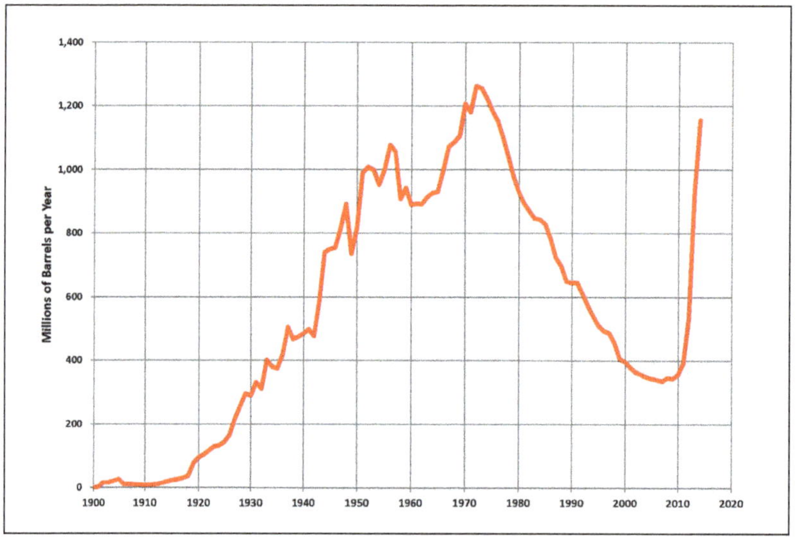

Texas oil field production decline curve.

The production peak in 1970 was predicted by one of the two projections put forward in 1956 by Hubbert. By 1972 all import quotas and controls on U.S. domestic production had been removed. Despite this, and despite the quadrupling of prices during the 1973 oil crisis, the production decline was not reversed in the lower 48 states until 2009. Crude oil production has since risen sharply from 2009 through 2014, so that the rate of US oil production in October 2014 was 81% higher than the average rate in 2008.

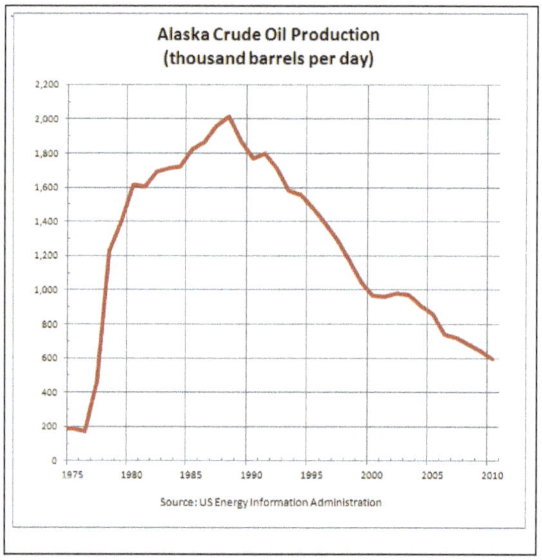

Alaska oil production decline curve.

The actual U.S. production curve deviates from Hubbert's 1956 curve in significant ways:

- When oil surpluses created a glut on the market and low prices began causing demand and production curves to rise, regulatory agencies such as the Texas Railroad Commission stepped in to restrain production.
- The curve peaked at a higher rate and sharper point than predicted.

- Production fell after 1970, but started to recover and reached a lower secondary peak in 1988. This occurred because the supergiant Prudhoe Bay field in Alaska was only discovered in 1968, and the Trans-Alaska Pipeline System (TAPS) was not completed until 1977. After 1988, Alaska production peaked and total U.S. production began to decline again. By 2005, Prudhoe Bay had produced over 75% of its oil.
- Production increases in the 2010s.

World Oil Production

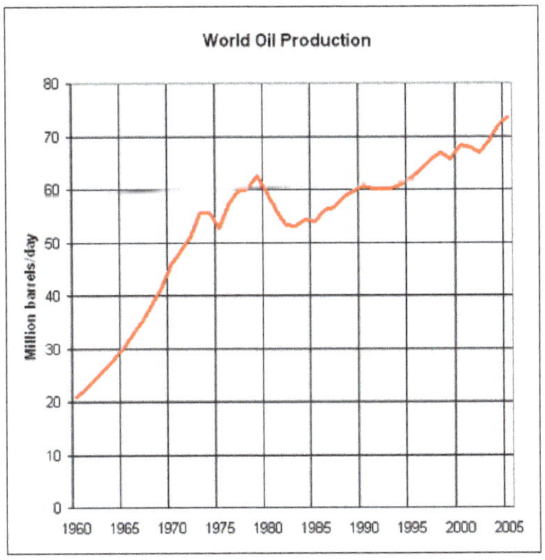

World oil field production curve.

The 1970 production peak in the U.S. caused many people to begin to question when the world production peak would occur. The peak of world production is known as Peak oil.

Implications of a world peak: A peak in oil production could result in a worldwide oil shortage, or it could not even be noticed as demand decreases in conjunction with increased prices. While past shortages stemmed from a temporary insufficiency of supply, crossing Hubbert's Peak would mean that the production of oil would continue to decline, and that demand for these products must be reduced to meet supply. The effects of such a shortage would depend on the rate of decline and the development and adoption of effective alternatives.

Catastrophe

The use of fossil fuels allows humans to participate in takedown, which is the consumption of energy at a greater rate than it is being replaced. The industrial economy is currently heavily dependent on oil as a fuel and chemical feedstock. For example, over 90% of transportation in the United States relies on oil.

Since the 1940s, agriculture has dramatically increased its productivity, due largely to the use of chemical pesticides, fertilizers, and increased mechanisation. This process has been called the Green Revolution. The increase in food production has allowed world population to grow dramatically over the last 50 years. Pesticides rely upon oil as a critical ingredient, and fertilizers require natural gas. Farm machinery also requires oil.

Most or all of the uses of fossil fuels in agriculture can be replaced with alternatives. For example, by far the biggest fossil fuel input to agriculture is the use of natural gas as a hydrogen source for the Haber-Bosch fertilizer-creation process. Natural gas is used simply because it is the cheapest currently available source of hydrogen; were that to change, other sources, such as electrolysis powered by solar energy, could be used to provide the hydrogen for creating fertilizer without relying on fossil fuels.

Oil shortages may force a move to lower input "organic agriculture" methods, which may be more labor-intensive and require a population shift from urban to rural areas, reversing the trend towards urbanisation which has predominated in industrial societies; however, some organic farmers using modern organic-farming methods have reported yields as high as those available from conventional farming, but without the use of fossil-fuel-intensive artificial fertilizers or pesticides.

Another possible effect would derive from modern transportation and housing infrastructure. A large proportion of the developed world's population live in suburbs, a type of low-density settlement designed with the automobile in mind. A movement to deal with this problem early, called "New Urbanism," seeks to develop the suburbs into higher density neighborhoods and use high density, mixed-use forms for new building projects.

Recession

A more modest scenario, assuming a slower rate of depletion or a smoother transition to alternative energy sources, could still cause substantial economic hardship such as a recession or depression due to higher energy prices. Inflation has also been linked to oil price spikes. However, economists disagree on the strength and causes of this association.

Rising Food Prices

Rising oil prices cause rising food prices in three ways. First, increased equipment fuel costs drive higher prices. Second, transportation costs increase retail prices. Third, higher oil prices are causing farmers to switch from producing food crops to producing biofuel crops. The law of supply and demand predicts that if fewer farmers are producing food the price of food will rise.

Replacement

An alternative considered likely by some is that oil will be replaced with renewable energy during the first half of the 21st century. The replacement fuel would likely be hydrogen. A hydrogen economy would then replace the current oil-based economy. Another possible replacement fuel is biogas, which is composed of methane. Methane has boiling point of −161 °C, rather than hydrogen's -252.87 °C, making methane a much easier fuel to condense.

Other people consider that the whole idea of "the hydrogen economy" is flawed. Compressed hydrogen has an energy density of only 5.6 megajoules per liter. Robert Zubrin looks at the practical problems of using hydrogen as an energy storage medium in *Energy Victory: Winning the War on Terror by Breaking Free of Oil.* He considers that hydrogen is a very poor form of storage, and that batteries, methanol or dimethyl ether would be better.

Geothermal power is one source of sustainable energy that can produce hydrogen. Note that David MacKay has shown in his book *Sustainable Energy: Without the Hot Air* that geothermal can only provide a tiny fraction of the world's needs sustainably. In some areas located over geological hotspots (such as Iceland), geothermal makes more sense.

Solar energy is a source of inexhaustible energy. There is more solar energy that reaches the surface of the Earth each hour than the amount of energy consumed by the world in a year. The challenges of using the sun's energy – energy which can be obtained either from wind power or from solar power – is that the energy needs to either be (1) stored in physical form of fuel for when it can be used in the future, or (2) transported directly as electricity, through transmission lines. Neither is dispatchable, as there is no control over when the sun will shine or when the wind will blow. There are, however, concentrated solar power plants using thermal storage that can store energy efficiently for up to 24 hours.

GAS DEPLETION

Gas depletion is the decline in natural gas production of a well, gas field, or geographic area.

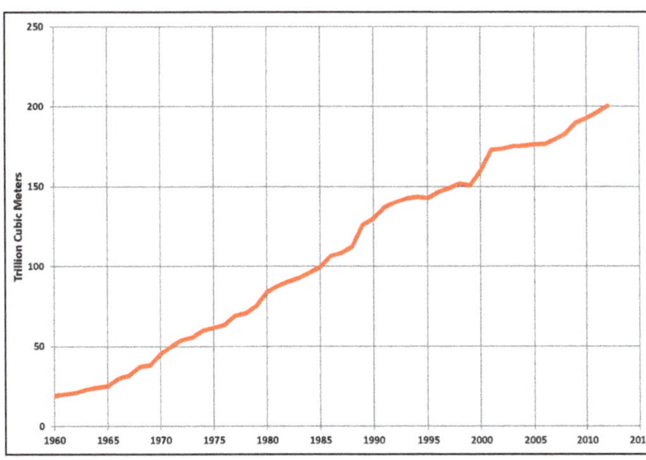

Proven global natural gas reserves between 1960 and 2012 (OPEC).

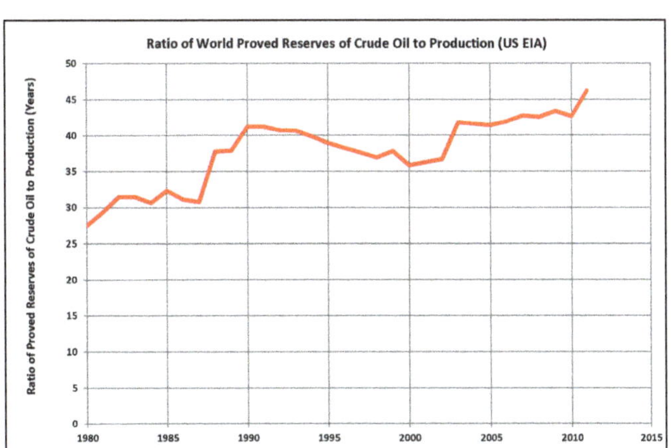

Ratio of world proved gas reserves to production, 1980-2011.

Depletion Date

According to the US Energy Information Administration, in 1980 the world had enough proved gas reserves to last 48 years at the 1980 rate of production. Cumulative world gas production from 1980 through 2011 was greater than the proved gas reserves in 1980. In 2011, world proved gas reserves were enough to last 58 years at 2011 production levels, even though the 2011 production rate was more than double the 1980 rate.

Role of New Technology

As new technologies for natural gas production are discovered, the world's ultimate reserves can grow. Although some predictions of ultimate reserve recovery include provisions for new technology, not every magnitude of breakthrough can be accurately accounted for.

More than half the increase in US natural gas production from 2006 to 2008 came from Texas, where production rose 15% between the first quarter of 2007 and the first quarter of 2008. This was mostly due to improved technology, which allowed the production of deepwater offshore and "unconventional" resources. Important new developments were horizontal drilling and fracking in a geologic formation known as the Barnett Shale, underlying the city of Fort Worth, which is a highly impermeable formation and difficult to produce by conventional means. The Barnett Shale now produces 6% of US natural gas. Other shale gas formations in the lower 48 states are widely distributed, and are known to contain large resources of natural gas.

GROUNDWATER DEPLETION

Groundwater depletion is a serious threat to the environment. The majority of our bodies and the Earth is made up of water. We may see the beautiful, flowing surface waters that make up the oceans, lakes and rivers, but this water is not always safe for consumption and is much more difficult to filter than groundwater. Consequently, water from the ground is especially valuable.

Groundwater is something that we need all over the world. Humans and animals need water in order to survive as our bodies could not function without it. We also need water to assist us in growing crops, powering equipment, and to keep us comfortable. Societies require much more clean water than we are afforded from precipitation and surface water, which is why groundwater is used so frequently.

If you were to see groundwater moving, you'll likely find it interesting that so much water lies beneath us. From a bird's eye view, you may even feel that there is more than enough water to go around. While we know that groundwater shortage is a serious issue, we should also know how water naturally finds its way into the aquifers we extract it from.

Nature goes through a unique process to provide us with groundwater. The surface water that we can see is heated by the Sun and goes into the atmosphere as evaporation. Water vapor then creates precipitation, water that falls from the sky as rain and snow. Once water falls from sky and onto the ground, it is absorbed into the Earth and is then stored as groundwater in aquifers.

Causes of Groundwater Depletion

1. Groundwater depletion most commonly occurs because of the frequent pumping of water from the ground. We pump the water more quickly than it can renew itself, leading to a dangerous shortage in the groundwater supply. As a growing world with a population that continues to rise, the more we pump water from the ground at a rapid rate, the more difficult it is for the groundwater to provide us with the amount of water that we need.

2. We continuously pump groundwater from aquifers and it does not have enough time to replenish itself. Water flows freely through the saturated rocks known as aquifers. There are large and small aquifers, and they are the underground water reserves that absorb water and hold it, enabling us to pump it for use.

The amount of water that aquifers hold is beyond impressive and can provide us with billions of gallons of water per day. While this amount of water seems plentiful, groundwater is a major contributor to the Earth's freshwater supply and is responsible for providing up to 40% of freshwater in the world. Therefore, it doesn't have the ability to recollect quickly enough to be continually sourced for our use.

3. Agricultural needs require a large amount of groundwater. It's frightening to think that there isn't very much groundwater left when you consider how much water we use on a daily basis to support our population of billions and our personal lifestyles. A large amount of groundwater goes to farming, but the availability of groundwater is steadily declining.

Without it, it will be extremely difficult to provide drinking water and water for crops and animals that would help communities during times of drought. The less water that is available, the less food we have and we will be faced with the issue of great demand and very little supply.

4. Groundwater depletion can also occur naturally. The problems we would face with freshwater shortage is sure to cause problems in every aspect of our lives. The activities that lead to groundwater depletion come mostly from humans, but a portion of it also comes from changes in our climate and can speed up the process.

Effects of Groundwater Depletion

1. Groundwater depletion will force us to pump water from deeper within the Earth. The more we extract groundwater right below the Earth's surface, the further down we have to go in order to get more. As we have to extract water from deeper within the Earth, we find that there is less water

available. Consequently, we will have to use even more resources to develop alternative methods to reach further into the ground.

2. Large bodies of water will become more shallow from groundwater depletion. A groundwater shortage keeps additional water from flowing into lakes, rivers and seas. This means that over time, less water will enter as the existing surface water continues to evaporate. As the water becomes less deep, it will affect everything in that particular region, including fish and wildlife.

3. Saltwater contamination can occur. We may pump groundwater instead of sourcing it from lakes and rivers, but that doesn't mean that it isn't connected to larger bodies of water. Groundwater that is deep within the ground often intermingles with saltwater that we shouldn't drink. When freshwater mixes with saltwater, it is called saltwater contamination. This sort of contamination would raise the prices of drinking water for everyone because it will cost much more to pump and filter.

4. As large aquifers are depleted, food supply and people will suffer. The depletion of the Colorado River and the Ogallala aquifer serve as examples of large groundwater reserves that are being depleted, despite how necessary they are to our economy and well-being. The Ogallala aquifer has been collecting groundwater for thousands of years, and its water resources have to be shared among farmers and citizens.

Water from the Ogallala aquifer is used for irrigation throughout the Great Plains. So much water is being taken from this aquifer that there is no time for it to refill. Unfortunately, strict orders are not in place to regulate how much water can be pumped from this reservoir, which could have a devastating effect on the crops and people who live there.

5. A lack of groundwater limits biodiversity and dangerous sinkholes result from depleted aquifers. Aquifers collect groundwater and are extremely important. For example, the residents near the Gulf of Mexico and Mexico City rely solely on aquifers. Wildlife, marine animals, and agriculture continues to suffer near the Gulf of Mexico because the Mississippi River runoff from industrial farming materials finds its way into the water. Parts of Mexico City are falling as the water table lowers and creates sinkholes that destroy buildings and homes.

Solutions to Groundwater Depletion

1. As individuals, one of the things we can do to make a difference is to use less water for luxury purposes. We must all address the issue of groundwater depletion. Considering the impending crisis of a mass water shortage, everyone should do their part to use less water whenever possible. Water is used so freely that it is often part of outdoor decor ideas and used for major attractions, such as amusement parks.

Throughout countless neighborhoods, large amounts of water are used for swimming pools while water hoses are kept running to wash cars and for other miscellaneous reasons. We conserve water when we turn off the faucet and reduce our usage of washing machines, dishwashers and similar appliances. Also, we save a massive amount of water by deciding not to use water for decorative and unnecessary reasons at home.

2. We should reduce our use of chemicals and dispose of them properly. Many people are not paying attention and are simply unaware of how important it is to keep pollution from occurring beneath the ground. The water from businesses and private residences that run into the streets and sewage systems are commonly laden with chemicals. These chemicals find their way into larger bodies of water and absorb into the ground, poisoning animals and the soil. By using less chemicals and discarding of them carefully, we keep them from adding toxic materials into our water supply.

3. More comprehensive research and additional funding can help with groundwater depletion. The best way to approach the topic of groundwater depletion and to find a solution is to think on both a personal and government level. Laws that are in place for the pumping of groundwater should be more strict and follow specific regulations.

There are many scientists, researchers, and sustainable companies that remind us how important it is to know the amount of groundwater we actually have. They also believe that many of the policies we have should be changed with the consideration of saving groundwater in mind instead of treating it like an endless resource.

4. One of the most effective ways to address the issue of groundwater depletion is to find alternative sources of water. Alternative water sources can be used to help replenish aquifers. Deriving water from other sources would also give aquifers time to refill instead of pumping too much water from them at once.

5. The pumping of groundwater should be regulated. If we don't have a better understanding of our groundwater supply, then we can easily use much more than we should. Understandably, more funding should be granted towards researching our groundwater supply instead of just pumping the water, so that we can set limits and better pace our usage. Additional funding should be given to support initiatives that not only study the supply of groundwater we have, but also seek to find sustainable ways to use less of it.

OZONE DEPLETION

Ozone depletion consists of two related events observed since the late 1970s: a steady lowering of about four percent in the total amount of ozone in Earth's atmosphere (the ozone layer), and a much larger springtime decrease in stratospheric ozone around Earth's polar regions. The latter phenomenon is referred to as the ozone hole. There are also springtime polar tropospheric ozone depletion events in addition to these stratospheric events.

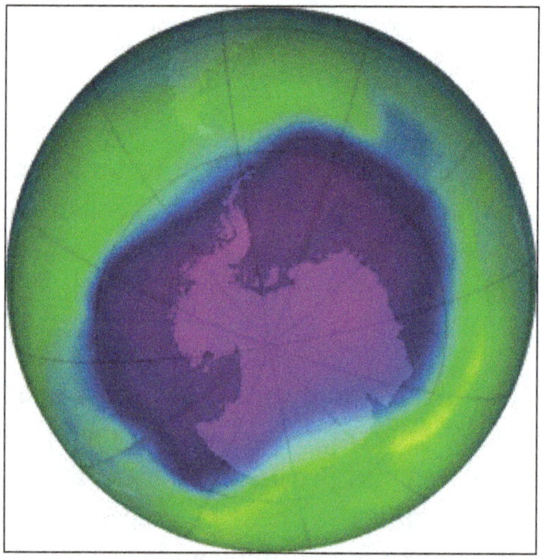

Image of the largest Antarctic ozone hole ever recorded over the South Pole in September 2006.

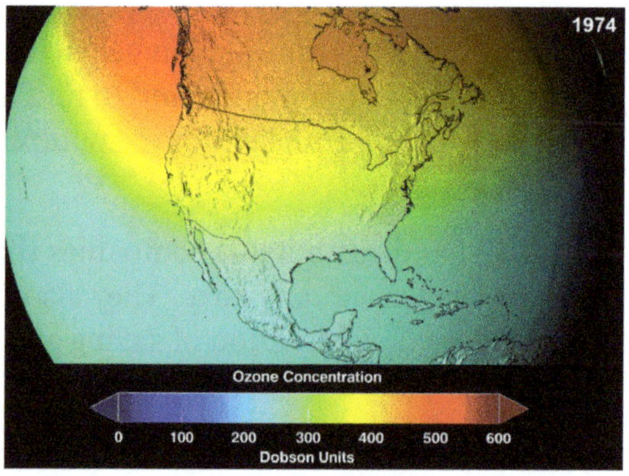

NASA projections of stratospheric ozone concentrations if chlorofluorocarbons had not been banned.

The main cause of ozone depletion and the ozone hole is manufactured chemicals, especially manufactured halocarbon refrigerants, solvents, propellants and foam-blowing agents (chlorofluorocarbons (CFCs), HCFCs, halons), referred to as ozone-depleting substances (ODS). These compounds are transported into the stratosphere by turbulent mixing after being emitted from the surface, mixing much faster than the molecules can settle. Once in the stratosphere, they release halogen atoms through photodissociation, which catalyze the breakdown of ozone (O_3) into oxygen (O_2). Both types of ozone depletion were observed to increase as emissions of halocarbons increased.

Ozone depletion and the ozone hole have generated worldwide concern over increased cancer risks and other negative effects. The ozone layer prevents most harmful UVB wavelengths of ultraviolet light (UV light) from passing through the Earth's atmosphere. These wavelengths cause skin cancer, sunburn and cataracts, which were projected to increase dramatically as a result of thinning ozone, as well as harming plants and animals. These concerns led to the adoption of the Montreal Protocol in 1987, which bans the production of CFCs, halons and other ozone-depleting chemicals.

The ban came into effect in 1989. Ozone levels stabilized by the mid-1990s and began to recover in the 2000s. Recovery is projected to continue over the next century, and the ozone hole is expected to reach pre-1980 levels by around 2075. The Montreal Protocol is considered the most successful international environmental agreement to date.

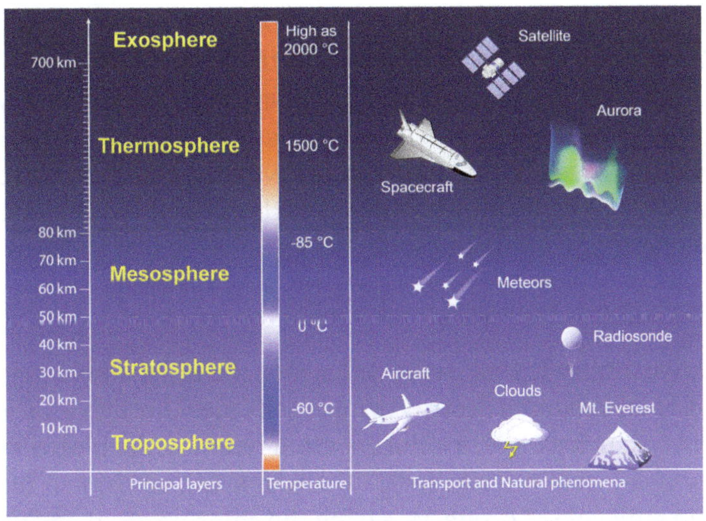

Layers of the atmosphere (not to scale). The Earth's ozone layer is mainly found in the lower portion of the stratosphere from approximately 20 to 30 km (12 to 19 mi).

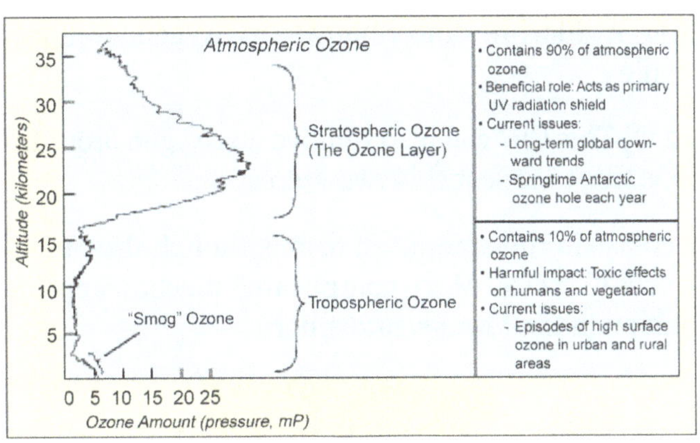

Ozone Hole.

Ozone Cycle

Three forms (or allotropes) of oxygen are involved in the ozone-oxygen cycle: oxygen atoms (O or atomic oxygen), oxygen gas (O_2 or diatomic oxygen), and ozone gas (O_3 or triatomic oxygen). Ozone is formed in the stratosphere when oxygen molecules photodissociate after absorbing ultraviolet photons. This converts a single O_2 into two atomic oxygen radicals. The atomic oxygen radicals then combine with separate O_2 molecules to create two O_3 molecules. These ozone molecules absorb ultraviolet (UV) light, following which ozone splits into a molecule of O_2 and an oxygen atom. The oxygen atom then joins up with an oxygen molecule to regenerate ozone. This is a continuing process that terminates when an oxygen atom recombines with an ozone molecule to make two O_2 molecules.

$$O + O_3 \rightarrow 2\,O_2$$

The total amount of ozone in the stratosphere is determined by a balance between photochemical production and recombination.

Ozone can be destroyed by a number of free radical catalysts; the most important are the hydroxyl radical (OH·), nitric oxide radical (NO·), chlorine radical (Cl·) and bromine radical (Br·). The dot is a notation to indicate that each species has an unpaired electron and is thus extremely reactive. All of these have both natural and man-made sources; at the present time, most of the OH· and NO· in the stratosphere is naturally occurring, but human activity has drastically increased the levels of chlorine and bromine. These elements are found in stable organic compounds, especially chlorofluorocarbons, which can travel to the stratosphere without being destroyed in the troposphere due to their low reactivity. Once in the stratosphere, the Cl and Br atoms are released from the parent compounds by the action of ultraviolet light, e.g:

$$CFCl_3 + \text{electromagnetic radiation} \rightarrow Cl\cdot + \cdot CFCl_2$$

Ozone is a highly reactive molecule that easily reduces to the more stable oxygen form with the assistance of a catalyst. Cl and Br atoms destroy ozone molecules through a variety of catalytic cycles. In the simplest example of such a cycle, a chlorine atom reacts with an ozone molecule (O_3), taking an oxygen atom to form chlorine monoxide (ClO) and leaving an oxygen molecule (O_2). The ClO can react with a second molecule of ozone, releasing the chlorine atom and yielding two molecules of oxygen. The chemical shorthand for these gas-phase reactions is:

- $Cl\cdot + O_3 \rightarrow ClO + O_2$ A chlorine atom removes an oxygen atom from an ozone molecule to make a ClO molecule
- $ClO + O_3 \rightarrow Cl\cdot + 2\,O_2$ This ClO can also remove an oxygen atom from another ozone molecule; the chlorine is free to repeat this two-step cycle

The overall effect is a decrease in the amount of ozone, though the rate of these processes can be decreased by the effects of null cycles. More complicated mechanisms have also been discovered that lead to ozone destruction in the lower stratosphere.

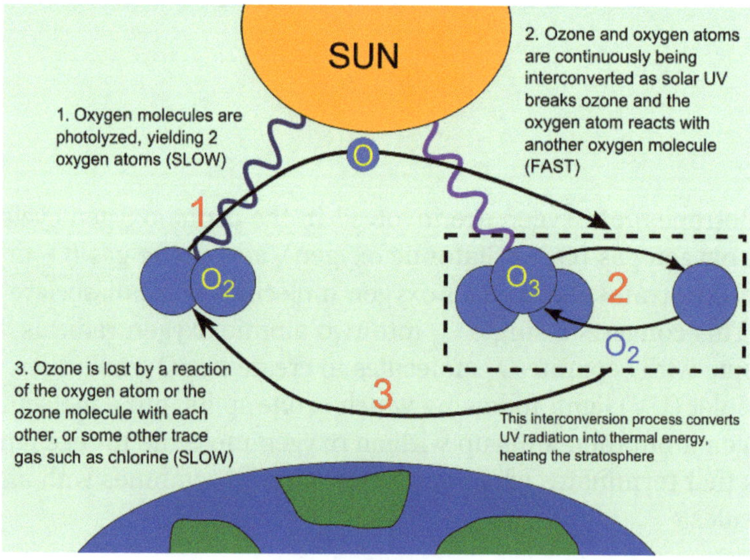

The ozone cycle.

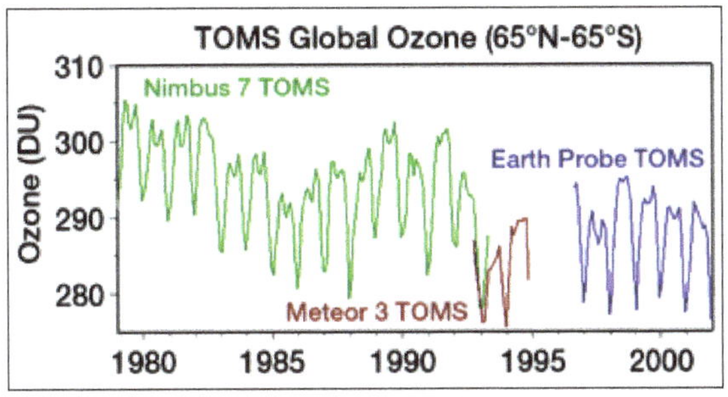

Global monthly average total ozone amount.

A single chlorine atom would continuously destroy ozone (thus a catalyst) for up to two years (the time scale for transport back down to the troposphere) were it not for reactions that remove them from this cycle by forming reservoir species such as hydrogen chloride (HCl) and chlorine nitrate ($ClONO_2$). Bromine is even more efficient than chlorine at destroying ozone on a per atom basis, but there is much less bromine in the atmosphere at present. Both chlorine and bromine contribute significantly to overall ozone depletion. Laboratory studies have also shown that fluorine and iodine atoms participate in analogous catalytic cycles. However, fluorine atoms react rapidly with water and methane to form strongly bound HF in the Earth's stratosphere, while organic molecules containing iodine react so rapidly in the lower atmosphere that they do not reach the stratosphere in significant quantities.

A single chlorine atom is able to react with an average of 100,000 ozone molecules before it is removed from the catalytic cycle. This fact plus the amount of chlorine released into the atmosphere yearly by chlorofluorocarbons (CFCs) and hydrochlorofluorocarbons (HCFCs) demonstrates the danger of CFCs and HCFCs to the environment.

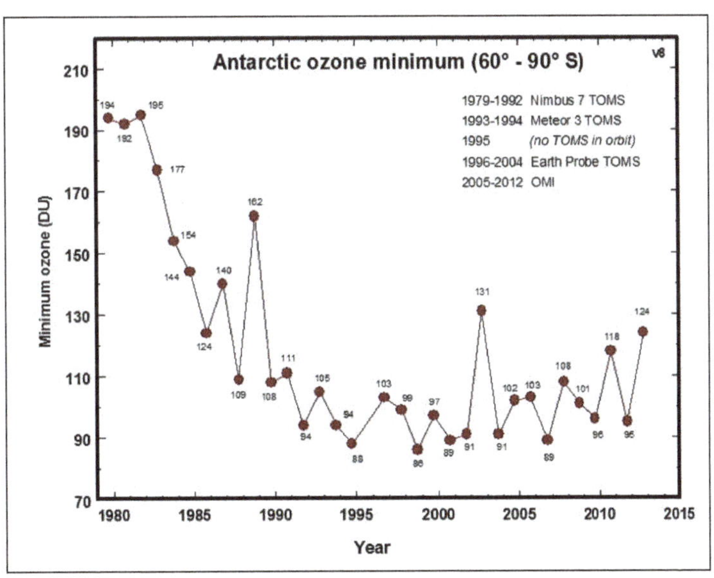

Lowest value of ozone measured by TOMS each year in the ozone hole.

Observations on Ozone Layer Depletion

The ozone hole is usually measured by reduction in the total *column ozone* above a point on the Earth's surface. This is normally expressed in Dobson units; abbreviated as "DU". The most prominent decrease in ozone has been in the lower stratosphere. Marked decreases in column ozone in the Antarctic spring and early summer compared to the early 1970s and before have been observed using instruments such as the Total Ozone Mapping Spectrometer (TOMS).

Reductions of up to 70 percent in the ozone column observed in the austral (southern hemispheric) spring over Antarctica and first reported in 1985 (Farman et al.) are continuing. Antarctic total column ozone in September and October have continued to be 40–50 percent lower than pre-ozone-hole values since the 1990s. A gradual trend toward "healing" was reported in 2016. In 2017, NASA announced that the ozone hole was the weakest since 1988 because of warm stratospheric conditions. It is expected to recover around 2070. The amount lost is more variable year-to-year in the Arctic than in the Antarctic. The greatest Arctic declines are in the winter and spring, reaching up to 30 percent when the stratosphere is coldest.

Reactions that take place on polar stratospheric clouds (PSCs) play an important role in enhancing ozone depletion. PSCs form more readily in the extreme cold of the Arctic and Antarctic stratosphere. This is why ozone holes first formed, and are deeper, over Antarctica. Early models failed to take PSCs into account and predicted a gradual global depletion, which is why the sudden Antarctic ozone hole was such a surprise to many scientists.

It is more accurate to speak of ozone depletion in middle latitudes rather than holes. Total column ozone declined below pre-1980 values between 1980 and 1996 for mid-latitudes. In the northern mid-latitudes, it then increased from the minimum value by about two percent from 1996 to 2009 as regulations took effect and the amount of chlorine in the stratosphere decreased. In the Southern Hemisphere's mid-latitudes, total ozone remained constant over that time period. There are no significant trends in the tropics, largely because halogen-containing compounds have not had time to break down and release chlorine and bromine atoms at tropical latitudes.

Large volcanic eruptions have been shown to have substantial albeit uneven ozone-depleting effects, as observed with the 1991 eruption of Mt. Pinotubo in the Philippines.

Ozone depletion also explains much of the observed reduction in stratospheric and upper tropospheric temperatures. The source of the warmth of the stratosphere is the absorption of UV radiation by ozone, hence reduced ozone leads to cooling. Some stratospheric cooling is also predicted from increases in greenhouse gases such as CO_2 and CFCs themselves; however, the ozone-induced cooling appears to be dominant.

Predictions of ozone levels remain difficult, but the precision of models' predictions of observed values and the agreement among different modeling techniques have increased steadily. The World Meteorological Organization Global Ozone Research and Monitoring Project—Report No. 44 comes out strongly in favor of the Montreal Protocol, but notes that a UNEP 1994 Assessment overestimated ozone loss for the 1994–1997 period.

Compounds in the Atmosphere

CFCs and Related Compounds in the Atmosphere

Chlorofluorocarbons (CFCs) and other halogenated ozone depleting substances (ODS) are mainly responsible for man-made chemical ozone depletion. The total amount of effective halogens (chlorine and bromine) in the stratosphere can be calculated and are known as the equivalent effective stratospheric chlorine (EESC).

CFCs were invented by Thomas Midgley, Jr. in the 1930s. They were used in air conditioning and cooling units, as aerosol spray propellants prior to the 1970s, and in the cleaning processes of delicate electronic equipment. They also occur as by-products of some chemical processes. No significant natural sources have ever been identified for these compounds—their presence in the atmosphere is due almost entirely to human manufacture. As mentioned above, when such ozone-depleting chemicals reach the stratosphere, they are dissociated by ultraviolet light to release chlorine atoms. The chlorine atoms act as a catalyst, and each can break down tens of thousands of ozone molecules before being removed from the stratosphere. Given the longevity of CFC molecules, recovery times are measured in decades. It is calculated that a CFC molecule takes an average of about five to seven years to go from the ground level up to the upper atmosphere, and it can stay there for about a century, destroying up to one hundred thousand ozone molecules during that time.

1,1,1-Trichloro-2,2,2-trifluoroethane, also known as CFC-113a, is one of four man-made chemicals newly discovered in the atmosphere by a team at the University of East Anglia. CFC-113a is the only known CFC whose abundance in the atmosphere is still growing. Its source remains a mystery, but illegal manufacturing is suspected by some. CFC-113a seems to have been accumulating unabated since 1960. Between 2010 and 2012, emissions of the gas jumped by 45 percent.

Computer Modeling

Scientists have attributed ozone depletion to the increase of man-made (anthropogenic) halogen compounds from CFCs by combining observational data with computer models. These complex chemistry transport models (e.g. SLIMCAT, CLaMS—Chemical Lagrangian Model of the Stratosphere) work by combining measurements of chemicals and meteorological fields with chemical reaction rate constants. They identify key chemical reactions and transport processes that bring CFC photolysis products into contact with ozone.

Ozone Hole and its Causes

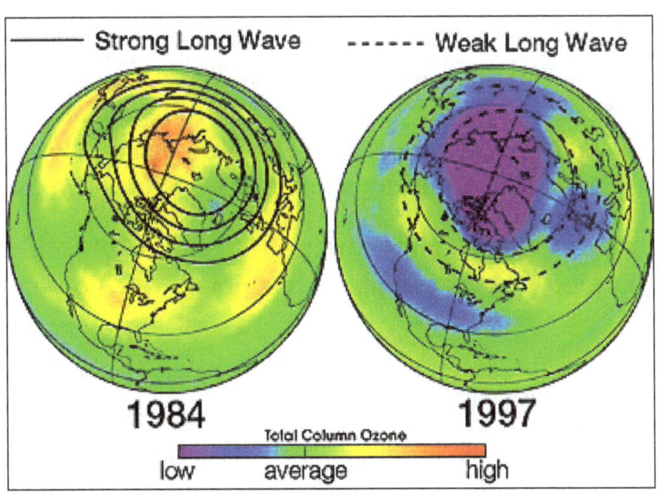

Ozone hole in North America during 1984 (abnormally warm reducing ozone depletion) and 1997 (abnormally cold resulting in increased seasonal depletion).

The Antarctic ozone hole is an area of the Antarctic stratosphere in which the recent ozone levels have dropped to as low as 33 percent of their pre-1975 values. The ozone hole occurs during the Antarctic spring, from September to early December, as strong westerly winds start to circulate around the continent and create an atmospheric container. Within this polar vortex, over 50 percent of the lower stratospheric ozone is destroyed during the Antarctic spring.

The primary cause of ozone depletion is the presence of chlorine-containing source gases (primarily CFCs and related halocarbons). In the presence of UV light, these gases dissociate, releasing chlorine atoms, which then go on to catalyze ozone destruction. The Cl-catalyzed ozone depletion can take place in the gas phase, but it is dramatically enhanced in the presence of polar stratospheric clouds (PSCs).

These polar stratospheric clouds form during winter, in the extreme cold. Polar winters are dark, consisting of three months without solar radiation (sunlight). The lack of sunlight contributes to a decrease in temperature and the polar vortex traps and chills air. Temperatures hover around or below −80 °C. These low temperatures form cloud particles. There are three types of PSC clouds—nitric acid trihydrate clouds, slowly cooling water-ice clouds, and rapid cooling water-ice (nacreous) clouds—provide surfaces for chemical reactions whose products will, in the spring lead to ozone destruction.

The photochemical processes involved are complex but well understood. The key observation is that, ordinarily, most of the chlorine in the stratosphere resides in "reservoir" compounds, primarily chlorine nitrate ($ClONO_2$) as well as stable end products such as HCl. The formation of end products essentially remove Cl from the ozone depletion process. The former sequester Cl, which can be later made available via absorption of light at shorter wavelengths than 400 nm. During the Antarctic winter and spring, however, reactions on the surface of the polar stratospheric cloud particles convert these "reservoir" compounds into reactive free radicals (Cl and ClO). The process by which the clouds remove NO_2 from the stratosphere by converting it to nitric acid in the PSC particles, which then are lost by sedimentation is called denitrification. This prevents newly formed ClO from being converted back into $ClONO_2$.

The role of sunlight in ozone depletion is the reason why the Antarctic ozone depletion is greatest during spring. During winter, even though PSCs are at their most abundant, there is no light over the pole to drive chemical reactions. During the spring, however, the sun comes out, providing energy to drive photochemical reactions and melt the polar stratospheric clouds, releasing considerable ClO, which drives the hole mechanism. Further warming temperatures near the end of spring break up the vortex around mid-December. As warm, ozone and NO_2-rich air flows in from lower latitudes, the PSCs are destroyed, the enhanced ozone depletion process shuts down, and the ozone hole closes.

Most of the ozone that is destroyed is in the lower stratosphere, in contrast to the much smaller ozone depletion through homogeneous gas phase reactions, which occurs primarily in the upper stratosphere.

Interest in Ozone Layer Depletion

Public misconceptions and misunderstandings of complex issues like the ozone depletion are common. The limited scientific knowledge of the public led to a confusion with global warming or the perception of global warming as a subset of the "ozone hole". In the beginning, classical green

NGOs refrained from using CFC depletion for campaigning, as they assumed the topic was too complicated. They became active much later, e.g. in Greenpeace's support for a CFC-free fridge produced by the former East German company VEB dkk Scharfenstein.

The metaphors used in the CFC discussion (ozone shield, ozone hole) are not "exact" in the scientific sense. The "ozone hole" is more of a *depression*, less "a hole in the windshield". The ozone does not disappear through the layer, nor is there a uniform "thinning" of the ozone layer. However they resonated better with non-scientists and their concerns. The ozone hole was seen as a "hot issue" and imminent risk as lay people feared severe personal consequences such as skin cancer, cataracts, damage to plants, and reduction of plankton populations in the ocean's photic zone. Not only on the policy level, ozone regulation compared to climate change fared much better in public opinion. Americans voluntarily switched away from aerosol sprays before legislation was enforced, while climate change failed to achieve comparable concern and public action. The sudden recognition in 1985 that there was a substantial "hole" was widely reported in the press. The especially rapid ozone depletion in Antarctica had previously been dismissed as a measurement error. Scientific consensus was established after regulation.

While the Antarctic ozone hole has a relatively small effect on global ozone, the hole has generated a great deal of public interest because:

- Many have worried that ozone holes might start appearing over other areas of the globe, though to date the only other large-scale depletion is a smaller ozone "dimple" observed during the Arctic spring around the North Pole. Ozone at middle latitudes has declined, but by a much smaller extent (a decrease of about 4–5 percent).
- If stratospheric conditions become more severe (cooler temperatures, more clouds, more active chlorine), global ozone may decrease at a greater pace. Standard global warming theory predicts that the stratosphere will cool.
- When the Antarctic ozone hole breaks up each year, the ozone-depleted air drifts out into nearby regions. Decreases in the ozone level of up to 10 percent have been reported in New Zealand in the month following the breakup of the Antarctic ozone hole, with ultraviolet-B radiation intensities increasing by more than 15 percent since the 1970s.

Consequences of Ozone Layer Depletion

Since the ozone layer absorbs UVB ultraviolet light from the sun, ozone layer depletion increases surface UVB levels (all else equal), which could lead to damage, including increase in skin cancer. This was the reason for the Montreal Protocol. Although decreases in stratospheric ozone are well-tied to CFCs and to increases in surface UVB, there is no direct observational evidence linking ozone depletion to higher incidence of skin cancer and eye damage in human beings. This is partly because UVA, which has also been implicated in some forms of skin cancer, is not absorbed by ozone, and because it is nearly impossible to control statistics for lifestyle changes over time.

Increased UV

Ozone, while a minority constituent in Earth's atmosphere, is responsible for most of the absorption of UVB radiation. The amount of UVB radiation that penetrates through the ozone layer decreases exponentially with the slant-path thickness and density of the layer. When stratospheric ozone levels decrease, higher levels of UVB reach the Earth's surface. UV-driven phenolic formation in tree rings has dated the start of ozone depletion in northern latitudes to the late 1700s.

In October 2008, the Ecuadorian Space Agency published a report called HIPERION. The study used ground instruments in Ecuador and the last 28 years' data from 12 satellites of several countries, and found that the UV radiation reaching equatorial latitudes was far greater than expected, with the UV Index climbing as high as 24 in Quito; the WHO considers 11 as an extreme index and a great risk to health. The report concluded that depleted ozone levels around the mid-latitudes of the planet are already endangering large populations in these areas. Later, the CONIDA, the Peruvian Space Agency, published its own study, which yielded almost the same findings as the Ecuadorian study.

Biological Effects

The main public concern regarding the ozone hole has been the effects of increased surface UV radiation on human health. So far, ozone depletion in most locations has been typically a few percent and, no direct evidence of health damage is available in most latitudes. If the high levels of depletion seen in the ozone hole were to be common across the globe, the effects could be substantially more dramatic. As the ozone hole over Antarctica has in some instances grown so large as to affect parts of Australia, New Zealand, Chile, Argentina, and South Africa, environmentalists have been concerned that the increase in surface UV could be significant.

Ozone depletion would magnify all of the effects of UV on human health, both positive (including production of vitamin D) and negative (including sunburn, skin cancer, and cataracts). In addition, increased surface UV leads to increased tropospheric ozone, which is a health risk to humans.

Basal and Squamous Cell Carcinomas

The most common forms of skin cancer in humans, basal and squamous cell carcinomas, have been strongly linked to UVB exposure. The mechanism by which UVB induces these cancers is well understood—absorption of UVB radiation causes the pyrimidine bases in the DNA molecule to form dimers, resulting in transcription errors when the DNA replicates. These cancers are relatively mild and rarely fatal, although the treatment of squamous cell carcinoma sometimes requires extensive reconstructive surgery. By combining epidemiological data with results of animal studies, scientists have estimated that every one percent decrease in long-term stratospheric ozone would increase the incidence of these cancers by two percent.

Malignant Melanoma

Another form of skin cancer, malignant melanoma, is much less common but far more dangerous, being lethal in about 15–20 percent of the cases diagnosed. The relationship between malignant melanoma and ultraviolet exposure is not yet fully understood, but it appears that both UVB and UVA are involved. Because of this uncertainty, it is difficult to estimate the effect of ozone depletion on melanoma incidence. One study showed that a 10 percent increase in UVB radiation was associated with a 19 percent increase in melanomas for men and 16 percent for women. A study of people in Punta Arenas, at the southern tip of Chile, showed a 56 percent increase in melanoma and a 46 percent increase in nonmelanoma skin cancer over a period of seven years, along with decreased ozone and increased UVB levels.

Cortical Cataracts

Epidemiological studies suggest an association between ocular cortical cataracts and UVB exposure, using crude approximations of exposure and various cataract assessment techniques. A detailed assessment of ocular exposure to UVB was carried out in a study on Chesapeake Bay Watermen, where increases in average annual ocular exposure were associated with increasing risk of cortical opacity. In this highly exposed group of predominantly white males, the evidence linking cortical opacities to sunlight exposure was the strongest to date. Based on these results, ozone depletion is predicted to cause hundreds of thousands of additional cataracts by 2050.

Increased Tropospheric Ozone

Increased surface UV leads to increased tropospheric ozone. Ground-level ozone is generally recognized to be a health risk, as ozone is toxic due to its strong oxidant properties. The risks are particularly high for young children, the elderly, and those with asthma or other respiratory difficulties. At this time, ozone at ground level is produced mainly by the action of UV radiation on combustion gases from vehicle exhausts.

Increased Production of Vitamin D

Vitamin D is produced in the skin by ultraviolet light. Thus, higher UVB exposure raises human vitamin D in those deficient in it. Recent research (primarily since the Montreal Protocol) shows that many humans have less than optimal vitamin D levels. In particular, in the U.S. population, the lowest quarter of vitamin D (<17.8 ng/ml) were found using information from the National Health and Nutrition Examination Survey to be associated with an increase in all-cause mortality in the general population. While blood level of vitamin D in excess of 100 ng/ml appear to raise blood calcium excessively and to be associated with higher mortality, the body has mechanisms that prevent sunlight from producing vitamin D in excess of the body's requirements.

Effects on Animals

A November 2010 report by scientists at the Institute of Zoology in London found that whales off the coast of California have shown a sharp rise in sun damage, and these scientists "fear that the thinning ozone layer is to blame". The study photographed and took skin biopsies from over 150 whales in the Gulf of California and found "widespread evidence of epidermal damage commonly associated with acute and severe sunburn", having cells that form when the DNA is damaged by UV radiation. The findings suggest "rising UV levels as a result of ozone depletion are to blame for the observed skin damage, in the same way that human skin cancer rates have been on the increase in recent decades."

Effects on Crops

An increase of UV radiation would be expected to affect crops. A number of economically important species of plants, such as rice, depend on cyanobacteria residing on their roots for the retention of nitrogen. Cyanobacteria are sensitive to UV radiation and would be affected by its increase. "Despite mechanisms to reduce or repair the effects of increased ultraviolet radiation, plants have a limited ability to adapt to increased levels of UVB, therefore plant growth can be directly affected by UVB radiation."

Public Policy

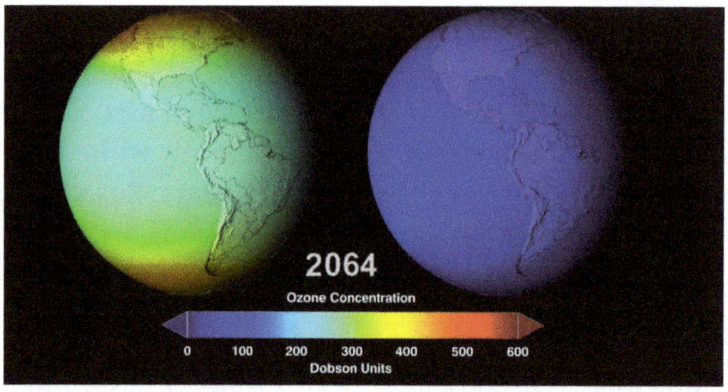

Comparsion of the projected (left sphere) and the world avoided (right sphere) if CFC and other ozone-depleting chemicals were not banned.

The full extent of the damage that CFCs have caused to the ozone layer is not known and will not be known for decades; however, marked decreases in column ozone have already been observed. The Montreal and Vienna conventions were installed long before a scientific consensus was established or important uncertainties in the science field were being resolved. The ozone case was understood comparably well by lay persons as e.g. *Ozone shield* or *ozone hole* were useful "easy-to-understand bridging metaphors". Americans voluntarily switched away from aerosol sprays, resulting in a 50 percent sales loss even before legislation was enforced.

After a 1976 report by the United States National Academy of Sciences concluded that credible scientific evidence supported the ozone depletion hypothesis a few countries, including the United States, Canada, Sweden, Denmark, and Norway, moved to eliminate the use of CFCs in aerosol spray cans. At the time this was widely regarded as a first step towards a more comprehensive regulation policy, but progress in this direction slowed in subsequent years, due to a combination of political factors (continued resistance from the halocarbon industry and a general change in attitude towards environmental regulation during the first two years of the Reagan administration) and scientific developments (subsequent National Academy assessments that indicated that the first estimates of the magnitude of ozone depletion had been overly large). A critical DuPont manufacturing patent for Freon was set to expire in 1979. The United States banned the use of CFCs in aerosol cans in 1978. The European Community rejected proposals to ban CFCs in aerosol sprays, and in the U.S., CFCs continued to be used as refrigerants and for cleaning circuit boards. Worldwide CFC production fell sharply after the U.S. aerosol ban, but by 1986 had returned nearly to its 1976 level. In 1993, DuPont Canada closed its CFC facility.

The U.S. government's attitude began to change again in 1983, when William Ruckelshaus replaced Anne M. Burford as Administrator of the United States Environmental Protection Agency. Under Ruckelshaus and his successor, Lee Thomas, the EPA pushed for an international approach to halocarbon regulations. In 1985 twenty nations, including most of the major CFC producers, signed the Vienna Convention for the Protection of the Ozone Layer, which established a framework for negotiating international regulations on ozone-depleting substances. That same year, the discovery of the Antarctic ozone hole was announced, causing a revival in public attention to the issue. In 1987, representatives from 43 nations signed the Montreal Protocol. Meanwhile, the halocarbon industry shifted its position and started supporting a protocol to limit CFC production. However, this shift was uneven with DuPont acting more quickly than its European counterparts. DuPont may have feared court action related to increased skin cancer, especially as the EPA had published a study in 1986 claiming that an additional 40 million cases and 800,000 cancer deaths were to be expected in the U.S. in the next 88 years. The EU shifted its position as well after Germany gave up its defence of the CFC industry and started supporting moves towards regulation. Government and industry in France and the UK tried to defend their CFC producing industries even after the Montreal Protocol had been signed.

At Montreal, the participants agreed to freeze production of CFCs at 1986 levels and to reduce production by 50 percent by 1999. After a series of scientific expeditions to the Antarctic produced convincing evidence that the ozone hole was indeed caused by chlorine and bromine from man-made organohalogens, the Montreal Protocol was strengthened at a 1990 meeting in London. The participants agreed to phase out CFCs and halons entirely (aside from a very small amount marked for certain "essential" uses, such as asthma inhalers) by 2000 in non-Article 5 countries and by 2010 in Article 5 (less developed) signatories. At a 1992 meeting in Copenhagen, the phase-out date was moved up to 1996. At the same meeting, methyl bromide (MeBr), a fumigant used primarily in agricultural production, was added to the list of controlled substances. For all substances controlled under the protocol, phaseout schedules were delayed for less developed ('Article 5(1)') countries, and phaseout in these countries was supported by transfers of expertise, technology, and money from non-Article 5(1) Parties to the Protocol. Additionally, exemptions from the agreed schedules could be applied for under the Essential Use Exemption (EUE) process for substances other than methyl bromide and under the Critical Use Exemption (CUE) process for methyl bromide.

Civil society including especially NGOs, played critical roles at all stages of policy development leading up to the Vienna Conference, the Montreal Protocol, and in assessing compliance afterwards. The major companies claimed that no alternatives to HFC existed. An ozone-safe hydrocarbon refrigerant was developed at a Hamburg technological institute in Germany, and in 1992 came to the attention of the non-governmental organization (NGO) Greenpeace. Greenpeace was given the patent, called it "Greenfreeze," and left the patent as open source. The NGO then worked successfully first with a small and struggling company to market an appliance beginning in Europe, then Asia and later Latin America, receiving a 1997 UNEP award. By 1995, Germany had already made CFC refrigerators illegal. Since 2004, corporations like Coca-Cola, Carlsberg, and IKEA have been forming a coalition to promote the ozone-safe Greenfreeze units. Production spread to companies like Electrolux, Bosch, and LG, with sales reaching some 300 million refrigerators by 2008. In Latin America, a domestic Argentinian company began Greenfreeze production in 2003, while the giant Bosch in Brazil began a year later. By 2013 it was being used by some 700 million refrigerators, making up about 40 percent of the market. In the U.S., however, change has been much slower. To some extent, CFCs were being replaced by the less damaging hydrochlorofluorocarbons (HCFCs), although concerns remain regarding HCFCs also. In some applications, hydrofluorocarbons (HFCs) were being used to replace CFCs. HFCs, which contain no chlorine or bromine, do not contribute at all to ozone depletion although they are potent greenhouse gases. The best known of these compounds is probably HFC-134a (R-134a), which in the United States has largely replaced CFC-12 (R-12) in automobile air conditioners. In laboratory analytics (a former "essential" use) the ozone depleting substances can be replaced with various other solvents. Chemical companies like Du Pont, whose representatives even disparaged Greenfreeze as "that German technology," maneuvered the EPA to block the technology in the U.S. until 2011. Ben & Jerry's of Unilever and General Electric, spurred by Greenpeace, had expressed formal interest in 2008 which figured in the EPA's final approval.

More recently, policy experts have advocated for efforts to link ozone protection efforts to climate protection efforts. Many ODS are also greenhouse gases, some thousands of times more powerful agents of radiative forcing than carbon dioxide over the short and medium term. Thus policies protecting the ozone layer have had benefits in mitigating climate change. In fact, the reduction of the radiative forcing due to ODS probably masked the true level of climate change effects of other greenhouse gases, and was responsible for the "slow down" of global warming from the mid-90s. Policy decisions in one arena affect the costs and effectiveness of environmental improvements in the other.

ODS Requirements in the Marine Industry

The IMO has amended MARPOL Annex VI Regulation 12 regarding ozone depleting substances. As from July 1, 2010, all vessels where MARPOL Annex VI is applicable should have a list of equipment using ozone depleting substances. The list should include name of ODS, type and location of equipment, quantity in kg and date. All changes since that date should be recorded in an ODS Record book on board recording all intended or unintended releases to the atmosphere. Furthermore, new ODS supply or landing to shore facilities should be recorded as well.

Prospects of Ozone Depletion

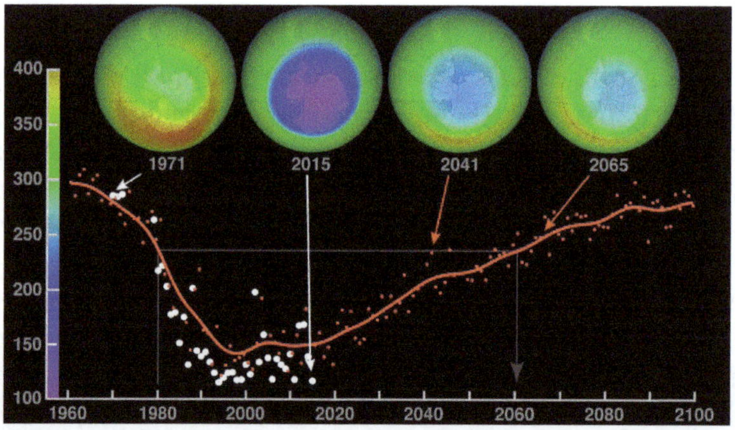

Ozone levels stabilized in the 1990s following the Montreal Protocol, and have started to recover. They are projected to reach pre-1980 levels before 2075.

Since the adoption and strengthening of the Montreal Protocol has led to reductions in the emissions of CFCs, atmospheric concentrations of the most-significant compounds have been declining. These substances are being gradually removed from the atmosphere; since peaking in 1994, the Effective Equivalent Chlorine (EECl) level in the atmosphere had dropped about 10 percent by 2008. The decrease in ozone-depleting chemicals has also been significantly affected by a decrease in bromine-containing chemicals. The data suggest that substantial natural sources exist for atmospheric methyl bromide (CH_3Br). The phase-out of CFCs means that nitrous oxide (N_2O), which is not covered by the Montreal Protocol, has become the most highly emitted ozone-depleting substance and is expected to remain so throughout the 21st century.

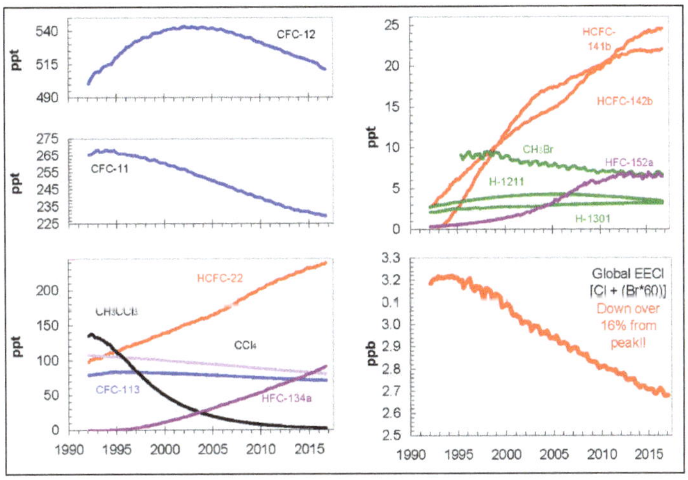

Ozone-depleting gas trends.

A 2005 IPCC review of ozone observations and model calculations concluded that the global amount of ozone has now approximately stabilized. Although considerable variability is expected from year to year, including in polar regions where depletion is largest, the ozone layer is expected to begin to recover in coming decades due to declining ozone-depleting substance concentrations, assuming full compliance with the Montreal Protocol.

The Antarctic ozone hole is expected to continue for decades. Ozone concentrations in the lower stratosphere over Antarctica will increase by 5–10 percent by 2020 and return to pre-1980 levels by about 2060–2075. This is 10–25 years later than predicted in earlier assessments, because of revised estimates of atmospheric concentrations of ozone-depleting substances, including a larger predicted future usage in developing countries. Another factor that may prolong ozone depletion is the drawdown of nitrogen oxides from above the stratosphere due to changing wind patterns. A gradual trend toward "healing" was reported in 2016.

The basic physical and chemical processes that lead to the formation of an ozone layer in the Earth's stratosphere were discovered by Sydney Chapman in 1930. Short-wavelength UV radiation splits an oxygen (O_2) molecule into two oxygen (O) atoms, which then combine with other oxygen molecules to form ozone. Ozone is removed when an oxygen atom and an ozone molecule "recombine" to form two oxygen molecules, i.e. $O + O_3 \rightarrow 2O_2$. In the 1950s, David Bates and Marcel Nicolet presented evidence that various free radicals, in particular hydroxyl (OH) and nitric oxide (NO), could catalyze this recombination reaction, reducing the overall amount of ozone. These free radicals were known to be present in the stratosphere, and so were regarded as part of the natural balance—it was estimated that in their absence, the ozone layer would be about twice as thick as it currently is.

In 1970 Paul Crutzen pointed out that emissions of nitrous oxide (N_2O), a stable, long-lived gas produced by soil bacteria, from the Earth's surface could affect the amount of nitric oxide (NO) in the stratosphere. Crutzen showed that nitrous oxide lives long enough to reach the stratosphere, where it is converted into NO. Crutzen then noted that increasing use of fertilizers might have led to an increase in nitrous oxide emissions over the natural background, which would in turn result in an increase in the amount of NO in the stratosphere. Thus human activity could affect the stratospheric ozone layer. In the following year, Crutzen and (independently) Harold Johnston suggested that NO emissions from supersonic passenger aircraft, which would fly in the lower stratosphere, could also deplete the ozone layer. However, more recent analysis in 1995 by David W. Fahey, an atmospheric scientist at the National Oceanic and Atmospheric Administration, found that the drop in ozone would be from 1–2 percent if a fleet of 500 supersonic passenger aircraft were operated. This, Fahey expressed, would not be a showstopper for advanced supersonic passenger aircraft development.

Rowland–Molina Hypothesis

In 1974 Frank Sherwood Rowland, Chemistry Professor at the University of California at Irvine, and his postdoctoral associate Mario J. Molina suggested that long-lived organic halogen compounds, such as CFCs, might behave in a similar fashion as Crutzen had proposed for nitrous oxide. James Lovelock had recently discovered, during a cruise in the South Atlantic in 1971, that almost all of the CFC compounds manufactured since their invention in 1930 were still present in the atmosphere. Molina and Rowland concluded that, like N_2O, the CFCs would reach the stratosphere where they would be dissociated by UV light, releasing chlorine atoms. A year earlier, Richard Stolarski and Ralph Cicerone at the University of Michigan had shown that Cl is even more efficient than NO at catalyzing the destruction of ozone. Similar conclusions were reached by Michael McElroy and Steven Wofsy at Harvard University. Neither group, however, had realized that CFCs were a potentially large source of stratospheric chlorine—instead, they had been investigating the possible effects of HCl emissions from the Space Shuttle, which are very much smaller.

The Rowland–Molina hypothesis was strongly disputed by representatives of the aerosol and halocarbon industries. The Chair of the Board of DuPont was quoted as saying that ozone depletion theory is "a science fiction tale a load of rubbish utter nonsense". Robert Abplanalp, the President of Precision Valve Corporation (and inventor of the first practical aerosol spray can valve), wrote to the Chancellor of UC Irvine to complain about Rowland's public statements. Nevertheless, within three years most of the basic assumptions made by Rowland and Molina were confirmed by laboratory measurements and by direct observation in the stratosphere. The concentrations of the source gases (CFCs and related compounds) and the chlorine reservoir species (HCl and $ClONO_2$) were measured throughout the stratosphere, and demonstrated that CFCs were indeed the major source of stratospheric chlorine, and that nearly all of the CFCs emitted would eventually reach the stratosphere. Even more convincing was the measurement, by James G. Anderson and collaborators, of chlorine monoxide (ClO) in the stratosphere. ClO is produced by the reaction of Cl with ozone—its observation thus demonstrated that Cl radicals not only were present in the stratosphere but also were actually involved in destroying ozone. McElroy and Wofsy extended the work of Rowland and Molina by showing that bromine atoms were even more effective catalysts for ozone loss than chlorine atoms and argued that the brominated organic compounds known as halons, widely used in fire extinguishers, were a potentially large source of stratospheric bromine. In 1976 the United States National Academy of Sciences released a report concluding that the ozone depletion hypothesis was strongly supported by the scientific evidence. In response the United States, Canada and Norway banned the use of CFCs in aerosol spray cans in 1978. Early estimates were that, if CFC production continued at 1977 levels, the total atmospheric ozone would after a century or so reach a steady state, 15 to 18 percent below normal levels. By 1984, when better evidence on the speed of critical reactions was available, this estimate was changed to 5 to 9 percent steady-state depletion.

Antarctic Ozone Hole

The discovery of the Antarctic "ozone hole" by British Antarctic Survey scientists Farman, Gardiner and Shanklin (first reported in a paper in *Nature* in May 1985) came as a shock to the scientific community, because the observed decline in polar ozone was far larger than anyone had anticipated. Satellite measurements showing massive depletion of ozone around the south pole were becoming available at the same time. However, these were initially rejected as unreasonable by data quality control algorithms (they were filtered out as errors since the values were unexpectedly low); the ozone hole was detected only in satellite data when the raw data was reprocessed following evidence of ozone depletion in *in situ* observations. When the software was rerun without the flags, the ozone hole was seen as far back as 1976.

Susan Solomon, an atmospheric chemist at the National Oceanic and Atmospheric Administration (NOAA), proposed that chemical reactions on polar stratospheric clouds (PSCs) in the cold Antarctic stratosphere caused a massive, though localized and seasonal, increase in the amount of chlorine present in active, ozone-destroying forms. The polar stratospheric clouds in Antarctica are only formed when there are very low temperatures, as low as −80 °C, and early spring conditions. In such conditions the ice crystals of the cloud provide a suitable surface for conversion of unreactive chlorine compounds into reactive chlorine compounds, which can deplete ozone easily.

Moreover, the polar vortex formed over Antarctica is very tight and the reaction occurring on the surface of the cloud crystals is far different from when it occurs in atmosphere. These conditions have led to ozone hole formation in Antarctica. This hypothesis was decisively confirmed, first by laboratory measurements and subsequently by direct measurements, from the ground and from high-altitude airplanes, of very high concentrations of chlorine monoxide (ClO) in the Antarctic stratosphere.

Alternative hypotheses, which had attributed the ozone hole to variations in solar UV radiation or to changes in atmospheric circulation patterns, were also tested and shown to be untenable.

Meanwhile, analysis of ozone measurements from the worldwide network of ground-based Dobson spectrophotometers led an international panel to conclude that the ozone layer was in fact being depleted, at all latitudes outside of the tropics. These trends were confirmed by satellite measurements. As a consequence, the major halocarbon-producing nations agreed to phase out production of CFCs, halons, and related compounds, a process that was completed in 1996.

Since 1981 the United Nations Environment Programme, under the auspices of the World Meteorological Organization, has sponsored a series of technical reports on the Scientific Assessment of Ozone Depletion, based on satellite measurements. The 2007 report showed that the hole in the ozone layer was recovering and the smallest it had been for about a decade. The 2010 report found, "Over the past decade, global ozone and ozone in the Arctic and Antarctic regions is no longer decreasing but is not yet increasing. The ozone layer outside the Polar regions is projected to recover to its pre-1980 levels some time before the middle of this century. In contrast, the springtime ozone hole over the Antarctic is expected to recover much later." In 2012, NOAA and NASA reported "Warmer air temperatures high above the Antarctic led to the second smallest season ozone hole in 20 years averaging 17.9 million square kilometres. The hole reached its maximum size for the season on Sept 22, stretching to 21.2 million square kilometres." A gradual trend toward "healing" was reported in 2016.

The hole in the Earth's ozone layer over the South Pole has affected atmospheric circulation in the Southern Hemisphere all the way to the equator. The ozone hole has influenced atmospheric circulation all the way to the tropics and increased rainfall at low, subtropical latitudes in the Southern Hemisphere.

Arctic Ozone Hole

On March 3, 2005, the journal *Nature* published an article linking 2004's unusually large Arctic ozone hole to solar wind activity.

On March 15, 2011, a record ozone layer loss was observed, with about half of the ozone present over the Arctic having been destroyed. The change was attributed to increasingly cold winters in the Arctic stratosphere at an altitude of approximately 20 km (12 mi), a change associated with global warming in a relationship that is still under investigation. By March 25, the ozone loss had become the largest compared to that observed in all previous winters with the possibility that it would become an ozone hole. This would require that the quantities of ozone to fall below 200 Dobson units, from the 250 recorded over central Siberia. It is predicted that the thinning layer would affect parts of Scandinavia and Eastern Europe on March 30–31.

On October 2, 2011, a study was published in the journal *Nature*, which said that between December 2010 and March 2011 up to 80 percent of the ozone in the atmosphere at about 20 kilometres (12 mi) above the surface was destroyed. The level of ozone depletion was severe enough that scientists said it could be compared to the ozone hole that forms over Antarctica every winter. According to the study, "for the first time, sufficient loss occurred to reasonably be described as an Arctic ozone hole." The study analyzed data from the Aura and CALIPSO satellites, and determined that the larger-than-normal ozone loss was due to an unusually long period of cold weather in the Arctic, some 30 days more than typical, which allowed for more ozone-destroying chlorine compounds to be created. According to Lamont Poole, a co-author of the study, cloud and aerosol particles on which the chlorine compounds are found "were abundant in the Arctic until mid March 2011—much later than usual—with average amounts at some altitudes similar to those observed in the Antarctic, and dramatically larger than the near-zero values seen in March in most Arctic winters".

Tibet Ozone Hole

As winters that are colder are more affected, at times there is an ozone hole over Tibet. In 2006, a 2.5 million square kilometer ozone hole was detected over Tibet. Also again in 2011 an ozone hole appeared over mountainous regions of Tibet, Xinjiang, Qinghai and the Hindu Kush, along with an unprecedented hole over the Arctic, though the Tibet one is far less intense than the ones over the Arctic or Antarctic.

Potential Depletion by Storm Clouds

Research in 2012 showed that the same process that produces the ozone hole over Antarctica occurs over summer storm clouds in the United States, and thus may be destroying ozone there as well.

Ozone Depletion and Global Warming

Among others, Robert Watson had a role in the science assessment and in the regulation efforts of ozone depletion and global warming. Prior to the 1980s, the EU, NASA, NAS, UNEP, WMO and the British government had dissenting scientific reports and Watson played a role in the process of unified assessments. Based on the experience with the ozone case, the IPCC started to work on a unified reporting and science assessment to reach a consensus to provide the IPCC Summary for Policymakers.

There are various areas of linkage between ozone depletion and global warming science:

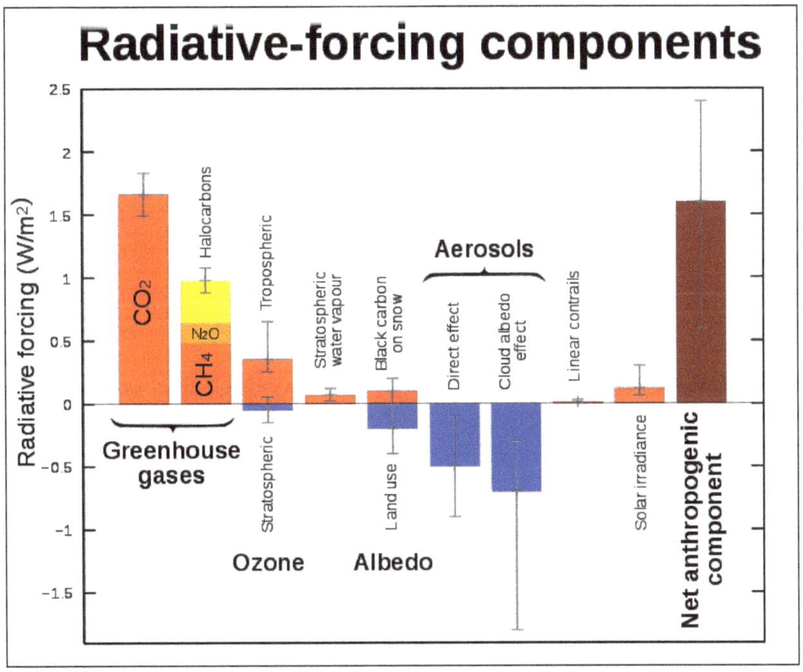

Radiative forcing from various greenhouse gases and other sources.

- The same CO_2 radiative forcing that produces global warming is expected to cool the stratosphere. This cooling, in turn, is expected to produce a relative *increase* in ozone (O_3) depletion in polar area and the frequency of ozone holes.

- Conversely, ozone depletion represents a radiative forcing of the climate system. There are two opposing effects: Reduced ozone causes the stratosphere to absorb less solar radiation, thus cooling the stratosphere while warming the troposphere; the resulting colder stratosphere emits less long-wave radiation downward, thus cooling the troposphere. Overall, the cooling dominates; the IPCC concludes "*observed stratospheric O_3 losses over the past two decades have caused a negative forcing of the surface-troposphere system*" of about -0.15 ± 0.10 watts per square meter (W/m^2).

- One of the strongest predictions of the greenhouse effect is that the stratosphere will cool. Although this cooling has been observed, it is not trivial to separate the effects of changes in the concentration of greenhouse gases and ozone depletion since both will lead to cooling. However, this can be done by numerical stratospheric modeling. Results from the National Oceanic and Atmospheric Administration's Geophysical Fluid Dynamics Laboratory show that above 20 km (12 mi), the greenhouse gases dominate the cooling.

- As noted under 'Public Policy', ozone depleting chemicals are also often greenhouse gases. The increases in concentrations of these chemicals have produced 0.34 ± 0.03 W/m² of radiative forcing, corresponding to about 14 percent of the total radiative forcing from increases in the concentrations of well-mixed greenhouse gases.
- The long term modeling of the process, its measurement, study, design of theories and testing take decades to document, gain wide acceptance, and ultimately become the dominant paradigm. Several theories about the destruction of ozone were hypothesized in the 1980s, published in the late 1990s, and are currently being investigated. Dr Drew Schindell, and Dr Paul Newman, NASA Goddard, proposed a theory in the late 1990s, using computational modeling methods to model ozone destruction, that accounted for 78 percent of the ozone destroyed. Further refinement of that model accounted for 89 percent of the ozone destroyed, but pushed back the estimated recovery of the ozone hole from 75 years to 150 years. (An important part of that model is the lack of stratospheric flight due to depletion of fossil fuels.)

Misconceptions

CFC Weight

Since CFC molecules are heavier than air (nitrogen or oxygen), it is commonly believed that the CFC molecules cannot reach the stratosphere in significant amount. However, atmospheric gases are not sorted by weight; the forces of wind can fully mix the gases in the atmosphere. Lighter CFCs are evenly distributed throughout the turbosphere and reach the upper atmosphere, although some of the heavier CFCs are not evenly distributed.

Percentage of Man-made Chlorine

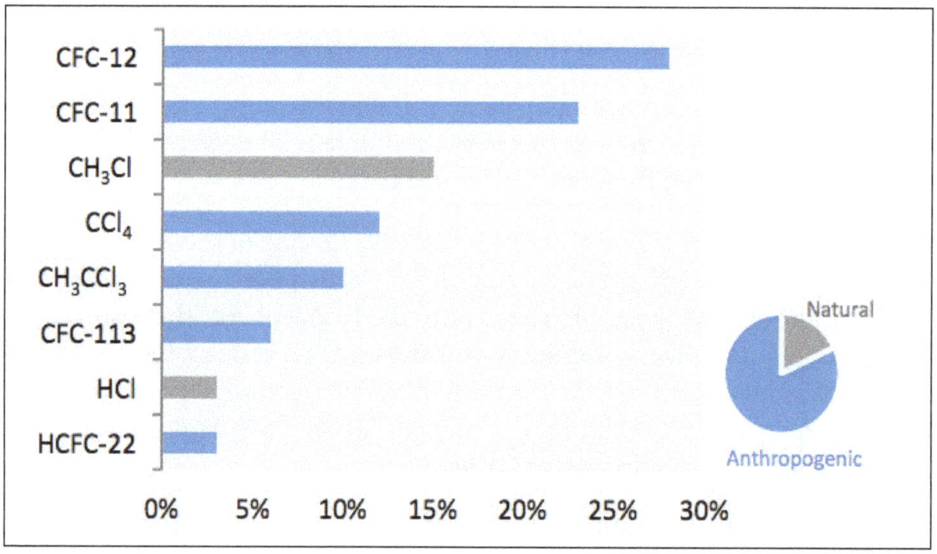

Sources of stratospheric chlorine.

Another misconception is that "it is generally accepted that natural sources of tropospheric chlorine are four to five times larger than man-made ones." While this statement is strictly true, *tropospheric* chlorine is irrelevant; it is *stratospheric* chlorine that affects ozone depletion. Chlorine from ocean spray is soluble and thus is washed by rainfall before it reaches the stratosphere. CFCs, in contrast, are insoluble and long-lived, allowing them to reach the stratosphere. In the lower atmosphere, there is much more chlorine from CFCs and related haloalkanes than there is in HCl from salt spray, and in the stratosphere halocarbons are dominant. Only methyl chloride, which is one of these halocarbons, has a mainly natural source, and it is responsible for about 20 percent of the chlorine in the stratosphere; the remaining 80 percent comes from manmade sources.

Very violent volcanic eruptions can inject HCl into the stratosphere, but researchers have shown that the contribution is not significant compared to that from CFCs. A similar erroneous assertion is that soluble halogen compounds from the volcanic plume of Mount Erebus on Ross Island, Antarctica are a major contributor to the Antarctic ozone hole.

Nevertheless, a 2015 study showed that the role of Mount Erebus volcano in the Antarctic ozone depletion was probably underestimated. Based on the NCEP/NCAR reanalysis data over the last 35 years and by using the NOAA HYSPLIT trajectory model, researchers showed that Erebus volcano gas emissions (including hydrogen chloride (HCl)) can reach the Antarctic stratosphere via high-latitude cyclones and then the polar vortex. Depending on Erebus volcano activity, the additional annual HCl mass entering the stratosphere from Erebus varies from 1.0 to 14.3 kt.

First Observation

G.M.B. Dobson mentioned that when springtime ozone levels in the Antarctic over Halley Bay were first measured in 1956, he was surprised to find that they were ~320 DU, or about 150 DU below spring Arctic levels of ~450 DU. These were at that time the only known Antarctic ozone values available. What Dobson describes is essentially the *baseline* from which the ozone hole is measured: actual ozone hole values are in the 150–100 DU range.

The discrepancy between the Arctic and Antarctic noted by Dobson was primarily a matter of timing: during the Arctic spring ozone levels rose smoothly, peaking in April, whereas in the Antarctic they stayed approximately constant during early spring, rising abruptly in November when the polar vortex broke down.

The behavior seen in the Antarctic ozone hole is completely different. Instead of staying constant, early springtime ozone levels suddenly drop from their already low winter values, by as much as 50 percent, and normal values are not reached again until December.

Location of Hole

Some people thought that the ozone hole should be above the sources of CFCs. However, CFCs are well mixed globally in the troposphere and stratosphere. The reason for occurrence of the ozone hole above Antarctica is not because there are more CFCs concentrated but because the low temperatures help form polar stratospheric clouds. In fact, there are findings of significant and localized "ozone holes" above other parts of the earth.

DEPLETION OF FRESHWATER RESOURCES

In many parts of the world people are extracting water from aquifers more quickly than the aquifers are replenished by recharge. In addition to draining aquifers, excessive groundwater pumping changes groundwater flow patterns around wells and can drain nearby rivers and streams. This happens because pumping changes the natural equilibrium that exists in an undeveloped aquifer with discharge balancing recharge. When pumping starts, groundwater stores are depleted in the vicinity of the well, creating a cone of depression in the hydraulic head. If a new water source such as a river or stream is available close by, the well may capture (draw water from) that source and increase its recharge rate until this inflow matches the pumping rate. If no such source is available and pumping draws the water table down far enough, it will dry up the aquifer or deplete it so far that is it not physically possible or affordable to pump out the last stores of water.

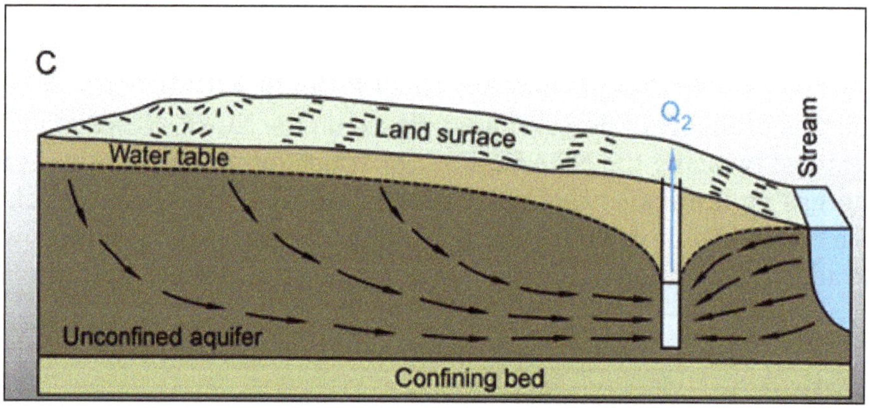

Effects of groundwater pumping.

Pumping quickly lowers the pressure within confined aquifers so that water no longer rises to the surface naturally. Fifty years ago artesian aquifers were common, but today they have become rare because of widespread groundwater withdrawals. In unconfined aquifers, air fills pores above the water table, so the water table falls much more slowly than in confined aquifers. As aquifers are depleted, water has to be lifted from much greater depths. In some parts of the world, the energy costs of lifting groundwater from deep beneath the surface have become prohibitive. Overuse of groundwater can also reduce the quality of the remaining water if wells draw from contaminated surface sources or if water tables near the coast drop below sea level, causing salt water to flow into aquifers. Serious groundwater depletion has occurred in major parts of North Africa, the Middle East, South and Central Asia, North China, North America, and Australia, along with other localized areas worldwide. In some cases, such as the Ogallala aquifer in the central United States, water tables are falling so low that wells can no longer produce water. In a draft plan issued in mid-2006, the Texas Water Development Board projected that the state's water supplies would fall by about 18 percent between 2010 and 2060, "primarily due to the accumulation of sediments in reservoirs and the depletion of aquifers," and that at the same time the state's population would more than double. If Texas did not implement the water management plan, the board estimated, water shortages could cost the state nearly $100 billion by 2060.

Many rivers around the globe have also been depleted by increasing water withdrawals. Some, such as the Colorado and Rio Grande, no longer reach the sea during much of the year because their flow levels have been reduced so drastically by dams and water diversion. This overuse destroys estuaries at river mouths, which are important habitats and breeding grounds for fish and birds.

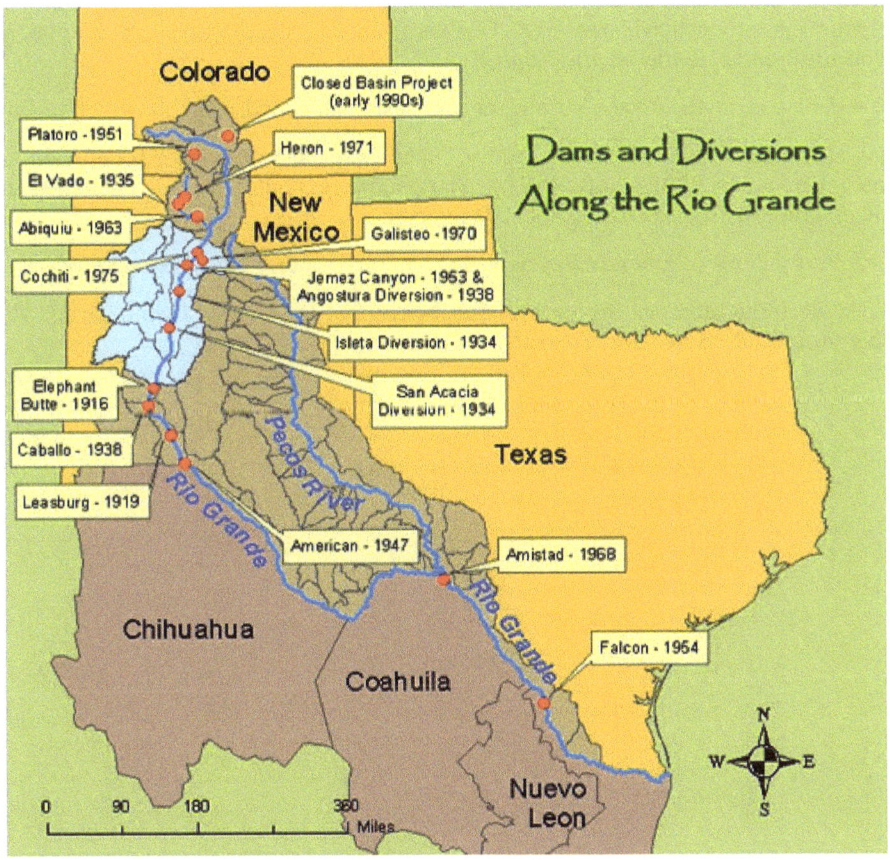

Dams and diversions along the Rio Grande.

Under normal conditions, most rivers are gaining rivers: groundwater flows into the rivers because the local water table sits at a higher elevation than the river water. However, with excessive groundwater pumping, water tables slowly decline and natural discharge to the rivers is reduced, so river flow declines. Over the long term, groundwater extraction may greatly reduce river flows in many regions. This connection between water levels in aquifers and river flows complicates the process of estimating sustainable yield from aquifers. If users pump more water from an aquifer than the natural rate of recharge, the aquifer may draw water from adjoining rivers and increase its rate of recharge. However, by doing so it will reduce surface water flows.

By regulating river flows to reduce floods and increase flows during dry periods, dams have major impacts on river ecosystems. Like forest fires, river floods play important ecological roles that we have only begun to appreciate and foster in recent decades. Among other services, floods scour out channels, deposit nutrient-rich sediments on flood plains, and help to replenish groundwater. In regions where rivers have been channeled between levees to prevent flooding, they no longer deposit sediments and nutrients on surrounding lands. Scientists widely agree that damage from Hurricane Katrina in August 2005 was magnified because levees and canals around New Orleans had directed the Mississippi River's flow straight into the Gulf of Mexico for decades. Without fresh water and sediment from the Mississippi, southern Louisiana's wetlands degraded and subsided, reducing their ability to buffer the region against storms and flooding.

References

- Causes-effects-solutions-depletion-natural-resources, conserve-energy-future.com, Retrieved 11 June, 2019
- "Is U.S. natural gas production increasing?". US Energy Information Administration. 2008. Archived from the original on 2008-06-12. Retrieved 2008-09-08
- Fossil-fuel-depletion, methodology, learning-center: sustainableminds.com, Retrieved 12 July, 2019
- Abarca, J. F.; Casiccia, C. C. (December 2002). "Skin cancer and ultraviolet-B radiation under the Antarctic ozone hole: southern Chile, 1987–2000". Photodermatol Photoimmunol Photomed. 18 (6): 294–302. Doi:10.1034/j.1600-0781.2002.02782.x. PMID 12535025
- Causes-effects-solutions-of-groundwater-depletion: conserve-energy-future.com, Retrieved 13 August, 2019
- "The Ozone Hole-The Montreal Protocol on Substances that Deplete the Ozone Layer". Theozonehole.com. September 16, 1987. Retrieved May 15, 2019

Conservation of Natural Resources

5 CHAPTER

Natural resources can be conserved by using various methods such as using alternative energy sources, rainwater harvesting, switching to biofuel, reducing the use of plastics, using hybrid vehicles, etc. This chapter discusses in detail these practices and concepts related to conservation of natural resources.

ALTERNATIVE ENERGY SOURCES

Alternative energy encompasses all those things that do not consume fossil fuel. They are widely available and environment friendly. They cause little or almost no pollution. There have been several alternative energy projects running in various countries to reduce our dependence on traditional fossil fuels. There are many impressive options that you can take into consideration such as solar tankless water heater reviews.

Solar Energy

Solar is the first energy source in the world. It was in use much earlier before humans even learn how to light a fire. Many living things are dependent on solar energy from plants, aquatic life and the animals. The solar is mostly used in generating light and heat. The solar energy coming down to the planet is affected by the orbital path of the sun and its variations within the galaxy. In addition, it is affected by activity taking place in space and on the sun. It was this energy that is believed to have been responsible for the breaking of ice during the ice age, which creates the separation of lands and sea.

Solar energy is one the alternative energy source that is used most widely across the globe. About 70% of the sunlight gets reflected back into the space and we have only 30% of sunlight to meet up our energy demands. While solar energy is used for producing solar energy, it is also used for drying clothes, used by plants during the process of photosynthesis and also used by human beings during winter seasons to make their body temperature warm. Solar energy can be extracted either by Solar Thermal or using Photovoltaic (PV) Cells.

There are two kinds of solar energy the active solar energy and the passive solar energy. Passive solar energy basically uses duration, position and sun's rays intensity to its advantage in heating a particular area. It also uses it to induce airflow from an area to the next. Active solar energy uses electrical technology and mechanical technology like collection panels in capturing, converting and storing of energy for future use.

Solar energy does not create any pollution and is widely used by many countries. It is renewable source of power since sun will continue to produce sunlight all the years. Solar panels, which are required to harness this energy can be used for long time and require little or no maintenance. Solar energy proves to be ineffective in colder regions which don't receive good sunlight. It cannot be used during night and not all the light from sun can be trapped by solar panels. Solar energy advantages are much more than its disadvantages which make it as a viable source of producing alternative energy.

Wind Energy

This is one of the energy sources that have been in use for a very long time and for centuries. It was used in powering sailing ships, which made it possible for explorers to sail around their trade routes in distant lands. A single windmill can power the crop irrigation, and the family energy needs, water pumping and electric lights. However, in the present time there are several windmills that are used to generate required energy mostly for industrial uses. Many of the wind turbines can capture much power all at once before feeding it to the power grid. This is commonly know as wind farms and has been in use for many years all round the world. It is only the United States that is going slow in terms of accepting this alternative energy source.

Wind power is renewable source of energy and reduces our alliance on foreign countries for supply of oil and gas. It does not cause any air pollution and have created several jobs in last few decades. Advancement in technologies has brought down the cost of setting up wind power plant. Wind energy can only be used in areas which experience high winds which mean that it cannot be used as a source to extract energy anywhere on earth. They sometimes create noise disturbances and cannot be used near residential areas. These disadvantages have made the use of wind energy to particular regions only.

Geothermal Energy

'Geo' means Earth and 'thermal' means energy. Geothermal energy means energy drawn or harnessed from beneath the earth. It is completely clean and renewable. Geothermal energy has been in used since last several years. The earth contains a molten rock called magma. Heat is continuously produced from there. The temperature increases about 3 degrees Celsius, for every 100 meters you go below ground. Below, 10,000 meters the temperature is so high, that it can be used to boil water. Water makes its way deep inside the earth and hot rock boils that water. The boiling water then produces steam which is captured by geothermal heat pumps. The steam turns the turbines which in turn activates generators.

ALTERNATIVE ENERGY PRODUCTION 2018	Billion BTU's
HYDROELECTRIC	18,213,033
NUCLEAR	14,711,238
WIND	3,499,942
BIOFUELS	1,391,457
SOLAR	696,655
GEOTHERMAL	190,838
TOTAL CONSUMPTION	282,120,615

Geothermal energy can be found anywhere on the earth. Most countries tap this energy to generate electricity, using thermal mass flowmeters, and power millions of homes. The areas which have high underground temperatures are the ones which are the ones which are prone to earthquakes and volcanoes. The United States produces more Geothermal electricity than any other country in the world. Most hot water geothermal reservoirs are located in the western states, Alaska, and Hawaii. Geothermal energy is totally renewable as earth will continue to produce heat as long as we are all are here. If these resources are tapped and are utilized effectively, they can provide solution to the world's power problems.

Geothermal energy produces no pollution, reduces our alliance on fossil fuels. It also results in significant cost savings as no fuel is required to harness energy from beneath the earth. These advantages make geothermal energy as one the best alternative energy source. But, geothermal has its downsides too. It is suitable to particular region and cannot be harnessed everywhere. The earth may release some harmful gases while releasing the heat which may prove adverse from mankind. Also, the areas where this energy is harnessed are prone to earthquakes and volcanoes. Apart from that, setting up of geothermal power stations requires huge installation cost. Here are some pros and cons of geothermal energy.

Hydroelectric Energy

Solar energy is produced by sun and wind energy is produced by moving of winds. The heat caused by sun drives the wind. The movement of winds is then captured by wind turbines. Both wind and sun cause water to evaporate. The water vapor then turns into rain or snow and flows down to sea or oceans through rivers or streams. The energy of the moving water can then be captured and called as hydroelectric power. Hydroelectric power stations capture the kinetic energy of moving water and give mechanical energy to turbines. The moving turbines then convert mechanical energy into electrical energy through generators. Dams around the world have been built for this purpose only. Hydropower is the largest producer of alternative energy in the world.

There are different types of hydropower plants. The selection of hydropower plant depends on many volume and flow of water. Hydropower is renewable, constant, predictable and controllable source of energy. They emit no greenhouse gases and are environment friendly. On the negative side, they may cause adverse effect on aquatic life, reduce flow of water which may affect agriculture, require huge costs to build and may cause havoc if they get breakdown.

Biomass Energy

This is the process by which an alternative energy is generated through conversion of biological materials and wastes into forms that can be used as energy sources for heating, power generation and transportation. Those carbon based substances or materials converted over a long period of time to fossil fuels are not regarded as biomass. However, in their original state they are regarded as biomass. This is because of the separation of the carbon they previously contained from the carbon cycle. This makes them figure differently affecting carbon dioxide levels in air.

Biomass energy has been around since ancient times when people use to burn wood or coal to heat their homes or prepare food. Wood still remains the most common source to produce biomass energy. Apart from wood, the other products that are used to create biomass energy include crops, plants, landfills, municipal and industrial waste, trees and agricultural waste. Biomass is renewable source of energy as we would be able to produce it as long as crops, plants and waste exist. It does not create any greenhouse gases and is can be easily extracted through the process of combustion. Another advantage of biomass is that it helps to reduce landfills. Biomass is comparatively ineffective as compared to fossil fuels. They release methane gases which can be harmful to the environment.

Ocean Energy

The earth promises many power sources. Just like the geothermal and solar energy, which have long been used in heating homes and lighting as well when harnessed. Even in the last century these forms of energy was in use. Due to massive size of oceans, this energy can be used on much wider scale than other alternative sources of energy. The waves produced by the ocean and tides that hit the sea shore has enormous potential in them. If they are harnessed with full capacity they can go a long way in reducing world's energy problems. There are 3 ways i.e. Tidal energy, Wave energy and Ocean thermal energy conversion (OTEC) via which ocean energy can be harnessed.

Tidal power basically involves using kinetic energy from the incoming and outgoing tides. The difference in high tides and low tides are also important in this respect. There is a lot of energy that can be harnessed from waves for use. It is another form of hydropower. The rise and fall of ocean tides are captured by tidal energy generators which turn turbines. The movement of turbines is responsible for producing electricity. In short, tidal energy generator captures the kinetic motion of the tides and converts them into electrical energy. The main advantage of tidal energy is that it is completely renewable and are much more predictable than wave energy.

Hydrogen Energy

Hydrogen is the most abundant element available on earth but it is rarely alone. Even water contains two third of hydrogen. It is usually available with other elements and have to separated before we can make use of it. Hydrogen has tremendous potential and can be used to power up homes, vehicles and even space rockets. It takes a lot of energy to separate hydrogen from other elements and therefore it proves to quite expensive to extract it.

The main benefit of hydrogen energy is that it is clean source of fuel and does not leave any waste elements behind except water. There are no harmful emissions and is environment friendly. It is completely renewable and can be produced over and over again on demand. Hydrogen can also be used to make bombs like the ones used by America on Hiroshima and Nagasaki which makes it highly inflammable. Dependency on fossil fuels still remains as we need them to extract hydrogen from other elements. Also, it is quite expensive to produce and store.

These are some of the alternative energy sources that can be taken into consideration when planning your energy production and usage. You can harness any of these and you will satisfy your power needs.

RAINWATER HARVESTING

Water is, undoubtedly, the top natural resource you need for your home use. It's glamorous to possess a stockpile of guns, gold, and jeweler, but without water, life might prove to be unbearable. Water shortages are sometimes inevitable, and so if you're not prepared for the eventuality, you might find yourself between a rock and a hard place. The best and cheapest alternative to the traditional water supply systems is rainwater harvesting. However, to be able to harvest rainwater, you'll need to install a rainwater harvesting system.

We all take water for granted. It is one of those natural resources that most people do not put a lot of thought into, but in order to continue enjoying that free supply of water for many more years, changes must be made. Rainwater harvesting is the process of collection of rainwater from surfaces on which rain falls, filtering it and storing it for multiple uses. Rainwater harvesting puts the supply of water back to normal levels. It is the collection and storage of water from surfaces that rain has fallen upon.

Rainwater harvesting is an innovative technique utilized to harvest rainwater from roofs and other above surfaces to be stored for later use. Rain harvested water can be used for garden and crop irrigation, watering livestock, laundry, and flushing toilets. However, you cannot use harvested rainwater for showering, bathroom sink or kitchen use because it's not really fit for consumption.

In a normal scenario the rainwater is collected from roof buildings and then stored inside of a special tank. Rainwater harvesting systems are designed after assessing site conditions that include rainfall pattern, incident rainfall, subsurface strata and their storage characteristics. Rainwater harvesting is popular all across the world, although in countries that are very dry, such as Australia, it is even more popular.

Rainwater can be harvested and used by those in the city who have running city water just as well as it can be used by those in more rural towns where adequate water supply may be unavailable. It is simple to replace many things that you are using regular city water with rainwater and enjoy numerous benefits when you do. Not only it helps you to conserve water but can also help you to save energy as the need to maintain centralized water system can be bypassed.

If you are worried about your roof being dirty, put that fear to the side. Many different tools are available to help you easily clean your roof. Hiring a roofer to com provide you with a cleaning is another option that you will have available.

Individuals are driven to harvest rainwater because of a wide range of factors such as unpredictable weather patterns, enhanced costs of infrastructure and explosion of water consumption. On top of that, most businesses and homes are looking to embrace green practices to become efficient and a lot more self-reliant. In this case, rainwater presents the obvious choice because it is the easiest and quickest method to minimize water consumption. Most homeowners that have embraced this practice have reported a reduction of about 50% in water bills. On top of helping to reduce water bills, rainwater harvesting helps the environment a lot.

Benefits of Rainwater Harvesting

The collection of rainwater and harvesting it for everyday use has an ample number of exciting benefits.

Provides Backup Source of Water

There are many uncertainties in water supply systems. Droughts may lead to shortage of water. Destruction of water supply systems may occur at specific locations. Major repairs and maintenance in water companies happen sporadically. All these variables lead to unavailability of water in your home. So, installing rainwater harvesting system is the best course of action to continue enjoying water supply in case any of the above variables occur.

The collected rainwater can be used for many different purposes around the home. This includes laundry, washing dishes and more. This would prevent groundwater depletion and augment ground water table.

Ecological Benefit

The ecological benefits of rainwater harvesting are immense. An activity like flushing the toilet, for instance, attributes to about 35% of home water usage. Add up the amount of water used to irrigate the lawn, do laundry, wash cars and the total amount water used is simply astronomical. For businesses, more so hospitality establishments that accommodate a big number of guests in a single location, require a lot of water to satisfy customers. Rainwater harvesting will simply help to fill this gap.

The ecological benefit rainwater harvesting systems bring is that there will be a significant reduction in the amount of water used from the mains. This, ideally, means that water companies will not have to artificially pump in water from rivers and lakes. This will help minimize the possibility of rivers drying up. Another great ecological benefit of rainwater harvesting systems is that they help reduced the load placed upon drainage systems, minimizing the impacts of flooding by funneling the runoff water into large tanks for recycling.

Easy to Maintain

Rainwater harvesting systems are considerably easy to maintain since they are not utilized for drinking, cooking or other sensitive uses. This means that they will not need installation of purification systems, which are usually expensive.

Rainwater harvesting systems are cost effective, provide high quality water, reduce dependence on wells. The surplus rainwater can also be used to recharge ground water aquifer through artificial recharge techniques.

Reduces Erosion and Flooding Around Buildings

Most buildings that utilize rainwater harvesting systems have a built-in catchment area on top of the roof, which is capable of collecting vast amounts of water in case of rain storms. It helps to reduce soil erosion as by capturing rainwater, the flow of storm water is reduced which can also prevent urban flooding. If the water were not collected efficiently, it could have resulted in serious soil erosion and flooding around the house.

Requires Low Upfront Capital Investment

Installation of rainwater harvesting system is not that expensive, plus it's a one-time installation, and that's it. The only routine maintenance required is cleaning out the tank. You will probably hire an expert technician to install the system for you. The technician won't quote a high price, plus he will offer free advice on the best rainwater system to buy. He will also help out when buying the system to ensure you get the best quality rainwater harvesting system. When you sum up the overall cost of installing the system, you'll find that it's actually manageable.

Once you begin using rainwater you will also appreciate a reduced amount of water consumption in the home, thus all of your utility bills will greatly shrink in size. How incredible would it be to slash as much as 50 to 60% off of your water bill each month? No complaints with having additional money in the pocket each and every month.

Rainwater Harvesting Methods

It is simple to collect rainwater from building roofs and numerous other sources. As long as you are ready and equipped with a couple of different items you have all that it takes to begin rainwater harvesting and enjoying naturally delicious, clean and useful water. Rainwater harvesting systems can be purchased complete from various home improvement stores. The cost of these systems will vary.

Rainwater Barrels

Barrel installation is the cheapest and easiest way to start harvesting rainwater in your home. A barrel is simply installed underneath the downspout of the guttering so that rain falling on the roof is funneled into the barrel. Usually, the container will consist of a spigot under it to enable you draw water and irrigate your garden. Better still; a hose can be connected to the spigot or to a drip irrigation system.

Barrels are advantageous because they can effortlessly be sourced whether recycled or new. If you opt for the recycled barrel, make a point to know exactly what the barrel was used for in order to be sure that no chemical residues remain inside. If you reside in a mosquito infested area, make sure to include a lid for your barrel to mitigate the possibility of mosquitoes breeding in your barrel.

When winter month knocks, it is advisable to disconnect your barrel to prevent freezing and cracking. The major disadvantage to rain water barrels is that they have limited capacity; meaning prolonged rains would result in flooding. The barrels are easy to use and readily available for purchase at many locations, all at reasonable prices.

Dry System

This is a well-known method of rainwater harvesting. It's basically an improvement to the rain water barrel technique in terms of size. A larger water storage container is situated just a few steps from the property. This container provides a much larger storage capacity compared to the barrel. The gutter is then diverted to channel water into the tank. It's also easy to implement and relatively cheap. The name "dry" comes from the fact that the collection pipe dries up after any rainy day because it's meant to empty into the top of tank. The dry system is ideal for areas with huge storms.

Wet System

The wet system is the exact opposite of the dry system. This is because the collection pipes are ever full of water since they are located underground. Here, numerous collection pipes are connected to multiple downspouts on the building and channeled to empty into the storage tank underground. When there is no rain, the level stays constant, and the pipes are always full. Due to the ever availability of water inside the pipes, it is recommended that they be watertight to mitigate the possibility of leaking into the soil. The underground piping makes it relatively expensive to install compared to the dry and wet systems.

Green Roof

This method of rainwater harvesting literally cuts out the middleman. Instead of directing rainwater for storage in the tank and then channel it to the garden; you could install a green roof on your house to enable plants use the water instantly. But you have to lay down a lining for your roof's protection and include a drainage system to take care of the runoffs. Installing garden beds with plants that require low maintenance is the surefire way of maximizing your plot's productive space and leveraging the rainwater where it falls. Also, installing a green roof will add insulation to your house and cushion your roof from damage.

ENERGY CONSERVATION

The consumption of fossil fuels has been going at a steady pace since last century and has contributed much to the degradation of our environment. Climate change, global warming, extinction of several endangered species, depletion of ozone layer, increase in air pollution are few of the effects from which our environment is suffering. Although many countries have taken steps to move toward clean and green energy sources like solar energy, wind energy and geothermal energy to save energy, still there is long way to go before we can leave fossil fuels behind and depend on these natural sources of energy for our daily needs.

Heating Systems

1. Inspect windows and ductwork for any air leakage. If you do feel air leaking at duct joints, use duct tape to seal them. Winterize windows with weather stripping (for all movable parts) and caulk (for non-moving parts). Eliminating these leaks can reduce heating costs up to 10%.

2. Use kitchen, bath and other ventilating fans sparingly. Leaving them on too long will suck away a tremendous amount of household heat. Turn them off when their job is complete.

3. Turn down your thermostat at night or when you're away for more than four hours during the day. Do not turn off your heating system entirely as this may cause pipes to freeze.

4. Keep heating supply registers and cold-air return registers clear of draperies and furniture to maintain proper air circulation.

5. Keep drapes and shades open during the day to let the sunshine in; close them at night.

6. Dust or vacuum radiator surfaces frequently. Dust and grime impede the flow of heat.

7. Keep lamps, TVs and other electrical appliances away from the thermostat. Heat from these appliances is sensed by the thermostat and could cause your furnace to shut off too soon and restart frequently.

8. Dress warmly to help retain body heat. Wear closely woven fabrics. Dressing in layers retains more heat than a single thick piece of clothing.

9. Keep garage doors closed in winter. An open garage door is just a giant hole that sucks warm air out of your home.

10. When having company, turn down the thermostat before your guests arrive. Their collective body heat will add to the room temperature.

11. Warm with a space heater. A portable space heater can heat a single room without using your furnace to heat the whole house. Using a space heater to heat all or most of your home costs more. Always follow the manufacturer's safety instructions when operating space heaters.

12. Use natural gas for heating. Consider switching to a natural gas heating system. Natural gas is less expensive than other heating fuels.

Kitchen

1. Boil water in a kettle or covered pan; the water will boil faster and use less energy.

2. Keep range-top burners and reflectors clean. They will reflect heat better and you will save energy.

3. Match the size of the pan to the heating element. More heat will get to the pan, and less will be dissipated.

4. Turn off the stove or oven five to 10 minutes before cooking time is up and let trapped heat finish the cooking.

5. Avoid opening the oven door repeatedly to check food while it cooks. This allows heat to escape and requires more energy to complete the job. Use a timer to let you know when food is ready.

6. Use small electric cooking appliances (such as portable grills and skillets) for small meals rather than the stove or oven.

7. Don't preheat the oven unless absolutely necessary and then for no more than 10 minutes.

8. Avoid using the broiler as much as possible; it uses a great deal of energy.

9. Thaw frozen foods thoroughly before cooking.

10. Barbecue outside as much as possible during warm weather months. Cooking inside raises the temperature forcing your refrigerator and central air to work harder to cool your rooms.

11. Cook during cooler hours (early morning and late evening) whenever possible.

12. Use a microwave to cook meals whenever possible; it uses about half the energy of a conventional oven.

13. Use crock pots and slow cookers; they can be as much at 75% more energy efficient than stoves and ovens.

14. After using your oven, leave it open a crack to let warm air escape into your kitchen. (Don't do this if you have children or pets around).

15. Use smaller kitchen appliances whenever possible. Microwaves, toaster ovens and slow-cookers can use 75 percent less energy than a large electric oven.

16. Water heaters should be close to kitchen so that it does not have to travel through a long distance of pipe and lose its heat.

Water Heater

1. Purchase an energy-efficient model. The initial cost may be more but operating costs are less in the long run. Consider a tank less or instantaneous water heater, which uses energy only when hot water is needed, rather than maintaining 40 gallons or more of hot water all the time.

2. Purchase the correct size. Consider your family's hot water needs. If your water heater is too large, it uses more energy than needed. If it is too small, you may run out of hot water.

3. Purchase a natural gas water heater. If you currently have an electric water heater, consider replacing it with a natural gas water heater. When it comes to heating water, natural gas is less expensive than electricity, and it heats more water faster during heavy use. Consider a sealed combustion or an on-demand water heater. Both types use less energy.

4. Install your water heater near the kitchen. The kitchen is where you use the hottest water. When the water heater is located near the kitchen, hot water doesn't have to travel as far and less heat is lost.

5. Insulate water pipes. Use half-inch foam or pipe tape for insulation wherever pipes are exposed. On cold water pipes, insulate four to five feet nearest to the water heater. Pipe insulation can save you up to $25 annually.

6. Set the water temperature to 120° F. It takes less energy to heat water to a lower temperature. If you have an electric water heater, you'll have to remove the cover plate of the thermostat to adjust the temperature. For safety reasons, remember to turn off the water heater at the circuit breaker/ fuse before changing the temperature.

7. Repair dripping faucets promptly. If the faucet leaks hot water, the energy used to heat it is costing you money. (One drop a second can waste up to 48 gallons a week.)

8. Install a heat loop or in-line trap. If you add a new water heater to your home, consider having a heat loop or in-line trap installed. These mechanisms can be inexpensive to install and keep hot water from moving into the piping system when you are not using hot water.

9. Insulate the outside of your electric water heater with an insulation blanket to reduce heat loss; this can easily save you $10 to $20 per year.

10. Turn down your hot water heater to its lowest setting when you go on vacation or are away from the house for an extended time period.

11. Drain a bucket of water out of the hot water heater once a year to remove sediment and dirty water and improve heating efficiency.

Fans and Lighting

1. Use Energy Star LED or compact fluorescent light bulbs. Energy Star light bulbs last longer and use up to 80 percent less energy than standard light bulbs.

2. Use LED lighting fixtures for outdoor lighting (spot lights, flood lights, security lights). They use up to 75% less energy than traditional incandescent luminaires.

3. Turn off lights in any room not being used. Turn on outdoor lights only when needed.

4. When using incandescent bulbs, use the lowest wattage possible or convenient. In many cases a lower wattage bulb can be substituted for the one currently being used.

5. Light-zone your home to save electricity. Concentrate lighting to areas where needed for reading, work and safety. Reduce lighting in little used areas.

6. Install lighting dimmer switches; they save energy by reducing the lighting intensity in a room, and work great with LED bulbs.

7. Keep light bulbs dust-free. Dust on bulbs could be reducing your light output by 50%.

8. Use timers, motion detectors, heat sensors or photocell controls for light fixtures when possible.

9. Use satin or semi-gloss paint on your walls will reflect more light and allow you to use lower watt bulbs.

10. Put your computer to sleep instead of using a screen saver.

11. Laser printers use an incredible amount of energy. Switch to ink-jet printers.

12. Get rid of your CRT monitor. CRT monitors are energy hogs. Get an LCD or LED monitor for your computer instead.

13. Dump your desktop computer. Laptops use a fraction of the electricity that desktop use.

Room Air Conditioner

1. Don't over-cool. The ideal thermostat setting is between 75 °F and 78 °F. Every degree you raise your thermostat can result in a 5% savings on the cost of cooling your home.

2. Keep lamps, televisions and other heat sources away from the air conditioner thermostat. Heat from these sources may cause the air conditioner unit to run longer than it should.

3. Make sure that no furniture or other obstacles are blocking ducts or fans. This will enable cooled air to circulate more freely.

4. When selecting a central air conditioning unit, be sure to choose one that is sized appropriately for your home and uses the minimal amount of electricity to complete its task. Air conditioners with high Seasonal Energy Efficiency Ratios (SEERs) – such as 13.0 SEER and above – provide the greatest energy efficiency.

5. Install a ventilating fan in your attic or in an upstairs window to help dissipate hot air and cool down your home.

6. Don't set your thermostat at a colder setting than normal when you turn your air conditioner on. It will not cool the room any faster, but it will use more energy.

7. Use a ceiling fan in conjunction with your air conditioner to spread cooled air to other rooms.

8. Clean the outside air conditioner condenser coil once a year. Turn off the unit and spray the coils with water at a low pressure to remove dirt, dust, leaves and grime.

9. Use duct tape to seal the cracks between each section of an air duct on your central air conditioning or forced heating system.

10. Close your blinds, curtains and shades during the hottest part of the day. Keep out the daytime sun with vertical louvers or awnings on the outside of your windows.

11. Keep lights low or off when not needed. Electric lights generate unnecessary room heat.

Refrigerators and Freezers

1. Vacuum the coils on your refrigerator at least every three months. Dust and dirt build-up makes the refrigerator work harder and uses more energy.

2. Set the refrigerator thermostat at 38 degrees F for fresh food compartments and 5 degrees F for the freezer compartment.

3. Regularly defrost your freezer. Frost buildup increases the amount of energy needed to keep the refrigerator at its proper temperature. Never allow frost to build up more than one quarter of an inch.

4. Don't place your refrigerator or freezer in direct sunlight or near the stove.

5. Make sure your refrigerator door seals airtight. Test them by closing the door on a piece of paper or dollar bill so it is half in and half out of the refrigerator. If you can pull the paper or dollar out easily, the hinge may need adjusting or the seal may need replacing.

6. Keep the refrigerator door closed. Each time you open the refrigerator, up to 1/4 of the cold air inside can leak out. Stop making unnecessary trips to the fridge.

7. Purchase an Energy Star, European EcoLabel, or Energy Saving Trust Recommended model. When buying a new refrigerator or freezer, look for the Energy Star, European EcoLabel, or Energy Saving Trust Recommended label. These refrigerators and freezers can save you hundreds of dollars on your electric bill over the life of the appliance. Remember, older refrigerators and freezers use two to three times more electricity than ones that are 10 years old or less.

8. Select the right size. Determine your household's needs before purchasing a refrigerator or freezer. One that is too large wastes energy.

9. Only use one refrigerator or freezer. You can spend up to $120 in electricity per year using a second refrigerator or freezer. If you want to use a second refrigerator or freezer during holidays or for special occasions, turn it on one to two days before you need it.

10. Defrost a manual-defrost unit regularly. Frost makes your unit work harder and wastes energy. Don't allow more than one-quarter inch of frost to build up.

11. Stay away from direct heat. Place the refrigerator or freezer away from direct sunlight and other heat sources such as ovens or ranges. Heat will cause the unit to use more energy to stay cold.

Dishwasher

1. When buying a dishwasher, look for an energy-efficient model with air power or overnight dry setting. These features automatically turn off the dishwasher after the rinse cycle. This can save you up to 10% of your dishwashing energy costs.

2. Scrape dishes and rinse with cold water before loading them into the dishwasher. Avoid using the dishwasher's pre-rinse cycle.

3. Don't use the "rinse-hold" on your machine for just a few soiled dishes. It uses several gallons of hot water each time you use it.

4. Run full loads. Always wait until you have a full load before running your dishwasher. Full loads use the same amount of hot water and energy as smaller loads. You run fewer loads and save energy.

5. Use short cycles. Select the shortest cycle that properly cleans your dishes. Shorter cycles use less hot water and less energy.

6. Skip rinsing the dishes. If you do rinse, use cold water.

7. Clean the filter. If your dishwasher has a filter screen, clean it regularly. A clean appliance runs more efficiently.

8. Don't bother pre-rinsing dishes with the idea that your dishwasher will work less hard.

Buying New Appliances

1. Remember that it pays to invest in energy efficiency. In some cases, the money you save in energy costs can pay back the purchase price in just a few years.

2. Always read the Energy Guide label carefully, and make sure you're comparing "apples to apples." Energy use can range significantly even within a single brand.

3. Choose the capacity that's right for your family. Whether it's a furnace or a refrigerator, it doesn't pay to purchase a unit that's too large or too small. Make sure you use the right filter even if you're tempted to buy one that's not quite right. If your unit requires 20x20x1 air filters then don't buy anything smaller.

4. In almost every case, a natural gas appliance is more economical to use than an electric model. The $50-75 price difference can be paid back in energy savings in less than a year.

5. Replace inefficient appliances – even if they're still working. An aging water heater or refrigerator could be costing you much more than you think. If your central air conditioner is more than 10 years old, replacing it with a high-efficiency new unit will cut your summer electric bills by about one-third. And make sure to RECYCLE the old appliance.

6. Shop during the off-season. Many heating and cooling manufacturers offer significant rebates during seasonal sales promotions, and dealers may charge less for installation.

7. Investigate new technology carefully. Some innovations, like convection ovens or argon-filled windows, may save energy and make life more convenient; others, such as commercial-grade kitchen appliances, might be merely expensive cosmetic enhancements.

8. Look for the "Energy Star," European EcoLabel," or "Energy Saving Trust Recommended" logo. This designation from the Environmental Protection Agency or the European Union means that the appliance exceeds minimum federal energy- use standards, usually by a significant amount.

9. Don't forget to ask about warranties, service contracts, and delivery and installation costs.

Washer, Dryer and Laundry

1. Wash clothes in warm or cold water instead of hot water. Rinse in cold water; this can save you about $50 per year.

2. Put a dry towel in the dryer with each load of wet clothes. The towel will absorb dampness and reduce drying time, thus saving energy and money.

3. Fill washers and clothes dryers but do not overload them.

4. Clean the lint screen after each load of laundry and check the exhaust regularly. Clogged, dirty lint screens and exhausts can increase drying time and energy usage.

5. Use a front-loading washing machine; they require less water and energy than other washing machines.

6. Use less detergent and skip the extra rinse cycle on your washing machine to save water and time. If your clothes need to be rinsed twice, you're using too much soap.

7. Adjust the water level. If you have a washer that allows you to control the load's water level, adjust the level according to laundry load size. You can save energy by using less hot water for small loads.

8. Run full loads. Always run a full load in your washer or dryer. Running a partial load uses the same amount of energy as a full load – but you get less done. Running full loads allows you to run your washer or dryer less often.

9. Dry your clothes on an outside clothesline whenever possible.

10. Rinse in cold water. Rinse water temperature has no effect on cleaning. Rinsing with cold water saves money by heating less water.

11. Place the washer close to the water heater. Water loses heat as it flows through pipes. When the washer is located near the water heater, hot water doesn't have to travel as far to reach the washer, and less heat is lost. Insulating the pipes between the water heater and washer helps retain heat, too.

For Travelers

1. Put indoor and outdoor lights on timers.

2. Don't leave your lights on 24/7 while you're away.

3. Put water heater on the vacation setting, if it has one.

4. Choose green-rated hotels when travelling for business or pleasure.

5. Pull the plug on battery chargers. Laptops, cell phones and digital cameras always draw power if they're plugged in.

6. If you travel at 105 km/h instead of 90 km/h, you are penalized by lowering your L/100 km 12.5 percent. If you get your vehicle up to 120 km/h, you're losing 25 percent compared with L/100 km at 90 km/h.

7. A loaded roof rack can decrease an SUV's fuel efficiency by 5 percent and that of a more aerodynamic car by 15 percent or more.

8. Stick with regular. If your car's manufacturer specifies regular gas, don't buy premium with the thought of going faster or operating more efficiently. Consider diesel over petrol when buying a new car. If petrol only option, consider a hybrid.

9. After starting the car in the morning, begin driving right away; don't let it sit and "warm up" for several minutes.

10. If your windows don't have a low-E coating, consider applying a self-adhesive film on the glass.

11. Use reusable containers for food storage instead of wrapping food in foil or plastic wrap.

12. Bring a reusable water bottle! Packaged bottled water is a waste and highly inefficient in most of the developed world.

At Office

1. Train myself or an employee to become an Energy Conservation Officer.

2. Making conservation someone's responsibility will set your business on the path of saving energy.

3. Participate in an OPA commercial demand response program.

4. Install effective automatic door closer. Doors can't save energy if they're not closed.

5. Educate and encourage employees who identify and implement energy savings.

6. Reward the people who work with me for their innovative, money-saving ideas.

7. Celebrate the implementation of successful energy efficiency measures.

8. Ensure meeting rooms are equipped with motion sensing light switches.

At Work- Employees

1. Turn off meeting room lights when not in use.

2. In the summer, unnecessary lighting can increase air conditioning load.

3. Dim, turn off or remove lights near windows in the daytime.

4. Use efficient task lighting where needed.

5. Unplug coffeemakers, toasters and microwaves. Make sure they're unplugged on weekends and before shutting the office down for the holidays.

6. Use the stairs instead of taking the elevator. It not only saves energy, it's good exercise too.

7. Consider double-sided printing, re-using paper, and using e-mail instead of mailing or faxing documents.

While Driving

1. When driving, avoid quick breaking and starting as it decreases mileage.

2. Don't run your car unnecessarily. Idling produces many pollutants and burns unnecessary fuel.

3. If you can travel at off peak hours or use public transport, do so. Traffic jams only create more pollution, waste fuel, and cause stress.

4. Keep your tires properly inflated-under-inflated tires will reduce mileage.

5. Use premium unleaded gasoline as it is more efficient. If possible, use clean burning diesel.

6. Use air conditioning only when it is necessary.

7. Open window or close them to adjust the heat instead of using the air conditioner.

8. Park in a shade to prevent your car from overheating and reliance on air-conditioning.

9. Service your air conditioner to ensure it works efficiently and it does not leak CFC's.

10. Turn off your engine if you are stopping for any more than 30 seconds.

11. Drive slowly, my L/100km indicator runs at highest efficiency at 90 km/h on motorways.

Other Energy Savers

1. Get rid of spare refrigerators or freezers. An extra appliance can add more than $100 to your energy bills every year, and it's a safety hazard for small children.

2. Keep outdoor hot tubs covered when not in use. If you have a pool, use a solar cover to use the natural warmth of the sun to heat the water.

3. Keep waterbeds covered with quilts or blankets to help retain their heat. You might also want to insulate the bottom with a sheet of rigid foam insulation.

4. Keep the garage door closed, especially during the winter.

5. If you need a new lawn mower, consider an electric model. They're less expensive to operate (about three cents of electricity per use), 75 percent quieter, and they significantly reduce toxic emissions.

6. Instead of air-polluting and expensive charcoal or propane, try an electric or natural gas grill. They're more economical and more convenient – you'll never run out of fuel.

7. Unplug any electrical device that's not being used. Many appliances, especially computers and televisions draw power even when turned off.

8. Place humidifiers and dehumidifiers away from walls and bulky furniture. These appliances work best when air circulates freely around them. Be sure to clean the unit often to prevent unhealthy mold and bacteria from developing.

9. If your home has no sidewall insulation, place heavy furniture like bookshelves, armoires and sofas along exterior walls, and use decorative quilts as wall hangings. This will help block cold air.

10. When you take a vacation, don't forget to give your appliances a rest too. Turn off and unplug everything you can, set your water heater to the lowest setting and shut off the water supply to the dishwasher and washing machine.

11. Use public transit whenever possible.

BIOFUEL

A biofuel is a fuel that is produced through contemporary processes from biomass, rather than a fuel produced by the very long-winded geological processes involved in the formation of fossil fuels, such as oil. Since biomass technically can be used as a fuel directly (e.g. wood logs), some people use the terms "biomass" and "biofuel" interchangeably. More often than not however, the word "biomass" simply denotes the biological raw material the fuel is made of, or some form of thermally/chemically altered solid end product, like torrefied pellets or briquettes. The word "biofuel" is usually reserved for liquid or gaseous fuels, used for transportation. The EIA (U.S. Energy Information Administration) follow this naming practice. If the biomass used in the production of biofuel can regrow quickly, the fuel is generally considered to be a form of renewable energy.

A bus fueled by biogas.

Biofuels can be produced from plants (i.e. energy crops), or from agricultural, commercial, domestic, and/or industrial wastes (if the waste has a biological origin). Renewable biofuels generally involve contemporary carbon fixation, such as those that occur in plants or microalgae through the process of photosynthesis.

Some argue that biofuel can be carbon-neutral because all biomass crops sequester carbon to a certain extent – basically all crops move CO_2 from above-ground circulation to below-ground storage in the roots and the surrounding soil. For instance, McCalmont et al. found below-ground carbon accumulation ranging from 0.42 to 3.8 tonnes per hectare per year for soils below Miscanthus x giganteus energy crops, with a mean accumulation rate of 1.84 tonne (0.74 tonnes per acre per year), or 20% of total harvested carbon per year.

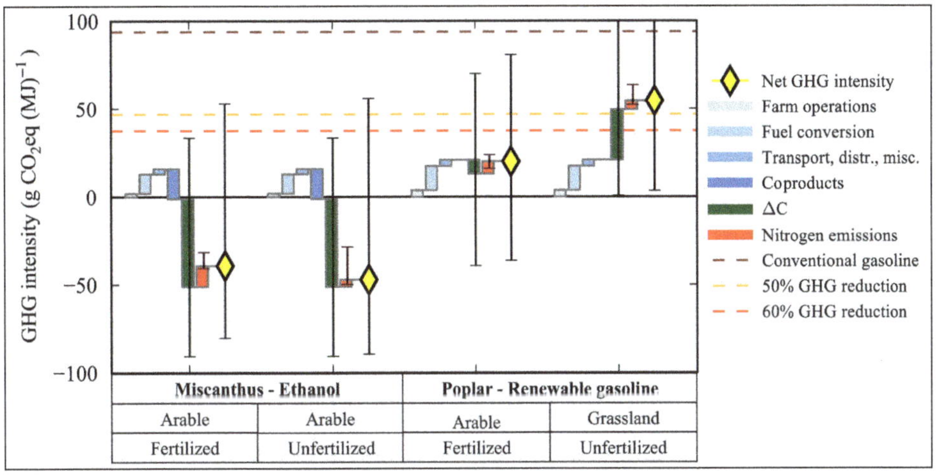

GHG/CO_2/carbon negativity for Miscanthus x giganteus production pathways.

Relationship between above-ground yield (diagonal lines), soil organic carbon (X axis), and soil's potential for successful/unsuccessful carbon sequestration (Y axis). Basically, the higher the yield, the more land is usable as a GHG mitigation tool (including relatively carbon rich land.) However, the simple proposal that biofuel is carbon-neutral almost by definition, has been superseded by the more nuanced proposal that for a particular biofuel project to be carbon neutral, the total carbon sequestered by the energy crop's root system must compensate for all the above-ground emissions (related to this particular biofuel project). This includes any emissions caused by direct or indirect land use change. Many first generation biofuel projects are not carbon neutral given these demands. Some have even higher total GHG emissions than some fossil based alternatives.

Some are carbon neutral or even negative, though, especially perennial crops. The amount of carbon sequestrated and the amount of GHG (greenhouse gases) emitted will determine if the total GHG life cycle cost of a biofuel project is positive, neutral or negative. A carbon negative life cycle is possible if the total below-ground carbon accumulation more than compensates for the total life-cycle GHG emissions above ground. In other words, to achieve carbon neutrality yields should be high and emissions should be low.

High-yielding energy crops are thus prime candidates for carbon neutrality. The graphic on the right displays two CO_2 negative Miscanthus x giganteus production pathways, represented in gram CO_2-equivalents per megajoule. The yellow diamonds represent mean values. Further, successful sequestration is dependent on planting sites, as the best soils for sequestration are those that are currently low in carbon. The varied results displayed in the graph highlights this fact. For the UK, successful sequestration is expected for arable land over most of England and Wales, with unsuccessful sequestration expected in parts of Scotland, due to already carbon rich soils (existing woodland) plus lower yields. Soils already rich in carbon includes peatland and mature forest. Grassland can also be carbon rich, however Milner et al. argues that the most successful carbon sequestration in the UK takes place below improved grasslands. The bottom graphic displays the estimated yield necessary to compensate for related lifecycle GHG-emissions. The higher the yield, the more likely CO_2 negativity becomes.

The two most common types of biofuel are bioethanol and biodiesel:

1. Bioethanol is an alcohol made by fermentation, mostly from carbohydrates produced in sugar or starch crops such as corn, sugarcane, or sweet sorghum. Cellulosic biomass, derived from non-food sources, such as trees and grasses, is also being developed as a feedstock for ethanol production. Ethanol can be used as a fuel for vehicles in its pure form (E100), but it is usually used as a gasoline additive to increase octane and improve vehicle emissions. Bioethanol is widely used in the United States and in Brazil.

2. Biodiesel is produced from oils or fats using transesterification and is the most common biofuel in Europe. It can be used as a fuel for vehicles in its pure form (B100), but it is usually used as a diesel additive to reduce levels of particulates, carbon monoxide, and hydrocarbons from diesel-powered vehicles.

In 2018, worldwide biofuel production reached 152 billion liters (40 billion gallons US), up 7% from 2017, and biofuels provided 3% of the world's fuels for road transport. The International Energy Agency want biofuels to meet more than a quarter of world demand for transportation fuels by 2050, in order to reduce dependency on petroleum. However, the production and consumption of biofuels are not on track to meet the IEA's sustainable development scenario. From 2020 to 2030 global biofuel output has to increase by 10% each year to reach IEA's goal. Only 3% growth annually is expected.

There are various social, economic, environmental and technical issues relating to biofuels production and use, which have been debated in the popular media and scientific journals.

Generations

First-generation Biofuels

"First-generation" or conventional biofuels are biofuels made from food crops grown on arable land. With this biofuel production generation, food crops are thus explicitly grown for fuel production, and not anything else. The sugar, starch, or vegetable oil obtained from the crops is converted into biodiesel or ethanol, using transesterification, or yeast fermentation.

Second-generation Biofuels

Second generation biofuels are fuels manufactured from various types of biomass. Biomass is a wide-ranging term meaning any source of organic carbon that is renewed rapidly as part of the carbon cycle. Biomass is derived from plant materials, but can also include animal materials.

Whereas first generation biofuels are made from the sugars and vegetable oils found in arable crops, second generation biofuels are made from lignocellulosic biomass or woody crops, agricultural residues or waste plant material (from food crops that have already fulfilled their food purpose). The feedstock used to generate second-generation biofuels thus either grows on arable lands, but are just byproducts of the actual harvest (main crop) or they are grown on lands which cannot be used to effectively grow food crops and in some cases neither extra water or fertilizer is applied to them. Non-human food second generation feedstock sources include grasses, jatropha and other seed crops, waste vegetable oil, municipal solid waste and so forth.

This has both advantages and disadvantages. The advantage is that, unlike with regular food crops, no arable land is used solely for the production of fuel. The disadvantage is that unlike with regular food crops, it may be rather difficult to extract the fuel. For instance, a series of physical and chemical treatments might be required to convert lignocellulosic biomass to liquid fuels suitable for transportation.

Third-generation Biofuels

From 1978 to 1996, the US NREL experimented with using algae as a biofuels source in the Aquatic Species Program. A self-published article by Michael Briggs, at the UNH Biofuels Group, offers estimates for the realistic replacement of all vehicular fuel with biofuels by using algae that have a natural oil content greater than 50%, which Briggs suggests can be grown on algae ponds at wastewater treatment plants. This oil-rich algae can then be extracted from the system and processed into biofuels, with the dried remainder further reprocessed to create ethanol. The production of algae to harvest oil for biofuels has not yet been undertaken on a commercial scale, but feasibility studies have been conducted to arrive at the above yield estimate. In addition to its projected high yield, algaculture – unlike crop-based biofuels – does not entail a decrease in food production, since it requires neither farmland nor fresh water. Many companies are pursuing algae bioreactors for various purposes, including scaling up biofuels production to commercial levels. Prof. Rodrigo E. Teixeira from the University of Alabama in Huntsville demonstrated the extraction of biofuels lipids from wet algae using a simple and economical reaction in ionic liquids.

Fourth-generation Biofuels

Similarly to third-generation biofuels, fourth-generation biofuels are made using non-arable land. However, unlike third-generation biofuels, they do not require the destruction of biomass. This class of biofuels includes electrofuels and photobiological solar fuels. Some of these fuels are carbon-neutral.

Types

The following fuels can be produced using first, second, third or fourth-generation biofuel production procedures. Most of these can even be produced using two or three of the different biofuel generation procedures.

Biogas

Biogas is methane produced by the process of anaerobic digestion of organic material by anaerobes. It can be produced either from biodegradable waste materials or by the use of energy crops fed into anaerobic digesters to supplement gas yields. The solid byproduct, digestate, can be used as a biofuel or a fertilizer.

Biogas can be recovered from mechanical biological treatment waste processing systems. Landfill gas, a less clean form of biogas, is produced in landfills through naturally occurring anaerobic digestion. If it escapes into the atmosphere, it is a potential greenhouse gas.

Farmers can produce biogas from manure from their cattle by using anaerobic digesters.

Pipes carrying biogas.

Syngas

Syngas, a mixture of carbon monoxide, hydrogen and other hydrocarbons, is produced by partial combustion of biomass, that is, combustion with an amount of oxygen that is not sufficient to convert the biomass completely to carbon dioxide and water. Before partial combustion, the biomass is dried, and sometimes pyrolysed. The resulting gas mixture, syngas, is more efficient than direct combustion of the original biofuel; more of the energy contained in the fuel is extracted.

Syngas may be burned directly in internal combustion engines, turbines or high-temperature fuel cells. The wood gas generator, a wood-fueled gasification reactor, can be connected to an internal combustion engine.

Syngas can be used to produce methanol, DME and hydrogen, or converted via the Fischer-Tropsch process to produce a diesel substitute, or a mixture of alcohols that can be blended into gasoline. Gasification normally relies on temperatures greater than 700 °C.

Lower-temperature gasification is desirable when co-producing biochar, but results in syngas polluted with tar.

Ethanol

Biologically produced alcohols, most commonly ethanol, and less commonly propanol and butanol, are produced by the action of microorganisms and enzymes through the fermentation of sugars or starches (easiest), or cellulose (which is more difficult). Biobutanol (also called biogasoline) is often claimed to provide a direct replacement for gasoline, because it can be used directly in a gasoline engine.

Neat ethanol on the left (A), gasoline on the right (G) at a filling station in Brazil.

Ethanol fuel is the most common biofuel worldwide, particularly in Brazil. Alcohol fuels are produced by fermentation of sugars derived from wheat, corn, sugar beets, sugar cane, molasses and any sugar or starch from which alcoholic beverages such as whiskey, can be made (such as potato and fruit waste, etc.). The ethanol production methods used are enzyme digestion (to release sugars from stored starches), fermentation of the sugars, distillation and drying. The distillation process requires significant energy input for heat (sometimes unsustainable natural gas fossil fuel, but cellulosic biomass such as bagasse, the waste left after sugar cane is pressed to extract its juice, is the most common fuel in Brazil, while pellets, wood chips and also waste heat are more common in Europe) Waste steam fuels ethanol factory – where waste heat from the factories also is used in the district heating grid.

Ethanol can be used in petrol engines as a replacement for gasoline; it can be mixed with gasoline to any percentage. Most existing car petrol engines can run on blends of up to 15% bioethanol with petroleum/gasoline. Ethanol has a smaller energy density than that of gasoline; this means it takes more fuel (volume and mass) to produce the same amount of work. An advantage of ethanol (CH_3CH_2OH) is that it has a higher octane rating than ethanol-free gasoline available at roadside gas stations, which allows an increase of an engine's compression ratio for increased thermal efficiency. In high-altitude (thin air) locations, some states mandate a mix of gasoline and ethanol as a winter oxidizer to reduce atmospheric pollution emissions.

Ethanol is also used to fuel bioethanol fireplaces. As they do not require a chimney and are "flueless", bioethanol fires are extremely useful for newly built homes and apartments without a flue. The downsides to these fireplaces is that their heat output is slightly less than electric heat or gas fires, and precautions must be taken to avoid carbon monoxide poisoning.

Corn-to-ethanol and other food stocks has led to the development of cellulosic ethanol. According to a joint research agenda conducted through the US Department of Energy, the fossil energy ratios (FER) for cellulosic ethanol, corn ethanol, and gasoline are 10.3, 1.36, and 0.81, respectively.

Ethanol has roughly one-third lower energy content per unit of volume compared to gasoline. This is partly counteracted by the better efficiency when using ethanol (in a long-term test of more than 2.1

million km, the BEST project found FFV vehicles to be 1–26% more energy efficient than petrol cars, but the volumetric consumption increases by approximately 30%, so more fuel stops are required).

With current subsidies, ethanol fuel is slightly cheaper per distance traveled in the United States.

Other Bioalcohols

Methanol is currently produced from natural gas, a non-renewable fossil fuel. In the future it is hoped to be produced from biomass as biomethanol. This is technically feasible, but the production is currently being postponed for concerns that the economic viability is still pending. The methanol economy is an alternative to the hydrogen economy, compared to today's hydrogen production from natural gas.

Butanol (C_4H_9OH) is formed by ABE fermentation (acetone, butanol, ethanol) and experimental modifications of the process show potentially high net energy gains with butanol as the only liquid product. Butanol will produce more energy and allegedly can be burned "straight" in existing gasoline engines (without modification to the engine or car), and is less corrosive and less water-soluble than ethanol, and could be distributed via existing infrastructures. DuPont and BP are working together to help develop butanol. *Escherichia coli* strains have also been successfully engineered to produce butanol by modifying their amino acid metabolism. One drawback to butanol production in E. coli remains the high cost of nutrient rich media, however, recent work has demonstrated E. coli can produce butanol with minimal nutritional supplementation.

Biodiesel

Biodiesel is the most common biofuel in Europe. It is produced from oils or fats using transesterification and is a liquid similar in composition to fossil/mineral diesel. Chemically, it consists mostly of fatty acid methyl (or ethyl) esters (FAMEs). Feedstocks for biodiesel include animal fats, vegetable oils, soy, rapeseed, jatropha, mahua, mustard, flax, sunflower, palm oil, hemp, field pennycress, *Pongamia pinnata* and algae. Pure biodiesel (B100, also known as "neat" biodiesel) currently reduces emissions with up to 60% compared to diesel Second generation B100.

Targray Biofuels Division railcar transporting Biodiesel.

Biodiesel can be used in any diesel engine when mixed with mineral diesel. It can also be used in its pure form (B100) in diesel engines, but some maintenance and performance problems may then occur during wintertime utilization, since the fuel becomes somewhat more viscous at lower temperatures, depending on the feedstock used. In some countries, manufacturers cover their diesel engines under warranty for B100 use, although Volkswagen of Germany, for example, asks drivers to check by telephone with the VW environmental services department before switching to B100. In most cases, biodiesel is compatible with diesel engines from 1994 onwards, which use 'Viton' (by DuPont) synthetic rubber in their mechanical fuel injection systems. Note however, that no vehicles are certified for using pure biodiesel before 2014, as there was no emission control protocol available for biodiesel.

Electronically controlled 'common rail' and 'unit injector' type systems from the late 1990s onwards may only use biodiesel blended with conventional diesel fuel. These engines have finely metered and atomized multiple-stage injection systems that are very sensitive to the viscosity of the fuel. Many current-generation diesel engines are made so that they can run on B100 without altering the engine itself, although this depends on the fuel rail design. Since biodiesel is an effective solvent and cleans residues deposited by mineral diesel, engine filters may need to be replaced more often, as the biofuel dissolves old deposits in the fuel tank and pipes. It also effectively cleans the engine combustion chamber of carbon deposits, helping to maintain efficiency. In many European countries, a 5% biodiesel blend is widely used and is available at thousands of gas stations. Biodiesel is also an oxygenated fuel, meaning it contains a reduced amount of carbon and higher hydrogen and oxygen content than fossil diesel. This improves the combustion of biodiesel and reduces the particulate emissions from unburnt carbon. However, using pure biodiesel may increase NO_x-emissions

Biodiesel is also safe to handle and transport because it is non-toxic and biodegradable, and has a high flash point of about 300 °F (148 °C) compared to petroleum diesel fuel, which has a flash point of 125 °F (52 °C).

In the US, more than 80% of commercial trucks and city buses run on diesel. The emerging US biodiesel market is estimated to have grown 200% from 2004 to 2005. "By the end of 2006 biodiesel production was estimated to increase fourfold [from 2004] to more than" 1 billion US gallons (3,800,000 m^3).

In France, biodiesel is incorporated at a rate of 8% in the fuel used by all French diesel vehicles. Avril Group produces under the brand Diester, a fifth of 11 million tons of biodiesel consumed annually by the European Union. It is the leading European producer of biodiesel.

Green Diesel

Green diesel is produced through hydrocracking biological oil feedstocks, such as vegetable oils and animal fats. Hydrocracking is a refinery method that uses elevated temperatures and pressure in the presence of a catalyst to break down larger molecules, such as those found in vegetable oils, into shorter hydrocarbon chains used in diesel engines. It may also be called renewable diesel, hydrotreated vegetable oil or hydrogen-derived renewable diesel. Unlike biodiesel, green diesel has exactly the same chemical properties as petroleum-based diesel. It does not require new engines, pipelines or infrastructure to distribute and use, but has not been produced at a cost that is competitive with petroleum. Gasoline versions are also being developed. Green diesel is being developed in

Louisiana and Singapore by ConocoPhillips, Neste Oil, Valero, Dynamic Fuels, and Honeywell UOP as well as Preem in Gothenburg, Sweden, creating what is known as Evolution Diesel.

Straight Vegetable Oil

Straight unmodified edible vegetable oil is generally not used as fuel, but lower-quality oil has been used for this purpose. Used vegetable oil is increasingly being processed into biodiesel, or (more rarely) cleaned of water and particulates and then used as a fuel.

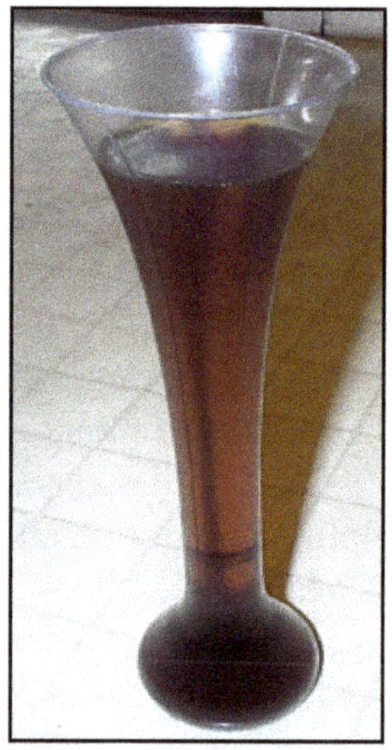

Filtered waste vegetable oil.

As with 100% biodiesel (B100), to ensure the fuel injectors atomize the vegetable oil in the correct pattern for efficient combustion, vegetable oil fuel must be heated to reduce its viscosity to that of diesel, either by electric coils or heat exchangers. This is easier in warm or temperate climates. MAN B&W Diesel, Wärtsilä, and Deutz AG, as well as a number of smaller companies, such as Elsbett, offer engines that are compatible with straight vegetable oil, without the need for after-market modifications.

This truck is one of 15 based at Walmart's Buckeye, Arizona distribution center that was converted to run on a biofuel made from reclaimed cooking grease produced during food preparation at Walmart stores.

Vegetable oil can also be used in many older diesel engines that do not use common rail or unit injection electronic diesel injection systems. Due to the design of the combustion chambers in indirect injection engines, these are the best engines for use with vegetable oil. This system allows the relatively larger oil molecules more time to burn. Some older engines, especially Mercedes, are driven experimentally by enthusiasts without any conversion, a handful of drivers have experienced limited success with earlier pre-"Pumpe Duse" VW TDI engines and other similar engines with direct injection. Several companies, such as Elsbett or Wolf, have developed professional conversion kits and successfully installed hundreds of them over the last decades.

Oils and fats can be hydrogenated to give a diesel substitute. The resulting product is a straight-chain hydrocarbon with a high cetane number, low in aromatics and sulfur and does not contain oxygen. Hydrogenated oils can be blended with diesel in all proportions. They have several advantages over biodiesel, including good performance at low temperatures, no storage stability problems and no susceptibility to microbial attack.

Bioethers

Bioethers (also referred to as fuel ethers or oxygenated fuels) are cost-effective compounds that act as octane rating enhancers."Bioethers are produced by the reaction of reactive iso-olefins, such as iso-butylene, with bioethanol." Bioethers are created from wheat or sugar beets. They also enhance engine performance, while significantly reducing engine wear and toxic exhaust emissions. Although bioethers are likely to replace petroethers in the UK, it is highly unlikely they will become a fuel in and of itself due to the low energy density. By greatly reducing the amount of ground-level ozone emissions, they contribute to air quality.

When it comes to transportation fuel there are six ether additives: dimethyl ether (DME), diethyl ether (DEE), methyl *tert*-butyl ether (MTBE), ethyl *tert*-butyl ether (ETBE), *tert*-amyl methyl ether (TAME), and *tert*-amyl ethyl ether (TAEE).

The European Fuel Oxygenates Association (EFOA) identifies methyl *tert*-butyl ether (MTBE) and ethyl *tert*-butyl ether (ETBE) as the most commonly used ethers in fuel to replace lead. Ethers were introduced in Europe in the 1970s to replace the highly toxic compound. Although Europeans still use bioether additives, the US no longer has an oxygenate requirement therefore bioethers are no longer used as the main fuel additive.

By Region

Bio Diesel Powered Fast Attack Craft Of Indian Navy patrolling during IFR 2016. The green bands on the side of the vessel are indicative of the fact that the vessel is powered by biodiesel.

There are international organizations such as IEA Bioenergy, established in 1978 by the OECD International Energy Agency (IEA), with the aim of improving cooperation and information exchange between countries that have national programs in bioenergy research, development and deployment. The UN International Biofuels Forum is formed by Brazil, China, India, Pakistan, South Africa, the United States and the European Commission. The world leaders in biofuel development and use are Brazil, the United States, France, Sweden and Germany. Russia also has 22% of world's forest, and is a big biomass (solid biofuels) supplier. In 2010, Russian pulp and paper maker, Vyborgskaya Cellulose, said they would be producing pellets that can be used in heat and electricity generation from its plant in Vyborg by the end of the year. The plant will eventually produce about 900,000 tons of pellets per year, making it the largest in the world once operational.

Biofuels currently make up 3.1% of the total road transport fuel in the UK or 1,440 million litres. By 2020, 10% of the energy used in UK road and rail transport must come from renewable sources – this is the equivalent of replacing 4.3 million tonnes of fossil oil each year. Conventional biofuels are likely to produce between 3.7 and 6.6% of the energy needed in road and rail transport, while advanced biofuels could meet up to 4.3% of the UK's renewable transport fuel target by 2020.

Air Pollution

Biofuels are similar to fossil fuels in that biofuels contribute to air pollution. Burning produces carbon dioxide, airborne carbon particulates, carbon monoxide and nitrous oxides. The WHO estimates 3.7 million premature deaths worldwide in 2012 due to air pollution. Brazil burns significant amounts of ethanol biofuel. Gas chromatograph studies were performed of ambient air in São Paulo, Brazil, and compared to Osaka, Japan, which does not burn ethanol fuel. Atmospheric Formaldehyde was 160% higher in Brazil, and Acetaldehyde was 260% higher.

The Environmental Protection Agency acknowledged in April 2007 that the increased use of bioethanol will lead to worse air quality. The total emissions of air pollutants such as nitrogen oxides will rise due the growing use of bioethanol. There is an increase in carbon dioxide from the burning of fossil fuels to produce the biofuels as well as nitrous oxide from the soil, which has most likely been treated with nitrogen fertilizer. Nitrous oxide is known to have a greater impact on the atmosphere in relation to global warming, as it is also an ozone destroyer.

Debates Regarding the Production and use of Biofuel

There are various social, economic, environmental and technical issues with biofuel production and use, which have been discussed in the popular media and scientific journals. These include: the effect of moderating oil prices, the "food vs fuel" debate, food prices, poverty reduction potential, energy ratio, energy requirements, carbon emissions levels, sustainable biofuel production, deforestation and soil erosion, loss of biodiversity, impact on water resources, the possible modifications necessary to run the engine on biofuel, as well as energy balance and efficiency. The International Resource Panel, which provides independent scientific assessments and expert advice on a variety of resource-related themes, assessed the issues relating to biofuel use in its first report *Towards sustainable production and use of resources: Assessing Biofuels*. "Assessing Biofuels" outlined the wider and interrelated factors that need to be considered when deciding on the relative merits of pursuing one biofuel over another. It concluded that not all biofuels perform equally in terms of their impact on climate, energy security and ecosystems, and suggested that environmental and social impacts need to be assessed throughout the entire life-cycle.

Another issue with biofuel use and production is the US has changed mandates many times because the production has been taking longer than expected. The Renewable Fuel Standard (RFS) set by congress for 2010 was pushed back to at best 2012 to produce 100 million gallons of pure ethanol (not blended with a fossil fuel).

Banning of First-generation Biofuels

In the EU, the revised renewable energy directive calls for a complete ban on first-generation biofuels by 2030. Particularly fuels made from such oils such as palm oil and soy oil are being targeted.

Sustainable Biofuels

Many of the biofuels that were being supplied in 2008 (using the first-generation biofuel production procedure) have been criticised for their adverse impacts on the natural environment, food security, and land use. In 2008, the Nobel-prize winning chemist Paul J. Crutzen published findings that the release of nitrous oxide (N_2O) emissions in the production of biofuels means that overall they contribute more to global warming than the fossil fuels they replace. In 2008, the challenge was to support biofuel development, including the development of new cellulosic technologies, with responsible policies and economic instruments to help ensure that biofuel commercialization is sustainable. Responsible commercialization of biofuels represented an opportunity to enhance sustainable economic prospects in Africa, Latin America and Asia. Biofuels in the form of liquid fuels derived from plant materials have entered the market, driven by the perception that they reduce climate gas emissions, and also by factors such as oil price spikes and the need for increased energy security.

According to the Rocky Mountain Institute, sound biofuel production practices would not hamper food and fibre production, nor cause water or environmental problems, and would enhance soil fertility. The selection of land on which to grow the feedstocks is a critical component of the ability of biofuels to deliver sustainable solutions. A key consideration is the minimisation of biofuel competition for prime cropland.

Greenhouse Gas Emissions

Some scientists have expressed concerns about land-use change in response to greater demand for crops to use for biofuel and the subsequent carbon emissions. The payback period, that is, the time it will take biofuels to pay back the carbon debt they acquire due to land-use change, has been estimated to be between 100 and 1000 years, depending on the specific instance and location of land-use change. However, no-till practices combined with cover-crop practices can reduce the payback period to three years for grassland conversion and 14 years for forest conversion.

A study conducted in the Tocantis State, in northern Brazil, found that many families were cutting down forests in order to produce two conglomerates of oilseed plants, the J. curcas (JC group) and the R. communis (RC group). This region is composed of 15% Amazonian rainforest with high biodiversity, and 80% Cerrado forest with lower biodiversity. During the study, the farmers that planted the

JC group released over 2193 Mg CO_2, while losing 53-105 Mg CO_2 sequestration from deforestation; and the RC group farmers released 562 Mg CO_2, while losing 48-90 Mg CO_2 to be sequestered from forest depletion. The production of these types of biofuels not only led into an increased emission of carbon dioxide, but also to lower efficiency of forests to absorb the gases that these farms were emitting. This has to do with the amount of fossil fuel the production of fuel crops involves. In addition, the intensive use of monocropping agriculture requires large amounts of water irrigation, as well as of fertilizers, herbicides and pesticides. This does not only lead to poisonous chemicals to disperse on water runoff, but also to the emission of nitrous oxide (NO_2) as a fertilizer byproduct, which is three hundred times more efficient in producing a greenhouse effect than carbon dioxide (CO_2).

Converting rainforests, peatlands, savannas, or grasslands to produce food crop–based biofuels in Brazil, Southeast Asia, and the United States creates a "biofuel carbon debt" by releasing 17 to 420 times more CO_2 than the annual greenhouse gas (GHG) reductions that these biofuels would provide by displacing fossil fuels. Biofuels made from waste biomass or from biomass grown on abandoned agricultural lands incur little to no carbon debt.

In addition to crop growth requiring water, biofuel facilities require significant process water.

Current Research

Specially bred mustard varieties can produce reasonably high oil yields and are very useful in crop rotation with cereals, and have the added benefit that the meal left over after the oil has been pressed out can act as an effective and biodegradable pesticide.

The NFESC, with Santa Barbara-based Biodiesel Industries, is working to develop biofuels technologies for the US navy and military, one of the largest diesel fuel users in the world. A group of Spanish developers working for a company called Ecofasa announced a new biofuel made from trash. The fuel is created from general urban waste which is treated by bacteria to produce fatty acids, which can be used to make biofuels. Before its shutdown, Joule Unlimited was attempting to make cheap ethanol and biodiesel from a genetically modified photosynthetic bacterium.

Ethanol Biofuels (Bioethanol)

As the primary source of biofuels in North America, many organizations are conducting research in the area of ethanol production. The National Corn-to-Ethanol Research Center (NCERC) is a research division of Southern Illinois University Edwardsville dedicated solely to ethanol-based biofuel research projects. On the federal level, the USDA conducts a large amount of research regarding ethanol production in the United States. Much of this research is targeted toward the effect of ethanol production on domestic food markets. A division of the US Department of Energy, the National Renewable Energy Laboratory (NREL), has also conducted various ethanol research projects, mainly in the area of cellulosic ethanol.

Cellulosic ethanol commercialization is the process of building an industry out of methods of turning cellulose-containing organic matter into fuel. Companies, such as Iogen, POET, and Abengoa, are building refineries that can process biomass and turn it into bioethanol. Companies, such as Diversa, Novozymes, and Dyadic, are producing enzymes that could enable a cellulosic ethanol future. The shift from food crop feedstocks to waste residues and native grasses offers significant opportunities for a range of players, from farmers to biotechnology firms, and from project developers to investors.

As of 2013, the first commercial-scale plants to produce cellulosic biofuels have begun operating. Multiple pathways for the conversion of different biofuel feedstocks are being used. In the next few years, the cost data of these technologies operating at commercial scale, and their relative performance, will become available.

In parts of Asia and Africa where drylands prevail, sweet sorghum is being investigated as a potential source of food, feed and fuel combined. The crop is particularly suitable for growing in arid conditions, as it only extracts one seventh of the water used by sugarcane. In India, and other places, sweet sorghum stalks are used to produce biofuel by squeezing the juice and then fermenting into ethanol.

A study by researchers at the International Crops Research Institute for the Semi-Arid Tropics (ICRISAT) found that growing sweet sorghum instead of grain sorghum could increase farmers incomes by US$40 per hectare per crop because it can provide fuel in addition to food and animal feed. With grain sorghum currently grown on over 11 million hectares (ha) in Asia and on 23.4 million ha in Africa, a switch to sweet sorghum could have a considerable economic impact.

Jatropha

Several groups in various sectors are conducting research on *Jatropha curcas*, a poisonous shrub-like tree that produces seeds considered by many to be a viable source of biofuels feedstock oil. Much of this research focuses on improving the overall per acre oil yield of Jatropha through advancements in genetics, soil science, and horticultural practices.

SG Biofuels, a San Diego-based jatropha developer, has used molecular breeding and biotechnology to produce elite hybrid seeds that show significant yield improvements over first-generation varieties. SG Biofuels also claims additional benefits have arisen from such strains, including improved flowering synchronicity, higher resistance to pests and diseases, and increased cold-weather tolerance.

Plant Research International, a department of the Wageningen University and Research Centre in the Netherlands, maintains an ongoing Jatropha Evaluation Project that examines the feasibility of large-scale jatropha cultivation through field and laboratory experiments. The Center for Sustainable Energy Farming (CfSEF) is a Los Angeles-based nonprofit research organization dedicated to jatropha research in the areas of plant science, agronomy, and horticulture. Successful exploration of these disciplines is projected to increase jatropha farm production yields by 200-300% in the next 10 years.

Fungi

A group at the Russian Academy of Sciences in Moscow, in a 2008 paper, stated they had isolated large amounts of lipids from single-celled fungi and turned it into biofuels in an economically efficient manner. More research on this fungal species, *Cunninghamella japonica*, and others, is likely to appear in the near future. The recent discovery of a variant of the fungus *Gliocladium roseum* (later renamed Ascocoryne sarcoides) points toward the production of so-called myco-diesel from cellulose. This organism was recently discovered in the rainforests of northern Patagonia, and has the unique capability of converting cellulose into medium-length hydrocarbons typically found in diesel fuel. Many other fungi that can degrade cellulose and other polymers have been observed to produce molecules that are currently being engineered using organisms from other kingdoms, suggesting that fungi may play a large role in the bioproduction of fuels in the future.

Animal Gut Bacteria

Microbial gastrointestinal flora in a variety of animals have shown potential for the production of biofuels. Recent research has shown that TU-103, a strain of *Clostridium* bacteria found in Zebra feces, can convert nearly any form of cellulose into butanol fuel. Microbes in panda waste are being investigated for their use in creating biofuels from bamboo and other plant materials. There has also been substantial research into the technology of using the gut microbiomes of wood-feeding insects for the conversion of lignocellulotic material into biofuel.

GOING GREEN

If you want to help your planet, do not think that there is nothing that can be done. Everyone plays an important part in keeping the environment clean and safe. This means you can do so much and probably more than you think that you can. In fact, we are sharing with you 40 ways that you can go green. These tips are easy and things that anyone can use.

1. Change your light bulbs. Changing just one of the light bulbs in your home to a florescent light could make a serious impact on your energy consumption. Imagine what can happen if you change them all.

2. Turn your computers off at night. Even on energy saving mode you are using a lot of energy.

3. Turn off lights in the home when they are not being used. This alone can cut energy costs greatly.

4. Stop rinsing dishes before you put them in the dishwasher. This is a great source of water and energy waste.

5. Take your own bags with you to the grocery store. You reduce the use of plastic, and we all know how dangerous plastic is to the environment.

6. Hang dry your clothes rather than use the clothes dryer.

7. Reduce, Reuse and Recycle. Reduce the usage of packaged food items. Reuse scrap paper. Recycle old jars.

8. Fix leaky faucets. This includes the toilet and the sinks in the home. Even a small leakage can cause good amount of wastage of water.

9. Check if you can sign up for green power from your utility company. Also, conduct a quick energy audit of your home and replace electrical appliances with energy efficient appliances.

10. When washing clothing, make sure that you use cold water or warm water. Using hot will take the machine longer to fill while consuming more water and using more energy.

11. Instead of drinking bottled water, install a water cleaning system on your sink. Plastic bottles are usually not recycled.

12. Cut the shower time in half and see your work into full swing.

13. Take small shower instead of taking a bath.

14. Plant a tree. Even one tree can make a serious impact and do great things for the environment.

15. Recycling cell phones is another awesome way to go green. The average cell phone lasts about 18 months, but after this time they can be recycled and given life again.

16. Use public transportation or carpooling to go to work. Better yet, walk when the weather is permitting.

17. Pay all of your bills online. This will not only save you time but will also help to reduce paper wastage.

18. Shop eco-friendly. Tons of environmentally friendly products are sold. Choose these items for benefits.

19. Use recycled products whenever you can. This includes printer ink, paper, cardboard, etc. Even a reusable mug is good to have when you want to go green.

20. Unplug all of your electronics when they are not being used.

21. Buying products in bulk reduces the amount of packaging needed, thus providing considerable benefits to the environment.

22. Do rainwater harvesting. Collect rainwater and use it to water your lawns and garden.

23. Reduce the amount of junk mail that you receive.

24. Go paperless. All bills have the option of being paid online, so take advantage of this option.

25. Buy energy-efficient appliances in your home. There are many of them available and they can greatly benefit you.

26. Buy organic food, make organic meals and try out new green recipes every other day.

27. Buy vegetables that are grown locally. Not only will they taste better they also help you go green and reduce the use of paper, plastics and shipping material.

28. Switch to cloth diapers instead of disposables. Even if you use one cloth diaper a day that will result in 365 fewer disposables in the landfill each year.

29. Take your vehicle into the repair shop for regular maintenance. This will reduce emissions and more.

30. If you have items around the home that you no longer need, do not throw them away. Instead give them to someone who would use them, donate to a thrift store or have a garage sale and put some cash in your pocket.

31. Open windows in the home during daytime to let sunlight and fresh air come in.

32. Set the thermostats at the proper temperatures.

33. Pre-heating the oven is often times not necessary and simply eats up energy costs.

34. Reuse scrap paper. Print on both sides of the paper to reduce paper wastage.

35 Keep your tires inflated. Tires that are low of pressure are going to cause more wear on the car and more harm to the environment.

36. Reduce your dependence on fossil fuels to reduce greenhouse gas emissions. The less we depend on them, the better.

37. When in office, turn off all the peripherals such as printers, speakers and scanners when not in use.

38. Try to put a cover on your pool when you are not using it. This will not only make the water cleaner but it will keep it from evaporating.

39. Get e-tickets for the movies instead of buying paper tickets. Even file your taxes electronically to cut back on paper usage.

40. Involve yourself in making your city clean and green. Encourage everyone in your neighborhood to join or start a recycling program and buy eco-friendly office products..

HYBRID VEHICLE

A hybrid vehicle uses two or more distinct types of power, such as internal combustion engine to drive an electric generator that powers an electric motor, e.g. in diesel-electric trains using diesel engines to drive an electric generator that powers an electric motor, and submarines that use diesels when surfaced and batteries when submerged. Other means to store energy include pressurized fluid in hydraulic hybrids.

The basic principle with hybrid vehicles is that the different motors work better at different speeds; the electric motor is more efficient at producing torque, or turning power, and the combustion engine is better for maintaining high speed (better than typical electric motor). Switching from one to the other at the proper time while speeding up yields a win-win in terms of energy efficiency, as such that translates into greater fuel efficiency.

A biodiesel hybrid bus in Montreal, Canada.

Vehicle Type

Two-wheeled and Cycle-type Vehicles

Mopeds, electric bicycles, and even electric kick scooters are a simple form of a hybrid, powered by an internal combustion engine or electric motor and the rider's muscles. Early prototype motorcycles in the late 19th century used the same principle.

- In a parallel hybrid bicycle human and motor torques are mechanically coupled at the pedal or one of the wheels, e.g. using a hub motor, a roller pressing onto a tire, or a connection to a wheel using a transmission element. Most motorized bicycles, mopeds are of this type.

- In a series hybrid bicycle (SHB) (a kind of chainless bicycle) the user pedals a generator, charging a battery or feeding the motor, which delivers all of the torque required. They are commercially available, being simple in theory and manufacturing.

The first published prototype of an SHB is by Augustus Kinzel in 1975. In 1994 Bernie Macdonalds conceived the Electrilite SHB with power electronics allowing regenerative braking and pedaling while stationary. In 1995 Thomas Muller designed and built a "Fahrrad mit elektromagnetischem Antrieb" for his 1995 diploma thesis. In 1996 Jürg Blatter and Andreas Fuchs of Berne University of Applied Sciences built an SHB and in 1998 modified a Leitra tricycle. Until 2005 they built several prototype SH tricycles and quadricycles. In 1999 Harald Kutzke described an "active bicycle": the aim is to approach the ideal bicycle weighing nothing and having no drag by electronic compensation.

- A series hybrid electric-petroleum bicycle (SHEPB) is powered by pedals, batteries, a petrol generator, or plug-in charger - providing flexibility and range enhancements over electric-only bicycles.

A SHEPB prototype made by David Kitson in Australia in 2014 used a lightweight brushless DC electric motor from an aerial drone and small hand-tool sized internal combustion engine, and a 3D printed drive system and lightweight housing, altogether weighing less than 4.5 kg. Active cooling keeps plastic parts from softening. The prototype uses a regular electric bicycle charge port.

Heavy Vehicle

Bus Rapid Transit of Metz, a diesel-electric hybrid driving system by Van Hool.

Hybrid power trains use diesel-electric or turbo-electric to power railway locomotives, buses, heavy goods vehicles, mobile hydraulic machinery, and ships. A diesel/turbine engine drives an electric generator or hydraulic pump, which powers electric/hydraulic motors - strictly an electric/hydraulic transmission (not a hybrid), unless it can accept power from outside. With large vehicles conversion losses decrease, and the advantages in distributing power through wires or pipes rather than mechanical elements become more prominent, especially when powering multiple drives — e.g. driven wheels or propellers. Until recently most heavy vehicles had little secondary energy storage, e.g. batteries/hydraulic accumulators – excepting non-nuclear submarines, one of the oldest production hybrids, running on diesels while surfaced and batteries when submerged. Both series and parallel setups were used in WW2 submarines.

Rail Transport

Europe

East Japan Railway Company HB-E300 series.

The new Autorail à grande capacité (AGC or high-capacity railcar) built by the Canadian company Bombardier for service in France is diesel/electric motors, using 1500 or 25000 V on different rail systems. It was tested in Rotterdam, the Netherlands with Railfeeding, a Genesse and Wyoming company.

China

The First Hybrid Evaluating locomotive was designed by rail research center MATRAI in 1999 and built in 2000. It was a G12 locomotive upgraded with batteries, a 200 kW diesel generator and 4 AC motors.

Japan

Japan's first hybrid train with significant energy storage is the KiHa E200, with roof-mounted lithium ion batteries.

India

Indian railway launched one of its kind CNG-Diesel hybrid trains in January 2015. The train has a 1400 hp engine which uses fumigation technology.The first of these train is set to run on the 81 km long Rewari-Rohtak route. CNG is less-polluting alternative for diesel and petrol and is popular as an alternative fuel in India. Already many transport vehicles such as auto-rickshaws and buses run on CNG fuel.

North America

In the US, General Electric made a locomotive with sodium - nickel chloride (Na-$NiCl_2$) battery storage. They expect ≥10% fuel economy.

Variant diesel electric locomotive include the Green Goat (GG) and Green Kid (GK) switching/yard engines built by Canada's Railpower Technologies, with lead acid (Pba) batteries and 1000 to 2000 hp electric motors, and a new clean burning ~160 hp diesel generator. No fuel is wasted for idling — ~60–85% of the time for these type locomotives. It is unclear if regenerative braking is used; but in principle it is easily utilized.

Since these engines typically need extra weight for traction purposes anyway the battery pack's weight is a negligible penalty.The diesel generator and batteries are normally built on an existing "retired" "yard" locomotive's frame. The existing motors and running gear are all rebuilt and reused. Fuel savings of 40–60% and up to 80% pollution reductions are claimed over a "typical" older switching/yard engine. The advantages hybrid cars have for frequent starts and stops and idle periods apply to typical switching yard use. "Green Goat" locomotives have been purchased by Canadian Pacific Railway, BNSF Railway, Kansas City Southern Railway, and Union Pacific Railroad among others.

Cranes

Railpower Technologies engineers working with TSI Terminal Systems are testing a hybrid diesel electric power unit with battery storage for use in Rubber Tyred Gantry (RTG) cranes. RTG cranes are typically used for loading and unloading shipping containers onto trains or trucks in ports and container storage yards. The energy used to lift the containers can be partially regained when they are lowered. Diesel fuel and emission reductions of 50–70% are predicted by Railpower engineers. First systems are expected to be operational in 2007.

Road Transport and Commercial Vehicles

GMC Yukon hybrid version.

Hybrid systems are coming into use for trucks, buses and other heavy highway vehicles. Small fleet sizes and installation costs are compensated by fuel savings. With advances such as higher capacity, lowered battery cost etc. Toyota, Ford, GM and others are introducing hybrid pickups and SUVs.

Kenworth Truck Company recently introduced the Kenworth T270 Class 6 that for city usage seems to be competitive. FedEx and others are investing in hybrid delivery vehicles – particularly for city use where hybrid technology may pay off first. As of December 2013 FedEx is trialling two delivery trucks with Wrightspeed electric motors and diesel generators; the retrofit kits are claimed to pay for themselves in a few years. The diesel engines run at a constant RPM for peak efficiency.

In 1978 students at Minneapolis, Minnesota's Hennepin Vocational Technical Center, converted a Volkswagen Beetle to a petro-hydraulic hybrid with off-the shelf components. A car rated at 32 mpg was returning 75 mpg with the 60 hp engine replaced by a 16 hp engine, and reached 70 mph. In the 1990s, engineers at EPA's National Vehicle and Fuel Emissions Laboratory developed a petro-hydraulic powertrain for a typical American sedan car. The test car achieved over 80 mpg on combined EPA city/highway driving cycles. Acceleration was 0-60 mph in 8 seconds, using a 1.9 liter diesel engine. No lightweight materials were used. The EPA estimated that produced in high volumes the hydraulic components would add only $700 to the cost. Under EPA testing, a hydraulic hybrid Ford Expedition returned 32 mpg (7.4 L/100 km) City, and 22 mpg (11 L/100 km) highway. UPS currently has two trucks in service using this technology.

Military Off-road Vehicles

Since 1985, the US military has been testing serial hybrid Humvees and have found them to deliver faster acceleration, a stealth mode with low thermal signature, near silent operation, and greater fuel economy.

Ships

Ships with both mast-mounted sails and steam engines were an early form of hybrid vehicle. Another example is the diesel-electric submarine. This runs on batteries when submerged and the batteries can be re-charged by the diesel engine when the craft is on the surface.

Newer hybrid ship-propulsion schemes include large towing kites manufactured by companies such as SkySails. Towing kites can fly at heights several times higher than the tallest ship masts, capturing stronger and steadier winds.

Aircraft

The Boeing Fuel Cell Demonstrator Airplane has a Proton Exchange Membrane (PEM) fuel cell/lithium-ion battery hybrid system to power an electric motor, which is coupled to a conventional propeller. The fuel cell provides all power for the cruise phase of flight. During takeoff and climb, the flight segment that requires the most power, the system draws on lightweight lithium-ion batteries.

The demonstrator aircraft is a Dimona motor glider, built by Diamond Aircraft Industries of Austria, which also carried out structural modifications to the aircraft. With a wing span of 16.3 meters (53 feet), the airplane will be able to cruise at about 100 km/h (62 mph) on power from the fuel cell.

Hybrid FanWings have been designed. A FanWing is created by two engines with the capability to autorotate and landing like a helicopter.

Engine Type

Hybrid Electric-petroleum Vehicles

When the term *hybrid vehicle* is used, it most often refers to a Hybrid electric vehicle. These encompass such vehicles as the Saturn Vue, Toyota Prius, Toyota Yaris, Toyota Camry Hybrid, Ford Escape Hybrid, Toyota Highlander Hybrid, Honda Insight, Honda Civic Hybrid, Lexus RX 400h and 450h, Hyundai Ioniq and others. A petroleum-electric hybrid most commonly uses internal combustion engines (using a variety of fuels, generally gasoline or Diesel engines) and electric motors to power the vehicle. The energy is stored in the fuel of the internal combustion engine and an electric battery set. There are many types of petroleum-electric hybrid drivetrains, from Full hybrid to Mild hybrid, which offer varying advantages and disadvantages.

Hybrid New Flyer Metrobus.

William H. Patton filed a patent application for a gasoline-electric hybrid rail-car propulsion system in early 1889, and for a similar hybrid boat propulsion system in mid 1889. There is no evidence that his hybrid boat met with any success, but he built a prototype hybrid tram and sold a small hybrid locomotive.

Hybrid Optare Solo.

In 1899, Henri Pieper developed the world's first petro-electric hybrid automobile. In 1900, Ferdinand Porsche developed a series-hybrid using two motor-in-wheel-hub arrangements with an internal combustion generator set providing the electric power; Porsche's hybrid set two speed records.While liquid fuel/electric hybrids date back to the late 19th century, the braking regenerative hybrid was invented by David Arthurs, an electrical engineer from Springdale, Arkansas in 1978–79. His home-converted Opel GT was reported to return as much as 75 mpg with plans still sold to this original design, and the "Mother Earth News" modified version on their website.

The plug-in-electric-vehicle (PEV) is becoming more and more common. It has the range needed in locations where there are wide gaps with no services. The batteries can be plugged into house (mains) electricity for charging, as well being charged while the engine is running.

Continuously Outboard Recharged Electric Vehicle (COREV)

Some battery electric vehicles (BEVs) can be recharged while the user drives. Such a vehicle establishes contact with an electrified rail, plate or overhead wires on the highway via an attached conducting wheel or other similar mechanism. The BEV's batteries are recharged by this process—on the highway—and can then be used normally on other roads until the battery is discharged. For example, some of the battery-electric locomotives used for maintenance trains on the London Underground are capable of this mode of operation.

Developing a BEV infrastructure would provide the advantage of virtually unrestricted highway range. Since many destinations are within 100 km of a major highway, BEV technology could reduce the need for expensive battery systems. Unfortunately, private use of the existing electrical system is almost universally prohibited. Besides, the technology for such electrical infrastructure is largely outdated and, outside some cities, not widely distributed. Updating the required electrical and infrastructure costs could perhaps be funded by toll revenue or by dedicated transportation taxes.

Hybrid Fuel (Dual Mode)

Ford Escape Plug-in Hybrid with a flexible fuel capability to run on E85 (ethanol).

In addition to vehicles that use two or more different devices for propulsion, some also consider vehicles that use distinct energy sources or input types ("fuels") using the same engine to be hybrids, although to avoid confusion with hybrids as described above and to use correctly the terms, these are perhaps more correctly described as dual mode vehicles:

- Some electric trolleybuses can switch between an on-board diesel engine and overhead electrical power depending on conditions. In principle, this could be combined with a battery subsystem to create a true plug-in hybrid trolleybus, although as of 2006, no such design seems to have been announced.
- Flexible-fuel vehicles can use a mixture of input fuels mixed in one tank — typically gasoline and ethanol, methanol, or biobutanol.
- Bi-fuel vehicle: Liquified petroleum gas and natural gas are very different from petroleum or diesel and cannot be used in the same tanks, so it would be impossible to build an (LPG or NG) flexible fuel system. Instead vehicles are built with two, parallel, fuel systems feeding one engine. For example, some Chevrolet Silverado 2500 HDs can effortlessly switch between petroleum and natural gas, offering a range of over 1000 km (650 miles). While the duplicated tanks cost space in some applications, the increased range, decreased cost of fuel, and flexibility where LPG or CNG infrastructure is incomplete may be a significant incentive to purchase. While the US Natural gas infrastructure is partially incomplete, it is increasing at a fast pace, and already has 2600 CNG stations in place. With a growing fueling station infrastructure, a large scale adoption of these bi-fuel vehicles could be seen in the near future. Rising gas prices may also push consumers to purchase these vehicles. When gas prices trade around $4.00, the price per MMBTU of gasoline is $28.00, compared to natural gas's $4.00 per MMBTU. On a per unit of energy comparative basis, this makes natural gas much cheaper than gasoline. All of these factors are making CNG-Gasoline bi-fuel vehicles very attractive.
- Some vehicles have been modified to use another fuel source if it is available, such as cars modified to run on autogas (LPG) and diesels modified to run on waste vegetable oil that has not been processed into biodiesel.
- Power-assist mechanisms for bicycles and other human-powered vehicles are also included.

Fluid Power Hybrid

Chrysler minivan, petro-hydraulic hybrid.

Hydraulic hybrid and pneumatic hybrid vehicles use an engine to charge a pressure accumulator to drive the wheels via hydraulic (liquid) or pneumatic (compressed air) drive units. In most cases the engine is detached from the drivetrain, serving solely to charge the energy accumulator. The transmission is seamless. Regenerative braking can be used to recover some of the supplied drive energy back into the accumulator.

Petro-air Hybrid

A French company, MDI, has designed and has running models of a petro-air hybrid engine car. The system does not use air motors to drive the vehicle, being directly driven by a hybrid engine. The engine uses a mixture of compressed air and gasoline injected into the cylinders. A key aspect of the hybrid engine is the "active chamber", which is a compartment heating air via fuel doubling the energy output. Tata Motors of India assessed the design phase towards full production for the Indian market and moved into "completing detailed development of the compressed air engine into specific vehicle and stationary applications".

French MDI petro-air hybrid car developed with Tata.

Petro-hydraulic Hybrid

Peugeot 2008 HYbrid air/hydraulic concept car.

Peugeot 2008 HYbrid air/hydraulic cutaway.

Petro-hydraulic configurations have been common in trains and heavy vehicles for decades. The auto industry recently focused on this hybrid configuration as it now shows promise for introduction into smaller vehicles.

In petro-hydraulic hybrids, the energy recovery rate is high and therefore the system is more efficient than electric battery charged hybrids using the current electric battery technology, demonstrating a 60% to 70% increase in energy economy in US Environmental Protection Agency (EPA) testing. The charging engine needs only to be sized for average usage with acceleration bursts using the stored energy in the hydraulic accumulator, which is charged when in low energy demanding vehicle operation. The charging engine runs at optimum speed and load for efficiency and longevity. Under tests undertaken by the US Environmental Protection Agency (EPA), a hydraulic hybrid Ford Expedition returned 32 miles per US gallon (7.4 L/100 km; 38 mpg_{imp}) City, and 22 miles per US gallon (11 L/100 km; 26 mpg_{imp}) highway. UPS currently has two trucks in service using this technology.

Although petro-hydraulic hybrid technology has been known for decades, and used in trains and very large construction vehicles, high costs of the equipment precluded the systems from lighter trucks and cars. In the modern sense an experiment proved the viability of small petro-hydraulic hybrid road vehicles in 1978. A group of students at Minneapolis, Minnesota's Hennepin Vocational Technical Center, converted a Volkswagen Beetle car to run as a petro-hydraulic hybrid using off-the shelf components. A car rated at 32 mpg_{US} (7.4 L/100 km; 38 mpg_{imp}) was returning 75 mpg_{US} (3.1 L/100 km; 90 mpg_{imp}) with the 60 hp engine replaced by a 16 hp engine. The experimental car reached 70 mph (110 km/h).

In the 1990s, a team of engineers working at EPA's National Vehicle and Fuel Emissions Laboratory succeeded in developing a revolutionary type of petro-hydraulic hybrid powertrain that would propel a typical American sedan car. The test car achieved over 80 mpg on combined EPA city/highway driving cycles. Acceleration was 0-60 mph in 8 seconds, using a 1.9 liter diesel engine. No lightweight materials were used. The EPA estimated that produced in high volumes the hydraulic components would add only $700 to the base cost of the vehicle.

The petro-hydraulic hybrid system has faster and more efficient charge/discharge cycling than petro-electric hybrids and is also cheaper to build. The accumulator vessel size dictates total energy storage capacity and may require more space than an electric battery set. Any vehicle space consumed by a larger size of accumulator vessel may be offset by the need for a smaller sized charging engine, in HP and physical size.

Research is underway in large corporations and small companies. Focus has now switched to smaller vehicles. The system components were expensive which precluded installation in smaller trucks and cars. A drawback was that the power driving motors were not efficient enough at part load. A British company (Artemis Intelligent Power) made a breakthrough introducing an electronically controlled hydraulic motor/pump, the Digital Displacement® motor/pump. The pump is highly efficient at all speed ranges and loads, giving feasibility to small applications of petro-hydraulic hybrids. The company converted a BMW car as a test bed to prove viability. The BMW 530i, gave double the mpg in city driving compared to the standard car. This test was using the standard 3,000 cc engine, with a smaller engine the figures would have been more impressive. The design of petro-hydraulic hybrids using well sized accumulators allows downsizing an engine to average power usage, not peak power usage. Peak power is provided by the energy stored in the accumulator. A smaller more efficient constant speed engine reduces weight and liberates space for a larger accumulator.

Current vehicle bodies are designed around the mechanicals of existing engine/transmission setups. It is restrictive and far from ideal to install petro-hydraulic mechanicals into existing bodies not designed for hydraulic setups. One research project's goal is to create a blank paper design new car, to maximize the packaging of petro-hydraulic hybrid components in the vehicle. All bulky hydraulic components are integrated into the chassis of the car. One design has claimed to return 130 mpg in tests by using a large hydraulic accumulator which is also the structural chassis of the car. The small hydraulic driving motors are incorporated within the wheel hubs driving the wheels and reversing to claw-back kinetic braking energy. The hub motors eliminates the need for friction brakes, mechanical transmissions, drive shafts and U joints, reducing costs and weight. Hydrostatic drive with no friction brakes are used in industrial vehicles. The aim is 170 mpg in average driving conditions. Energy created by shock absorbers and kinetic braking energy that normally would be wasted assists in charging the accumulator. A small fossil fuelled piston engine sized for average power use charges the accumulator. The accumulator is sized at running the car for 15 minutes when fully charged. The aim is a fully charged accumulator which will produce a 0-60 mph acceleration speed of under 5 seconds using four wheel drive.

In January 2011 industry giant Chrysler announced a partnership with the US Environmental Protection Agency (EPA) to design and develop an experimental petro-hydraulic hybrid powertrain suitable for use in large passenger cars. In 2012 an existing production minvan was adapted to the new hydraulic powertrain for assessment.

PSA Peugeot Citroën exhibited an experimental "Hybrid Air" engine at the 2013 Geneva Motor Show. The vehicle uses nitrogen gas compressed by energy harvested from braking or deceleration to power a hydraulic drive which supplements power from its conventional gasoline engine. The hydraulic and electronic components were supplied by Robert Bosch GmbH. Mileage was estimated to be about 118 mpg_{US} (2 L/100 km; 142 mpg_{imp}) on the Euro test cycle if installed in a Citroën

C3 type of body. PSA Although the car was ready for production and was proven and feasible delivering the claimed results, Peugeot Citroën were unable to attract a major manufacturer to share the high development costs and are shelving the project until a partnership can be arranged.

Electric-human Power

Electric-human power hybrid vehicle: Another form of hybrid vehicle are human power-electric vehicles. These include such vehicles as the Sinclair C5, Twike, electric bicycles, and electric skateboards.

Hybrid Vehicle Power Train Configurations

Parallel Hybrid

Honda Insight, Mild Parallel Hybrid.

In a parallel hybrid vehicle an electric motor and an internal combustion engine are coupled such that they can power the vehicle either individually or together. Most commonly the internal combustion engine, the electric motor and gear box are coupled by automatically controlled clutches. For electric driving the clutch between the internal combustion engine is open while the clutch to the gear box is engaged. While in combustion mode the engine and motor run at the same speed.

Toyota Prius, series-parallel hybrid.

The first mass production parallel hybrid sold outside Japan was the 1st generation Honda Insight.

Mild Parallel Hybrid

These types use a generally compact electric motor (usually <20 kW) to provide auto-stop/start features and to provide extra power assist during the acceleration, and to generate on the deceleration phase (aka regenerative braking).

On-road examples include Honda Civic Hybrid, Honda Insight 2nd generation, Honda CR-Z, Honda Accord Hybrid, Mercedes Benz S400 BlueHYBRID, BMW 7 Series hybrids, General Motors BAS Hybrids, Suzuki S-Cross, Suzuki Wagon R and Smart fortwo with micro hybrid drive.

Power-split or Series-parallel Hybrid

In a power-split hybrid electric drive train there are two motors: a traction electric motor and an internal combustion engine. The power from these two motors can be shared to drive the wheels via a power split device, which is a simple planetary gear set. The ratio can be from 100% for the combustion engine to 100% for the traction electric motor, or anything in between, such as 40% for the electric motor and 60% for the combustion engine. The combustion engine can act as a generator charging the batteries.

Ford Escape Hybrid, a series-parallel drivetrain.

Modern versions such as the Toyota Hybrid Synergy Drive have a second electric motor/generator connected to the planetary gear. In cooperation with the traction motor/generator and the power-split device this provides a continuously variable transmission.

On the open road, the primary power source is the internal combustion engine. When maximum power is required, for example to overtake, the traction electric motor is used to assist. This increases the available power for a short period, giving the effect of having a larger engine than actually installed. In most applications, the combustion engine is switched off when the car is slow or stationary thereby reducing curbside emissions.

Passenger car installations include Toyota Prius, Ford Escape and Fusion, as well as Lexus RX400h, RX450h, GS450h, LS600h, and CT200h.

Series Hybrid

Chevrolet Volt, a series hybrid plug-in hybrid, also called extended range electric vehicle (EREV).

A series- or serial-hybrid vehicle is driven by an electric motor, functioning as an electric vehicle while the battery pack energy supply is sufficient, with an engine tuned for running as a generator when the battery pack is insufficient. There is typically no mechanical connection between the engine and the wheels, and the primary purpose of the range extender is to charge the battery. Series-hybrids have also been referred to as extended range electric vehicle, range-extended electric vehicle, or electric vehicle-extended range (EREV/REEV/EVER).

The BMW i3 with Range Extender is a production series-hybrid. It operates as an electric vehicle until the battery charge is low, and then activates an engine-powered generator to maintain power, and is also available without the range extender. The Fisker Karma was the first series-hybrid production vehicle.

When describing cars, the battery of a series-hybrid is usually charged by being plugged in - but a series-hybrid may also allow for a battery to only act as a buffer (and for regeneration purposes), and for the electric motor's power to be supplied constantly by a supporting engine. Series arrangements have been common in diesel-electric locomotives and ships. Ferdinand Porsche effectively invented this arrangement in speed-record-setting racing cars in the early 20th century, such as the Lohner-Porsche Mixte Hybrid. Porsche named his arrangement "System Mixt" and it was a wheel hub motor design, where each of the two front wheels was powered by a separate motor. This arrangement was sometimes referred to as an *electric transmission*, as the electric generator and driving motor replaced a mechanical transmission. The vehicle could not move unless the internal combustion engine was running.

In 1997 Toyota released the first series-hybrid bus sold in Japan. GM introduced the Chevy Volt series plug-in hybrid in 2010, aiming for an all-electric range of 40 mi (64 km), though this car also has a mechanical connection between the engine and drivetrain. Supercapacitors combined with a lithium ion battery bank have been used by AFS Trinity in a converted Saturn Vue SUV vehicle. Using supercapacitors they claim up to 150 mpg in a series-hybrid arrangement.

Plug-in Hybrid Electric Vehicle (PHEV

The Toyota Prius Prime has an all-electric range of 25 mi (40 km).

The Ford Fusion Energi is a plug-in hybrid with an all-electric range of 21 mi (34 km).

Another subtype of hybrid vehicles is the plug-in hybrid electric vehicle (PHEV). The plug-in hybrid is usually a general fuel-electric (parallel or serial) hybrid with increased energy storage capacity, usually through a lithium-ion battery, which allows the vehicle to drive on all-electric mode a distance that depends on the battery size and its mechanical layout (series or parallel). It may be connected to mains electricity supply at the end of the journey to avoid charging using the on-board internal combustion engine.

This concept is attractive to those seeking to minimize on-road emissions by avoiding – or at least minimizing – the use of ICE during daily driving. As with pure electric vehicles, the total emissions saving, for example in CO_2 terms, is dependent upon the energy source of the electricity generating company.

For some users, this type of vehicle may also be financially attractive so long as the electrical energy being used is cheaper than the petrol/diesel that they would have otherwise used. Current tax systems in many European countries use mineral oil taxation as a major income source. This is generally not the case for electricity, which is taxed uniformly for the domestic customer, however that person uses it. Some electricity suppliers also offer price benefits for off-peak night users, which may further increase the attractiveness of the plug-in option for commuters and urban motorists.

Road Safety for Cyclists and Pedestrians

The Nissan Leaf was the first plug-in electric car equipped with Nissan's Vehicle Sound for Pedestrians.

A 2009 National Highway Traffic Safety Administration report examined hybrid electric vehicle accidents that involved pedestrians and cyclists and compared them to accidents involving internal combustion engine vehicles (ICEV). The findings showed that, in certain road situations, HEVs are more dangerous for those on foot or bicycle. For accidents where a vehicle was slowing or stopping, backing up, entering or leaving a parking space (when the sound difference between HEVs and ICEVs is most pronounced), HEVs were twice as likely to be involved in a pedestrian crash than ICEVs. For crashes involving cyclists or pedestrians, there was a higher incident rate for HEVs than ICEVs when a vehicle was turning a corner. But there was no statistically significant difference between the types of vehicles when they were driving straight.

Several automakers developed electric vehicle warning sounds designed to alert pedestrians to the presence of electric drive vehicles such as hybrid electric vehicle, plug-in hybrid electric vehicles and all-electric vehicles (EVs) travelling at low speeds. Their purpose is to make pedestrians, cyclists, the blind, and others aware of the vehicle's presence while operating in all-electric mode.

Vehicles in the market with such safety devices include the Nissan Leaf, Chevrolet Volt, Fisker Karma, Honda FCX Clarity, Nissan Fuga Hybrid/Infiniti M35, Hyundai ix35 FCEV, Hyundai Sonata Hybrid, 2012 Honda Fit EV, the 2012 Toyota Camry Hybrid, 2012 Lexus CT200h, and all Prius family cars recently introduced, including the standard 2012 model year Prius, the Toyota Prius v, and the Toyota Prius Plug-in Hybrid.

Environmental Issues

Fuel Consumption and Emissions Reductions

The hybrid vehicle typically achieves greater fuel economy and lower emissions than conventional internal combustion engine vehicles (ICEVs), resulting in fewer emissions being generated. These savings are primarily achieved by three elements of a typical hybrid design:

- Relying on both the engine and the electric motors for peak power needs, resulting in a smaller engine size more for average usage rather than peak power usage. A smaller engine can have less internal losses and lower weight.
- Having significant battery storage capacity to store and reuse recaptured energy, especially in stop-and-go traffic typical of the city driving cycle.
- Recapturing significant amounts of energy during braking that are normally wasted as heat. This regenerative braking reduces vehicle speed by converting some of its kinetic energy into electricity, depending upon the power rating of the motor/generator.

Other techniques that are not necessarily 'hybrid' features, but that are frequently found on hybrid vehicles include:

- Using Atkinson cycle engines instead of Otto cycle engines for improved fuel economy.
- Shutting down the engine during traffic stops or while coasting or during other idle periods.
- Improving aerodynamics; (part of the reason that SUVs get such bad fuel economy is the drag on the car. A box shaped car or truck has to exert more force to move through the air causing more stress on the engine making it work harder). Improving the shape and aerodynamics of a car is a good way to help better the fuel economy and also improve vehicle handling at the same time.
- Using low rolling resistance tires (tires were often made to give a quiet, smooth ride, high grip, etc., but efficiency was a lower priority). Tires cause mechanical drag, once again making the engine work harder, consuming more fuel. Hybrid cars may use special tires that are more inflated than regular tires and stiffer or by choice of carcass structure and rubber compound have lower rolling resistance while retaining acceptable grip, and so improving fuel economy whatever the power source.
- Powering the a/c, power steering, and other auxiliary pumps electrically as and when needed; this reduces mechanical losses when compared with driving them continuously with traditional engine belts.

These features make a hybrid vehicle particularly efficient for city traffic where there are frequent stops, coasting and idling periods. In addition noise emissions are reduced, particularly at idling and low operating speeds, in comparison to conventional engine vehicles. For continuous high speed highway use these features are much less useful in reducing emissions.

Hybrid Vehicle Emissions

Hybrid vehicle emissions today are getting close to or even lower than the recommended level set by the EPA (Environmental Protection Agency). The recommended levels they suggest for a typical passenger vehicle should be equated to 5.5 metric tons of CO_2. The three most popular hybrid vehicles, Honda Civic, Honda Insight and Toyota Prius, set the standards even higher by producing 4.1, 3.5, and 3.5 tons showing a major improvement in carbon dioxide emissions. Hybrid vehicles can reduce air emissions of smog-forming pollutants by up to 90% and cut carbon dioxide emissions in half.

More fossil fuel is needed to build hybrid vehicles than conventional cars but reduced emissions when running the vehicle more than outweigh this.

Environmental Impact of Hybrid Car Battery

Though hybrid cars consume less fuel than conventional cars, there is still an issue regarding the environmental damage of the hybrid car battery. Today most hybrid car batteries are one of two types: 1) nickel metal hydride, or 2) lithium ion; both are regarded as more environmentally friendly than lead-based batteries which constitute the bulk of petrol car starter batteries today. There are many types of batteries. Some are far more toxic than others. Lithium ion is the least toxic of the two mentioned above.

The toxicity levels and environmental impact of nickel metal hydride batteries—the type currently used in hybrids—are much lower than batteries like lead acid or nickel cadmium according to one source. Another source claims nickel metal hydride batteries are much more toxic than lead batteries, also that recycling them and disposing of them safely is difficult. In general various soluble and insoluble nickel compounds, such as nickel chloride and nickel oxide, have known carcinogenic effects in chick embryos and rats. The main nickel compound in NiMH batteries is nickel oxyhydroxide (NiOOH), which is used as the positive electrode.

The lithium-ion battery has attracted attention due to its potential for use in hybrid electric vehicles. Hitachi is a leader in its development. In addition to its smaller size and lighter weight, lithium-ion batteries deliver performance that helps to protect the environment with features such as improved charge efficiency without memory effect. The lithium-ion batteries are appealing because they have the highest energy density of any rechargeable batteries and can produce a voltage more than three times that of nickel–metal hydride battery cell while simultaneously storing large quantities of electricity as well. The batteries also produce higher output (boosting vehicle power), higher efficiency (avoiding wasteful use of electricity), and provides excellent durability, compared with the life of the battery being roughly equivalent to the life of the vehicle. Additionally, use of lithium-ion batteries reduces the overall weight of the vehicle and also achieves improved fuel economy of 30% better than petro-powered vehicles with a consequent reduction in CO_2 emissions helping to prevent global warming.

Charging

There are two different levels of charging. Level one charging is the slower method as it uses a 120 V/15 A single-phase grounded outlet. Level two is a faster method; existing Level 2 equipment offers charging from 208 V or 240 V (at up to 80 A, 19.2 kW). It may require dedicated equipment and a connection installation for home or public units, although vehicles such as the Tesla have the power electronics on board and need only the outlet. The optimum charging window for Lithium ion batteries is 3-4.2 V. Recharging with a 120 volt household outlet takes several hours, a 240 volt charger takes 1–4 hours, and a quick charge takes approximately 30 minutes to achieve 80% charge. Three important factors—distance on charge, cost of charging, and time to charge In order for the hybrid to run on electrical power, the car must perform the action of braking in order to generate some electricity. The electricity then gets discharged most effectively when the car accelerates or climbs up an incline. In 2014, hybrid electric car batteries can run on solely electricity for 70–130 miles (110–210 km) on a single charge. Hybrid battery capacity currently ranges from 4.4 kWh to 85 kWh on a fully electric car. On a hybrid car, the battery packs currently range from 0.6 kWh to 2.4 kWh representing a large difference in use of electricity in hybrid cars.

Raw Materials Increasing Costs

There is an impending increase in the costs of many rare materials used in the manufacture of hybrid cars. For example, the rare earth element dysprosium is required to fabricate many of the advanced electric motors and battery systems in hybrid propulsion systems. Neodymium is another rare earth metal which is a crucial ingredient in high-strength magnets that are found in permanent magnet electric motors.

Nearly all the rare earth elements in the world come from China, and many analysts believe that an overall increase in Chinese electronics manufacturing will consume this entire supply by 2012. In addition, export quotas on Chinese rare earth elements have resulted in an unknown amount of supply.

A few non-Chinese sources such as the advanced Hoidas Lake project in northern Canada as well as Mount Weld in Australia are currently under development; however, the barriers to entry are high and require years to go online.

How Hybrid-electric Vehicles Work?

Hybrids-Electric vehicles (HEVs) combine the advantage of gasoline *engines* and electric *motors*. The key areas for efficiency or performance gains are regenerative braking, dual power sources, and less idling.

- Regenerate Braking: The drivetrain can be used to convert kinetic energy (from the moving car) into stored electrical energy (batteries). The same electric motor that powers the drivetrain is used to resist the motion of the drivetrain. This applied resistance from the electric motor causes the wheel to slow down and simultaneously recharge the batteries.
- Dual Power: Power can come from either the engine, motor or both depending on driving circumstances. Additional power to assist the engine in accelerating or climbing might be provided by the electric motor. Or more commonly, a smaller electric motor provides all of the power for low-speed driving conditions and is augmented by the engine at higher speeds.
- Automatic Start/Shutoff: It automatically shuts off the engine when the vehicle comes to a stop and restarts it when the accelerator is pressed down. This automation is much simpler with an electric motor.

Alternative Green Vehicles

Other types of green vehicles include other vehicles that go fully or partly on alternative energy sources than fossil fuel. Another option is to use alternative fuel composition (i.e. biofuels) in conventional fossil fuel-based vehicles, making them go partly on renewable energy sources.

Other approaches include personal rapid transit, a public transportation concept that offers automated on-demand non-stop transportation, on a network of specially built guideways.

Peugeot/Citroën Hybrid Vehicle

Peugeot and Citroën have announced that they too are building a car that uses compressed air as an energy source. However, the car they are designing uses a hybrid system which also uses a gasoline engine (which is used for propelling the car over 70 km/h, or when the compressed air tank has been depleted.

Marketing

Automakers spend around $US8 million in marketing Hybrid vehicles each year. With combined effort from many car companies, the Hybrid industry has sold millions of Hybrids.Hybrid car companies like Toyota, Honda, Ford and BMW have pulled together to create a movement of Hybrid vehicle sales pushed by Washington lobbyist to lower the worlds emissions and become less reliant on our petroleum consumption.In 2005, sales went beyond 200,000 Hybrids, but in retrospect that only reduced the global use for gasoline consumption by 200,000 gallons per day – a tiny fraction of the 360 million gallons used per day.According to Bradley Berman author of Driving Change—One Hybrid at a time, "Cold economics shows that in real dollars, except for a brief spike in the 1970s, gas prices have remained remarkably steady and cheap. Fuel continues to represent a small part of the overall cost of owning and operating a personal vehicle". Other marketing tactics include greenwashing which is the "unjustified appropriation of environmental virtue." Temma Ehrenfeld explained in an article by Newsweek. Hybrids may be more efficient than many other gasoline motors as far as gasoline consumption is concerned but as far as being green and good for the environment is completely inaccurate. Hybrid car companies have a long time to go if they expect to really go green.

According to Harvard business professor Theodore Levitt states "managing products" and "meeting customers' needs", "you must adapt to consumer expectations and anticipation of future desires." This means people buy what they want, if they want a fuel efficient car they buy a Hybrid without thinking about the actual efficiency of the product. This "Green Myopia" as Ottman calls it, fails because marketers focus on the greenness of the product and not on the actual effectiveness. Researchers and analysts say people are drawn to the new technology, as well as the convenience of fewer fill ups. Secondly, people find it rewarding to own the better, newer, flashier, and so called greener car. In the beginning of the Hybrid movement car companies reached out to the young people, by using top celebrities, astronauts, and popular TV shows to market Hybrids. This made the new technology of Hybrids a status to obtain for many people and a must to be cool or even the practical choice for the time. With the many benefits and status of owning a Hybrid it is easy to think it's the right thing to do, but in fact may not be as green as it appears.

In 2019 the term "Self-Charging Hybrid" became popular in advertising, though cars referred to by this name do not offer any different functionality than a standard hybrid vehicle provides. The only self-charging effect is in energy recovery via regenerative braking, which is also true of plug-in hybrids, fuel cell electric vehicles and battery electric vehicles.

Adoption Rate

While the adoption rate for hybrids in the US is small today (2.2% of new car sales in 2011), this compares with a 17.1% share of new car sales in Japan in 2011, and it has the potential to be very large over time as more models are offered and incremental costs decline due to learning and scale benefits. However, forecasts vary widely. For instance, Bob Lutz, a long-time skeptic of hybrids, indicated he expects hybrids "will never comprise more than 10% of the US auto market." Other sources also expect hybrid penetration rates in the US will remain under 10% for many years.

More optimistic views as of 2006 include predictions that hybrids would dominate new car sales in the US and elsewhere over the next 10 to 20 years. Another approach, taken by Saurin Shah, examines the penetration rates (or S-curves) of four analogs (historical and current) to hybrid and electrical vehicles in an attempt to gauge how quickly the vehicle stock could be hybridized and/or electrified in the United States. The analogs are (1) the electric motors in US factories in the early 20th century, (2) diesel electric locomotives on US railways in the 1920–1945 period, (3) a range of new automotive features/technologies introduced in the US over the past fifty years, and 4) e-bike purchases in China over the past few years. These analogs collectively suggest it would take at least 30 years for hybrid and electric vehicles to capture 80% of the US passenger vehicle stock.

REDUCING PLASTIC USE

1. Say NO to plastic straws:

We use more than 500 MILLION plastic straws *every single day*. Think about it: when you order coffee at a restaurant or cafe, you don't use a straw to drink it. So why do you need a straw for your water or soda? Saying NO to single-use straws is easier than you think. Restaurants and bars have the tendency to give you a plastic straw even before you have the chance to let them know you'd rather not have one, so make sure upon ordering drinks that you let your waiter or bartender know you are okay with no straw. If you would prefer to use a straw, there are great alternatives such as steel, bamboo, and glass straws that you can carry with you and can use them time and time again.

2. Bring a reusable shopping bag with you:

More than 1 million bags are used across the globe every day and annually, about 500 billion plastic bags are produced. Whether you are going grocery shopping at the supermarket or going on a shopping spree at the mall, bring your own bag with you. Most reusable bags are only about 99 cents - a small investment to help out our planet.

3. Get rid of the plastic water bottle:

Most stores and many companies make a variety of reusable water bottles. Made in all sizes, shapes, and materials, there is no reason to continue to use plastic water bottles. A single person using a reusable, refillable water bottle instead of single-use plastic water bottles can save as much as 170 bottles from being produced each year. If a family of 5 all hopped on board with this greener practice, that means as a family they would stop about 850 water bottles from having to be produced.

4. Pack your lunch in glass containers instead of plastic:

Ditch the plastic Ziplock baggie and use something more eco-friendly than single-use plastic. There are many brands that make glass containers with lids for all of your packed-food needs. Mason jars are also another creative and hip way to pack your foods for lunch.

5. Avoid snacks/food with excess packaging:

We're all guilty of this. You buy a huge plastic bag filled with even smaller plastic bags of snack-size chips. Think of all the unnecessary packing that goes into the food on the shelf. Also, some supermarkets will wrap each fruit or vegetable individually in plastic wrap. Instead of throwing it away, leave the plastic wrap with your grocer so that they can reuse it for other products.

6. Stop using plastic cutlery:

When you get a take-out order, you will automatically be given a set of plastic cutlery. Before you take your food, make sure to ask for no plastic fork, spoon, or knife. Chances are if you are taking the food home, you have silverware readily available and do not need to waste the plastic cutlery. If you are taking your food to-go and bringing it back to work, keep a cheaper set of silverware at work that you can wash off and use over and over again. This also guarantees that you will never be utensil-less for another lunch again.

7. Choose cardboard over plastic when you can:

Cardboard can be more easily recycled and unlike plastic, will biodegrade over time. While plastics can be recycled as well, buying products when you can that are in cardboard boxes such as laundry detergent will help to reduce the plastic that needs to be produced.

8. Swap out your plastic toothbrush:

Whether you believe it or not, every single toothbrush affects the environment. One billion plastic toothbrushes are thrown out every single year, creating about 50 million pounds of waste annually. There have not been any scientific research results that plastic toothbrushes perform better over bamboo ones. Just like plastic toothbrushes, bamboo brushes needed to be replaced just as often, about every 3 months, but the handle of a bamboo toothbrush only takes about 6 months to biodegrade back into the soil. On the other hand, a plastic toothbrush will never biodegrade and will remain in the environment forever.

9. Avoid cosmetic products that contain microbeads:

Countries are making this easier to do as more and more countries are putting a ban on the production of plastic microbeads in most cosmetic items. The UK is the latest country to issue a ban which will become effective beginning in July of this year. Millions of plastic microbeads are washed down the drain each year, posing a serious threat to marine life who mistake these small plastic particles for food. Choose bath and shower soaps that do not contain microbeads the next time you go to purchase one of these items.

10. Choose metal over plastic razors:

Sure, a metal razor may be a little heavier to hold than a plastic one, but the long-term result of discarded plastic razors is even heavier on the heart. 2 BILLION plastic razors are discarded every year - and discarded does *not* mean they were recycled. Invest a little more into a reusable metal razor and ditch the plastic - but in a recycle bin.

11. Get the hang of using wire hangers:

Almost any other type of hanger is better than plastic. Almost 90% of the clothes sold in the USA are imported from overseas. Unfortunately, almost every single garment sent over also comes on its own individual hanger - meaning 30-40 billion hangers are sent to the US every year. If you laid out all of these hangers, they would stretch 8 million miles, far beyond the orbit of *the moon*. Even worse? 85% of these hangers do not get reused or recycled but instead, end up in a landfill. Switch to metal, steel hangers instead. Steel hangers are 100% recyclable and not to mention, usually last longer than most flimsy plastic hangers.

12. While you're at it, get rid of the plastic hampers too:

Speaking of flimsy, we move on to plastic hampers. Another plastic commodity that we can all live without. So what can we use instead of plastic hampers? Try bamboo! Bamboo products are typically sturdy and pose no serious threat to the environment. You can place a cloth burlap bag inside the bamboo hamper and easily take the bag out to do laundry.

13. Switch to e-billing:

It's 2018 and you still get your bills mailed to you? E-billing may very well be one of the most overlooked green practices that we could all be doing. While there may not be a whole lot of plastic involved with receiving bills in the mail, there are many over ecological benefits for signing up for e-billing. The average American household can save 6.6 pounds of paper each year and avoid producing 171 pounds of greenhouse emissions. Call your billing provider today to get started on a more eco-friendly way to pay bills.

14. Paper newspapers are a thing of the past:

That newspaper that sits on your driveway may seem convenient, wrapped in the unnecessary plastic wrapping. However, chances are, whatever headlining story will be on the front page of the newspaper has already aired on every televised news station and you've already read about it online. If you don't want to give up the joy of reading a newspaper, sign up for an electronic one! Companies make it easy not with iPads, Kindles, and all other forms of tablets to receive the news you want when you want it.

15. If it's plastic, think twice:

While this last point is not a specific item, we realize that there are many other ways to help reduce your plastic intake than the 14 listed on this blog. Everything from the toys that kids are playing with to the many plastic supplies used for a birthday party, plastic items are all around us. While we understand that avoiding plastic at all costs is near impossible, we encourage you to avoid it when possible and to think twice before purchasing a plastic item that can easily be replaced.

SWITCH TO REUSABLE BAGS

The definition of "Reusable Bag" has become a very important topic in drafting plastic bag laws. Reusable bags are sturdy enough to withstand several uses (e.g. hundreds) and are machine-washable.

Types of Reusable Bags

Fabric Reusable Bags

There are a wide range of fabric reusable bags on the market, including natural fibre bags like cotton and canvas, jute, hemp. There are also petroleum-based fabric bags (nylon and polyester, known as PET).

Each bag material has advantages and disadvantages. Some of the options on the market today:

Cotton and Canvas Bags

- Cotton and canvas bags are the most common bags made with natural-fibres.
- They might be made from traditional cotton, organic cotton or recycled cotton bags.
- Traditional cotton is made from a renewable crop source, but requires chemicals and pesticides and consumes huge quantities of water.

- Organic cotton is grown without pesticides, which is helpful in reducing the negative environmental footprint of cotton production.
- Recycled cotton consists of reclaimed organic and traditional cotton "scrap" which is spun into new yarn.
- To match the efficiency of using a plastic shopping bag just once, each cotton bag must be reused 131 times to compensate for its large carbon footprint/global warming potential.

Advantages

- Biodegradable/natural plant fibre.
- Renewable resource.
- Strong and durable (bags are typically 8-12 ounces).
- Soft fabric.
- Can be machine washed in cold water.

Disadvantages

- Heavy environmental footprint and global warming potential.
- Traditional (non-organic) cotton production accounts for 16% of the world's pesticide use.
- High water consumption crop.
- Bags are not moisture resistant, unless chemically treated.
- Heavy, bulky and expensive to ship.
- Not sterile and needs to be washed regularly to prevent bacterial cross contamination of food.

Calico Reusable Bags

- Calico is a cotton fibre that is unbleached and not fully processed.
- Since this is essentially a cotton bag, it is very resource intensive, giving it a high carbon footprint.
- Has to be used hundreds of times to match the environmental performance of alternatives.

Advantages

- Lack of bleaching and processing makes this type of cotton bag kinder to the environment than traditional cotton.
- The fabric is relatively cheap to produce.
- These bags are strong and durable, but subject to shrinking when washed in warm or hot water.

Disadvantages

- Not water resistant unless chemically treated.
- Unless organically grown, this cotton requires heavy pesticide use.
- Very water-intensive crop.
- Needs to be washed regularly to prevent bacterial cross contamination of food.

Hemp Reusable Bags

- Hemp is a natural fibre that is several times stronger than cotton.
- Hemp is used for textiles and industrial applications.
- This is a different plant from the same family of hallucinogenic marijuana.
- The crop can grow in poor soils, is drought tolerant and grows well without pesticides or fertilizers.

Advantages

- Extremely strong, durable, and rot resistant.
- Can grow in poor soils with little water.
- Most hemp reusable bags can be machine washed and dried.
- Hemp can be blended with other materials to make highly desirable, high end fabrics with a texture similar to linen.
- Hemp is typically blended with cotton, or recycled PET.

Disadvantages

- Currently cannot be grown domestically (hemp products in the western world are imported).
- Can be expensive.
- Can be grainy, though most is refined.
- Refined hemp uses more water to cultivate.
- Needs to be washed regularly to prevent bacterial cross contamination of food.

Jute Reusable Bags

- Jute is a natural plant fibre that can be spun into coarse, strong threads.
- Grows in high rainfall areas and requires little to no pesticides or irrigation.
- Often referred to as hessian in Europe and burlap in North America.

Advantages

- Natural renewable resource.
- Biodegradable and compostable.
- Relatively cheap to purchase.
- Durable.
- Can be blended with other fabrics (like Jute made with Nonwoven Polypropylene).

Disadvantages

- Scarcity of supply as used primarily to store crops.
- The bags are not very resistant to moisture unless chemically treated or laminated.
- Grainy texture.
- Not easily branded—print capability is clunky and limited—so fewer organizations choose this material for their bags.
- Needs to be washed regularly to prevent bacterial cross contamination of food.

Reusable Paper Bags

- Paper bags are often used by specialty and non-grocery stores, but reuse of the bags is problematic.
- There is no significant reuse of the bags.
- They lose strength and tear when wet.

Advantages

- Biodegradable.
- Made from a renewable resource.
- Recyclable.
- As a litter item they are less persistent in the environment.
- Good colour printing.

Disadvantages

- Not durable—tears and loses strength when wet, so these bags curtail reusability.
- The bags are also anywhere from six to ten times heavier than lightweight plastic bags.
- Their heavier weight adds costs to municipal waste management.
- Their weight adds to transportation distribution costs and greenhouse gas emissions.

- Their greater volume also adds costs to inventory space.

Reusable Plastic Bags

There are a number of options available, made from different polymers:

Recycled PET Reusable Bag

- It looks and feels like a fabric bag but is made from plastic (PET#1 bottles recycled into fabric, e.g. Loblaws' resuable bag).
- Recycled PET is a durable, eco-friendly fabric made from post-consumer recycled plastic bottles and containers.
- Reusable bags made from recycled PET create a market for post-consumer recycled materials.

Advantages

- Using recycled PET materials reduces waste and conserves a non-renewable resource.
- Strong and durable.
- Requires 2/3 less energy to manufacture products made out of PET.
- Can be blended with other fabrics, like hemp or polyester to make a nice material for reusable bags.

Disadvantages

- Typically manufactured off shore.
- Recyclable.
- Not recommended for machine washing (hand wash only).

Polypropylene Reusable Bags (PP)

- Made from spun, bonded, non-woven polypropylene.
- Non-woven polypropylene is a form of plastic—a flexible resin polymer used to make rope, chairs and the tops of Tic-Tac containers.
- This type of bag is very popular in Canada because of its strength and slightly rigid, sturdy profile.
- A semi-rigid insert is put into the bottom of the bag to provide stability.

Advantages

- Very strong and durable.
- Can be made from recycled materials.
- Easy to wipe clean.

- Wide variety of material color and printing options.

Disadvantages

- Made off shore.
- Not biodegradable or compostable.
- Made from a non-renewable resource.
- Not recommended for machine washing (hand wash or spray clean only).
- Problems with lead in the inks and bag bottom inserts have led to a number of recalls.
- Needs to be washed regularly to prevent bacterial cross contamination of food.

Nylon Reusable Bags

- Nylon is a type of synthetic polymer originally made to replace silk in fabrics.
- Material compacts into a small ball for storage and ease of use.

Advantages

- Nylon is strong and durable.
- Lightweight material.
- Compacts easily.
- Easily dyed which creates interesting material colour options.
- Water resistant.

Disadvantages

- Not recyclable.
- Slow to break down.
- Made from a non-renewable resource.
- Needs to be washed regularly to prevent bacterial cross contamination of food.

Low density Polyethylene Reusable Bags (LDPE)/Bags-for-Life

- These are thick gauged, heavy duty plastic bags often referred to as "Bags-for-Life".
- They are highly recyclable, convenient and can be reused as kitchen catchers.
- The LCBO used to offer consumers a heavy gauge LDPE bag with 30% recycled content .
- A UK Environment Agency study of supermarket bags found that the LDPE "Bag-for-Life" has to be used five times to match the environmental impact of using a conventional plastic shopping bag (HDPE) once.

Advantages

- Recyclable (with the exception of the bag with some prodegradant additives).
- Can be recycled.
- High reuse.
- Does not biodegrade (excepting bags with the additive), making it useful for landfill.

Disadvantages

- Litter concerns for most of the bags because of their somewhat lightweight nature.
- Made from a non-renewable resource.
- Does not biodegrade.

Conventional Polyethylene Reusable Bags—the Multi-purpose Reusable

There are a number of different polyethylene reusable bags on the market – conventional high density (HDPE#2), polyethylene with prodegradant additive, and low density (LDPE#4) bags.

- High density polyethylene and Low density polyethylene bags:
    - These are multi-purpose, shorter life bags.
    - The conventional polyethylene plastic shopping bags have been included because of their high reuse rates of 40-60%.
    - This reuse is predominately as bin liners for household garbage - and in the case of Toronto, to recycle organics in the green bin.
    - However, the conventional bag, is also reused for a multitude of other purposes like carrying groceries, to manage pet waste, as lunch bags, for storage, for packaging, for travel, and so on.
- High Density Polyethylene Bags with a Prodegradant Additive:
    - This is similar in purpose and configuration to the conventional plastic shopping bag but it has an additive to accelerate the degradation process when exposed to natural daylight, heat, mechanical stress and weathering.
    - These bags have been introduced into the marketplace in response to litter concerns.
    - These plastics undergo accelerated degradation under the right conditions.
    - There are concerns some of these bags resins may not be compatible with the recycling of film plastics and may contaminate the recycling stream.

Reasons to use Reusable Bags

Using less resources and producing less waste is not only something for big corporations and factories to worry about. Each of us can make a huge difference in how we impact the environment around us. We can continue to use excessively and create billions of pounds of waste each year, or we can make changes to adopt a more environmentally friendly lifestyle.

Plastic bags are not easily decomposed and contribute towards the degradation of the environment. A plastic bag can take from 15 to 1,000 years to break down, depending on environment. Moreover, cost to recycle plastic bags outweighs their value. This is another reason why most of the plastic bags find their way to landfill sites. This results in huge pile of garbage that can be seen across the city releasing foul smell throughout the day and serving as distraction for the tourists.

Its high time for us to use alternative sources so as to reduce the impact of plastic bags on the environment. One such change is to ditch plastic bags altogether and use reusable bags.

Costs

While some stores still offer free plastic bags, most now charge around five cents per bag in the United States and Canada. Other countries, such as Ireland, now have a 15 cent charge per bag. A few dollars for reusable bags that last for years, or 25 to 50 dollars for plastic bags each year?

Production

A lot of oil and natural gas go into the production of plastic bags, which are not recyclable. Choosing reusable bags saves on these non-renewable resources and protects the environment.

Recycling and Garbage Costs

Even if you use paper bags, it costs money to recycle them. Similarly, plastic bags have to be taken into landfills and processed each year.

Degradation

If a plastic bag sits in a landfill, it will take around 1,000 years to properly degrade. They continue to break down into small toxic parts, which is bad for the environment.

Excess

Everywhere you go, you will see plastic bags. Sometimes they are lying on the street, or slipping out of garbage cans. They are a great symbol of our rapidly increasing consumerism.

Environmental Impact

If you believe in global warming or climate change, you are actively contributing to this phenomenon each time you use a plastic bag. In fact, paper bags are even worse for the environment because you are cutting down trees to make them, and using resources to recycle them.

Petroleum

It takes the same amount of petroleum to drive one kilometer in your car, as it takes to make seven plastic bags. This is another example of unnecessary waste, because reusable bags are just as effective as plastic ones, if not more.

Landfills

We already talked about the problems with plastic bag decomposition, but think about how much space they take in landfills. Many cities and countries already have issues with landfill space, with plastic bags only adding to the problem.

Ecosystem

The ecosystem around us is distributed by plastic bags, because they often fly away into trees or other animals' homes. Sometimes animals even try to eat these bags, thinking they are part of nature, which leads to their death.

Marine Life

Incredibly, around 100,000 marine animals perish every single year because of plastic bags. Some of the marine life most impacted are water birds and sea turtles, who often mistake them for food or get tangled up in them and cannot escape.

City-wide Litter

Plastic bags rarely stay where you put them. Even if you are careful about dumping them in a trash can, they will escape when the can is opened and the wind is blowing. This leads to bags all around cities and towns, making the area aesthetically unappealing.

No Recycling

Plastic bags are rarely recycled, because of the associated costs. It takes around $5,000 to recycle just one ton of these bags, while that amount only sells for around $30. No one is going to waste that much money recycling these bags, which is why they are always thrown out.

Contamination

Even if you try and recycle these bags, you are risking contamination when certain plastics mix together.

Oil Politics

Tired of your country bowing to foreign interests, or interfering in their conflicts, because of oil? Plastic bags are a direct reason for this political situation, because of how much petroleum is used to create them.

Never-Ending

Think about this for a second: every plastic bag you ever touched or used is probably still lying around somewhere on this planet. It might not be near you, but it is somewhere on the planet you call home.

Long-Lasting

A reusable bag is not going to tear for a long time. These bags are incredibly durable. You can probably use them to carry your groceries for years before needing a replacement.

Environmentally Conscious

It is easy to tell other people how to conserve energy and resources, but a lot harder to follow through yourself. Switching to reusable bags is your way of following through on your beliefs.

Discounts and Incentives

Many stores offer discounts and other incentives to shoppers who use these bags. While you may only save a few cents per trip, this adds up to a lot of money in a few years.

More Efficient

When checking out at the grocery store, it is a lot quicker to put your items into a reusable bag. They carry more items and retain their shape. Even when you are taking out and putting away your items at home, you will save time.

Comfort

If you have to walk a few blocks from the grocery store, you will often notice your fingers in a lot of pain by the time you get home. This is not the case with reusable bags, because they are a lot more comfortable to carry, especially for long distances.

Items do not Fall out

The worst feeling after a grocery-store trip happens when your bag rips and items fall out on the sidewalk. Sometimes an item breaks or gets damaged, while other times it is just frustrating and inconvenient. This never happens with reusable bags.

Less Germs

Do you know where plastic bags have been before they enter your home and touch your food? No. With reusable bags, you know exactly where the bag is sitting, which leads to far fewer germs.

Cleanliness

Expanding on the previous point, reusable bags are easy to wash or wipe down with a damp cloth. This keeps them clean, even if food gets on them on occasion.

Leaks

It is not uncommon for ice-cream to melt and leak out of the container, or the juices from vegetables to seep out of their plastic bags. When this stuff gets on your car seat, it is a problem to clean. With reusable bags, all leaks stay within the bag.

Multi-purpose

You can use these bags for anything, such as storing old clothes and papers around the house or keeping dirty clothes in one place before adding them to the laundry machine.

Education

This is often overlooked, but seeing someone use these bags makes others want to join in. It becomes more socially acceptable to care about the environment.

Less Bags

Reusable bags can carry a lot more items than a plastic bag, which means less hassle when you have a big load of groceries. Instead of ten different bags, you probably only need a few reusable bags to get the job done.

Easy to Store

Stack the bags up on top of each other and keep them in a corner of your pantry, or a kitchen drawer. This way you can easily access them before your weekly grocery trip.

Recycling

If you need to take a bunch of cans and bottles to your local recycling spot, use these bags to transport the items. This is a lot easier than picking up a few items at a time, and better for the environment than using plastic bags.

Sorting

If you can carry fewer bags out the grocery store, it is easier to store your items. Use one bag for perishables, while another can contain all your packaged groceries.

REDUCE, REUSE AND RECYCLE

If you have heard of something called the "waste hierarchy" you may be wondering what that means. It is the order of priority of actions to be taken to reduce the amount of waste generated, and to improve overall waste management processes and programs. The waste hierarchy consists of 3 R's as follows:

- Reduce,
- Reuse,
- Recycle.

Called the "three R's" of waste management, this waste hierarchy is the guidance suggested for creating a sustainable life. You might be wondering as to how can you incorporate these principles in your daily life. They are not hard to implement. All you need is to bring a small change in your daily lifestyle to reduce waste so that less amount of it goes to the landfill that can reduce your carbon footprint.

By refusing to buy items that you don't need, reusing items more than once and disposing the items that are no longer in use at appropriate recycling centers, you can contribute towards a healthier planet.

The First 'R' – Reduce

The concept of reducing what is produced and what is consumed is essential to the waste hierarchy. The logic behind it is simple to understand – if there is less waste, then there is less to recycle or reuse. The process of reducing begins with an examination of what you are using, and what it is used for. There are three simple steps to assessing the reduction value of an item or process:

- Is there something else that can be used for this purpose? Using multi-use items is essential to beginning reduction. One example would be a coffeepot and a cappuccino maker. Both of them do distinctly different things, but you can buy a coffeepot that has a steaming attachment on it so it can do both. The purchase of the one item means that you don't use two. It reduces the amount of production, and the amount of waste packaging material that will be generated.

- Is this something that needs to be done? A lot of our waste material comes from items that are considered to be "disposable." Not in the sense that you use something once and then throw it away, that can actually be a part of environmental responsibility when you are working with medical items – disposable in this sense means whether or not what the item allows you to do has any real meaning or purpose.
- Is the item a part of something that you need to do, or want to do in your life? There is a limit to what you need to be prepared for in life. Chances are you won't need a car that is equipped to handle a sandstorm in the desert. Buying one encourages production, wastes your resources and creates more generative waste than you can imagine. Always make sure that what you consume, or keep in your life as preparation – matches the reality of potential opportunity in your life.

Here are some of things you can do to reduce the waste:

- Print on both sides of the paper to reduce paper wastage.
- Use electronic mail to reach out to people instead of sending paper mail.
- Remove your name from the mailing lists that you no longer want to receive.
- Use cloth napkins instead of paper napkins.
- Avoid using disposable plates, spoons, glass, cups and napkins. They add to the problem and result in large amount of waste.
- Avoid buying items that are over-packaged with foil, paper, and plastic. This excess packaging goes to waste.
- Buy durable goods that have long warranty. They generally run longer and save landfill space.

Number 3 deals with the problems created by living within a culture of consumerism. This type of consumption driven culture also makes fulfilling the second "R" difficult, but it is getting easier to do.

The Second 'R' – Reuse

You may have a box of things you keep that are broken or that you don't have a use for that you hang on to in-case you find another use for them; or you may find bargains on old furniture or go trash picking and get things that you can refinish – in either case you are working towards reusing the item. Learning to reuse items, or re-purpose them for a use different then what they are intended for is essential in waste hierarchy.

One of the best examples for how this is being done today is the modular construction of homes and office buildings that is being created out of discarded shipping containers. These large, semi-truck sized metal containers represent a huge waste problem. Repurposing them as homes and offices saves them from the landfills and doesn't require the additional expenditure of nature resources to melt down and reconfigure the metals used to create them.

You may either reuse those items for your own use or donate so that others can use them. You can reuse below items like:

- Old jars and pots: Old jars and pots can be used to store items in kitchen. They can also be used to store loose items together such as computer wires.
- Tyres: Old tyres can either be sent to recycling station or can be used to make tyre-swing.
- Used wood: Used wood can be used as firewood or can be used woodcrafts.
- Newspaper: Old newspapers can be used to pack items when you're planning to move to another home or store old items.
- Envelopes: Old and waste envelopes can be used by children to make short notes.
- Waste paper: Waste paper can be used to make notes and sketches and can be send to recycling center when you don't need them anymore.

Items that can be donated to others include:

- Old books: Your old books can be used by poor children or can be donated to public libraries.
- Old clothes: Your unwanted clothes can be used by street children or can be donated to charity institutions.
- Old electric equipment: Old electric equipment can be donated to schools or NGO's so that they can use them.
- Rechargeable batteries: Rechargeable batteries can be used again and again and helps to reduce unnecessary wastage as opposed to regular batteries.

Apart from this, you can build a compost bin and reuse many waste items like used tea bags. The waste then degrades and turns into compost that help your plants grow and shine.

The Third 'R' – Recycling

The last stage of the waste hierarchy is to recycle. To recycle something means that it will be transformed again into a raw material that can be shaped into a new item. There are very few materials on the earth that cannot be recycled. One of the issues facing communities that want to become more involved with a recycling effort is that while the relying collection and sorting process may be affordable to implement, there still has to be a facility to receive and transform the discarded waste into a raw material. More progress is being made toward uniting recycling plants with industries that can process the waste material through agreements and incentive credits.

One need to learn as to what products can be recycled and what not. By carefully choosing the products that can be recycled, can be a first step towards efficient recycling:

- Buy products from market that are made up of recycled materials i.e. the product should be environment friendly.

- Buy products that can be recycled such as glass jars.
- Invent new ways to recycle different items.
- Avoid buying hazardous materials that could pose difficulty for you to recycle. Buy non-toxic products, whenever possible.
- Buy products that have been made from recycled material.
- Use recycled paper for printing or making paper handicrafts.

ECOFRIENDLY ABIOTIC RESOURCE EXTRACTION

Various approaches are used to keep environmental pollution attributable to raw material extraction within reasonable bounds. We need to use raw materials more efficiently and judiciously in the manufacturing and consumption domains. Waste management and product stewardship laws also make a key contribution in this regard, in that they allow primary raw materials to be replaced by secondary raw materials. Another possible approach is to intervene in actual primary raw material extraction processes, which often generate massive amounts of pollution. As an industrialized nation that exports large numbers of cars and machines, Germany is highly dependent on imported primary raw materials. A large portion of Germany's non-ferrous, mineral raw materials (sand, gravel, certain industrial minerals) are obtained within Germany, thus ensuring a reliable domestic supply of these elements in whole or in part. But on the other hand, Germany is highly dependent on imported metallic raw materials, certain industrial minerals, and energy raw materials, as well as the products derived from these elements.

Any given raw materials extraction project normally entails a series of life cycle phases (exploration, development, extraction, closure and rehabilitation) each of which impacts the environment very differently. The key factors in this regard are the impact on local ecosystems and biodiversity, the impact on the water balance, handling mining wastes, energy consumption, and water, soil and air emissions. The nature and extent of each of these vary greatly depending on factors related to the following:

- The raw materials that come into play,
- Technology,
- Policies and institutions society,
- Ecology.

The environmental impact of raw materials extraction unfolds over a long stretch of time, and during the extraction phase along a concurrently unfolding but often spatially distributed process chain extending from extraction to processing to refining. The environmental impact normally becomes considerably more severe during exploration, development and extraction operations. On the other hand, the environmental impact tapers off during the extraction site shutdown and cleanup/rehabilitation phases.

Exploration

This phase involves determining, using geological, geochemical and geophysical techniques, whether extracting raw materials from the target site is technically and economically feasible. The ecosphere interventions comprise exploratory drilling, sampling, initial mining, and processing tests. The environmental impact of this phase is relatively minor.

Development

During the development phase, which is relatively brief, preparations are made to extract materials from the target site. This involves the construction of the necessary project infrastructure elements such as roadways, conduits, buildings and installations. Conveyor and processing apparatuses are also installed, and basins for tailings are dug if necessary. The exact infrastructure elements needed for a given site can vary greatly depending on the location and surroundings of the deposit, whereby these elements mainly comprise the following: construction of a project infrastructure; building railroad lines, highways, ports, airports, power plants, water treatment plants, and even whole cities replete with schools and hospitals. And of course the environmental impact of the development phases varies accordingly.

During the open-cast mining development phase, the upper rock layer (which is of little or no value) is stripped away so as to expose the actual deposit and allow for raw materials extraction. This process normally generates massive amounts of mine waste that is dumped to form mounds, which of course permanently alter the landscape and occupy land and natural areas. Mine dumps can cause water, soil and air pollution, depending on the aforesaid parameters. They can also generate dust emissions, provoke acid mine drainage, and mobilize heavy metals and radionucleides. In underground mining, shafts and tunnels are dug into a mountain so as to expose the deposits. These operations can engender residues (albeit to a lesser extent than open-cast mining) in the guise of valueless waste rock, which needs to be dumped above ground.

Extraction Phase

During the extraction phase, the deposit's raw materials are extracted over a period extending from a number of years to decades. The oftentimes extremely severe environmental impact of raw material extraction and the subsequent processing of converting the extracted raw materials into a finished raw material.

Shutdown and Rehabilitation Phase

During the rehabilitation phase, the mine is closed and the various installations are usually dismantled. Mining often results in chronic environmental problems, irreversible environmental changes, and land that is rendered irreversibly unusable. The extent to which this occurs is mainly determined by the practices that were used during the extraction phase, as well as the nature and scope of the cleanup and recultivation measures. In order for site rehabilitation operations to achieve success, the project's mining permit should specify exactly which rehabilitation measures are to be carried out (recultivation, site stabilization, cleanup).

Ore Mining

Environmental impact along the supply chain: from rough raw material to refined raw material (ore mining).

Extraction

Extraction (i.e. removing raw materials from nature) is the phase in the raw materials supply chain that entails the most extensive intrusion into the natural environment. However, the environmental impact of extraction is largely determined by the type of mining involved and the mining techniques used. Open-cast mining usually has a more severe environmental impact than underground mining, since the former requires more space, the impact on the water balance is greater, and larger amounts of earth and rock are moved around.

The first step in ore mining involves the use of explosives to dislodge the rock and ore. The rock is loaded using electric or diesel driven equipment, for transport to the processing installation. To this end (and depending on the properties of the extracted ore) the ore is conveyed either continuously on belts or via pipes, or is conveyed non-continuously by vehicles. The waste rock, which is of little or no value, is piled in aboveground mounds, or is used as backfill for the mine. Such mounds can cause severe environmental damage, depending on the precautionary measures that were taken and how the ore was extracted. Acid mine drainage can occur, and toxic or radioactive substances can be released into waterbodies or the soil. Acid mine drainage can be prevented or at least minimized by separately processing residues entailing differing hazards, and by covering mine waste that can potentially cause acid mine drainage. If acid mine drainage cannot be prevented, control measures can be taken, or the acid components can perhaps be treated.

Processing

In the processing phase, the ore is converted to a commercial product (ore concentrate). The raw material processing method used is determined by factors such as the type of raw material involved, the mineralogical conditions of its extraction, the nature of the target commercial product, and the subsequent processing steps. The following main process steps come into play for metal ore:

The ore is crushed using crushers and mills (which consume considerable amounts of energy), so as to allow for subsequent separation of the ore and waste rock. This is done via a series of processes whose nature is determined by the physical or physicochemical properties of the ore. The amounts of water, energy and chemicals used vary greatly depending on the process or combination of processes involved (e.g. sedimentation, flotation, adsorption, filtration, leaching). These factors also determine the amount of wastewater, solid waste and air and water emissions that occur. Processing, which is often carried out at the mine site, consumes massive amounts of water and energy (particularly for low-concentration metal ores) and generates greenhouse gas and air emissions. The large amounts of processing sludge (some of it toxic) are taken to massive sedimentation basins, where the sludge is stabilized and then dumped in mounds. Terrestrial and/or waterbody ecosystems can be contaminated in the event of a dike breach, faulty sedimentation basin sealing, or sludge instability. The practice, now common, of extracting materials with ever lower ore concentrations in large open-cut mines has in recent decades resulted in a dramatic increase in processing residues and mining material.

Smelting and refining of the now processed raw material (ore concentrate) is partly carried out at the mine site, but is also performed at metal foundries and refineries around the world, depending on transport costs and target value creation. Depending on the technique and raw material that come into play, these final process steps in the raw material to refined material supply chain generate waste such as slag, result in air and greenhouse gas emissions, and release toxic substances into waterbodies, soil and the air.

References

- Alternativeenergysources: conserve-energy-future.com, Retrieved 14 January, 2019
- "Perstop Press release: Verdis Polaris Aura – second generation B100 – The advanced green one". Archived from the original on 4 August 2014. Retrieved 21 June 2014
- Methods-of-rainwater-harvesting: conserve-energy-future.com, Retrieved 15 February, 2019
- Ways-to-save-energy-151: conserve-energy-future.com, Retrieved 16 March, 2019
- Farrell, A.E.; et al. (2006). "Ethanol can Contribute to Energy and Environmental Goals". Science. 311 (5760): 506–8. Doi:10.1126/science.1121416. PMID 16439656
- Various-ways-to-go-green: conserve-energy-future.com, Retrieved 17 April, 2019
- "Greetings Ecological Transportation Futurist". MCN.org. Archived from the original on 2005-11-10. Retrieved 2013-04-30
- 15-ways-to-reduce-your-plastic-use-4ocean: 4ocean.com, Retrieved 18 May, 2019
- Typesofbags: allaboutbags.ca, Retrieved 19 June, 2019
- 30-breathtaking-reasons-to-switch-to-reusable-bags: conserve-energy-future.com, Retrieved 20 July, 2019
- Reduce-reuse-recycle: conserve-energy-future.com, Retrieved 21 August, 2019
- Ecofriendly-abiotic-resource-extraction, resource-conservation-in-the-manufacturing, topics: umweltbundesamt.de, Retrieved 22 January, 2019

Environmental Protection and Natural Resource Management

CHAPTER 6

The practice of protecting the natural environment by individuals, organizations and governments is termed as environmental protection. Natural resource management involves the management of natural resources such soil, water, land, etc. All the diverse principles of environmental protection and natural resource management have been carefully analyzed in this chapter.

ENVIRONMENTAL PROTECTION

Environmental protection refers to any measure that is taken to conserve, maintain or preserve the state of the environment. Protection of the environment can be done through reducing pollutants or anything that leads to its degradation. Conservation of the environment aims at keeping it safe and healthy. It aims at the reduction of overusing the natural resources. It is the taking care of all the components that make up the environment.

Preserving is also used hand in hand with the term conserving. Environmental preservation refers practices that do not alter the environment. It aims at keeping the environment unchanged so as to leave it intact. Protection of the environment can also mean that the environmental practices that the human race indulge in are sustainable to help avoid damaging or harming the ecosystem. The animals are also part of the environment and when we talk about protection, animals are a key factor. For animals, it is more about conservation. It has to do with protecting the endangered species from extinction by discouraging activities such as poaching.

When the environment is protected it serves to benefit all those who rely on it. It serves in the maintenance of life for the plants, humans and animals.

Importance of Environmental Protection

To Protect/Save our Lives

The environment supports the life of each and every living thing on earth. We rely on the environment for life. When it is protected we are assured of better health. Food, quality air and so much more. As the late professor Wangari Mathai said and I quote, "if we destroy the environment, the environment will destroy us." This is so true because it is the environment that sustains our life.

Environment has Suffered due to the Scientific Inventions

A lot has been discovered over the years. Many of these inventions tend to be harmful to the environment, though it is a way of the human race trying to make their life better. Factories have been built in so many places around the world. The emission of harmful gases into the air is on the increase. The dredging of oil in the sea is also another case. Trees are being cut down to create space for more land. With all this going on, the environment remains at or mercy for protection.

Discharge of Carbon Gases

The first thing everyone with a good amount of money is thinking about is how to get a car. The purchase of cars has grown over the years. The worst part is that there are not many cars that are environment friendly. Most of them use fuel which when burnt, releases carbon into the air. Factories are also playing a role in this. Carbon gases are not in any way friendly to the environment and this is why we need to protect it.

Use of Low Grade Plastics

The chemicals that go into making plastics is highly toxic and it poses serious threats to the environment. Burning of plastics during their production and even after use releases toxic fumes into the air. The toxins can also leak into the soil and ground water causing contamination. This makes it difficult to grow plants and even pose a challenge to hormones in many living things.

Biodiversity is Important

For the environment to be a better place to live, biodiversity has to be a part of it. In science it is said that during the day, plants use carbon dioxide, while humans breathe in oxygen and breathe out carbon dioxide. This is a form of exchange plan. Plants help to reduce carbon dioxide in the air, which in turn benefits humans. Each living has a role to play in the environment. It makes the world a better place to live in.

It is our Moral Obligation

We owe our existence to the environment. It is our role to ensure that the environment supports us and other living species in a comfortable way. The only way we can pay it back is by protecting it in all ways possible.

Environmental Hazards are Dangerous

When we look at our water bodies, they have become dumping grounds for dangerous chemicals. Most factories throw their waste into the lakes and oceans. These chemicals end up in the food web such as mercury in fish. These foods end up on our plates and the end result could be serious diseases. The air we breathe in and what our skin comes into contact with is crucial. When we have harmful gases in the air it is a threat to life.

How to Protect the Environment?

The following protective and control measures are aimed at environmental protection.

Reforestation

Trees are very important. They play a great role in air purification, they are water catchment areas and a home to many other living species. The more trees we have the purer the air and the less the chances of having water problems. Animals also have their own habitat in the forests.

Use Green Technologies

Factories should try to go green. Use more environmentally friendly gases that are not harmful. Wind energy is one way to go about it. Solar energy is also an applicable method. Use of renewable energy will reduce the harmful chemicals.

Use Less Chemicals in Factories

When the chemicals are less, this means that waste is also minimal. Not only the factories but also those who do farming. Most of the pesticides and fertilizers used in farms end up in water bodies. It is important to use a reasonable amount that will not be harmful.

Share your Car or use Public Transport

Since cars are a major air pollutant, trying to minimize the number of cars on the road is important. People can choose to use more of public transport. Families can share cars rather than each member of the family having a car or use bicycles where possible.

Create Awareness

It is important to educate people on the importance of environmental protection. The little things people do will do a long way in environmental protection. Encourage them on the importance of reusing and recycling. Encourage use of energy savers as well as collecting rain water. It is also important to educate on animal conservation as well as taking part in tree planting programs. There are so many organizations all over the world that are planting trees in the aim of saving the world.

Be Sustainable

Try as much as possible to reduce or eliminate waste and use the environment is an eco-friendly way. Sustainability means reducing the use of natural resources so as to reduce the chances of depleting them. Use more of fluorescent tubes, use rechargeable batteries, use renewable energy, and use renewable bags for shopping are some of the ways to be sustainable.

Plant Trees along Sea-beach

Sea beaches are low-lying lands that are bear. Planting trees in these areas will play a great role in protecting the environment. They can serve as air purifiers and reduce the chances of harmful waste reaching the sea and oceans. They will also serve the purpose of preventing dunes.

In the industrial countries, voluntary environmental agreements often provide a platform for companies to be recognized for moving beyond the minimum regulatory standards and thus support the development of best environmental practice. For instance, in India, Environment

Improvement Trust (EIT) has been working for environmental and forest protection since 1998. A group of Green Volunteers get a goal of Green India Clean India concept. CA Gajendra Kumar Jain a Chartered Accountant, is the founder of Environment Improvement Trust in Sojat city a small village of State of Rajasthan in India In developing countries, such as Latin America, these agreements are more commonly used to remedy significant levels of non-compliance with mandatory regulation. The challenges that exist with these agreements lie in establishing baseline data, targets, monitoring and reporting. Due to the difficulties inherent in evaluating effectiveness, their use is often questioned and, indeed, the whole environment may well be adversely affected as a result. The key advantage of their use in developing countries is that their use helps to build environmental management capacity.

Ecosystems Approach

An ecosystems approach to resource management and environmental protection aims to consider the complex interrelationships of an entire ecosystem in decision making rather than simply responding to specific issues and challenges. Ideally the decision-making processes under such an approach would be a collaborative approach to planning and decision making that involves a broad range of stakeholders across all relevant governmental departments, as well as representatives of industry, environmental groups and community. This approach ideally supports a better exchange of information, development of conflict-resolution strategies and improved regional conservation. Religions also play an important role in the conservation of the environment.

International Environmental Agreements

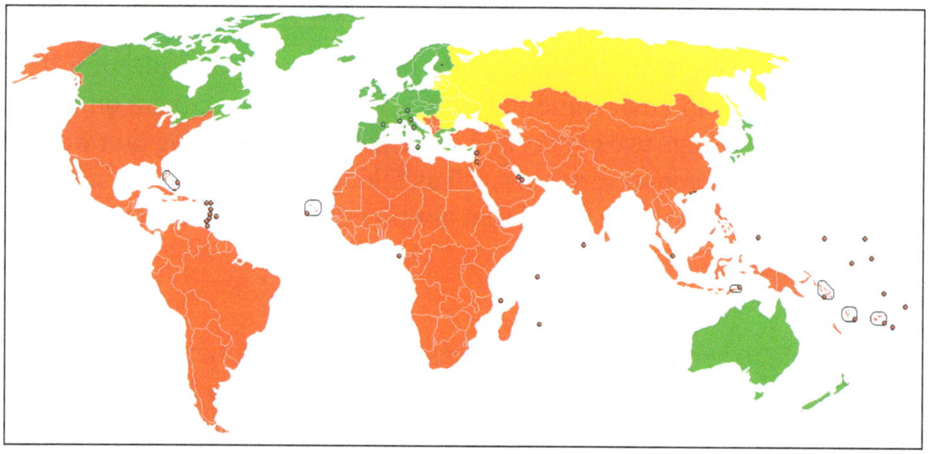

Kyoto Protocol Commitment map 2010.

Many of the earth's resources are especially vulnerable because they are influenced by human impacts across many countries. As a result of this, many attempts are made by countries to develop agreements that are signed by multiple governments to prevent damage or manage the impacts of human activity on natural resources. This can include agreements that impact factors such as climate, oceans, rivers and air pollution. These international environmental agreements are sometimes legally binding documents that have legal implications when they are not followed and, at other times, are more agreements in principle or are for use as codes of conduct. These agreements have a long history with some multinational agreements being in place from as early as 1910 in Europe, America and Africa. Some of the most well-known international agreements include the Kyoto Protocol.

Government

Discussion concerning environmental protection often focuses on the role of government, legislation, and law enforcement. However, in its broadest sense, environmental protection may be seen to be the responsibility of all the people and not simply that of government. Decisions that impact the environment will ideally involve a broad range of stakeholders including industry, indigenous groups, environmental group and community representatives. Gradually, environmental decision-making processes are evolving to reflect this broad base of stakeholders and are becoming more collaborative in many countries.

Many constitutions acknowledge the fundamental right to environmental protection and many international treaties acknowledge the right to live in a healthy environment. Also, many countries have organizations and agencies devoted to environmental protection. There are international environmental protection organizations, such as the United Nations Environment Programme.

Although environmental protection is not simply the responsibility of government protection acts, most people view these agencies as being of prime importance in establishing and maintaining basic standards that protect both the environment and the people interacting with it.

Tanzania

Tanzania is recognised as having some of the greatest biodiversity of any African country. Almost 40% of the land has been established into a network of protected areas, including several national parks. The concerns for the natural environment include damage to ecosystems and loss of habitat resulting from population growth, expansion of subsistence agriculture, pollution, timber extraction and significant use of timber as fuel.

Zebras at the Serengeti savana plains in Tanzania.

Environmental Protection

Environmental protection in Tanzania began during the German occupation of East Africa — colonial conservation laws for the protection of game and forests were enacted, whereby restrictions were placed upon traditional indigenous activities such as hunting, firewood collecting and cattle grazing. In year 1948, Serengeti was officially established the first national park for wild cats in East Africa. Since 1983, there has been a more broad-reaching effort to manage environmental issues at a national level, through the establishment of the National Environment Management Council (NEMC) and the development of an environmental act. In 1998 Environment Improvement Trust

(EIT) start working for environment & forest protection in India from a small city Sojat. Founder of Environment Improvement Trust is CA Gajendra Kumar Jain working with volunteers.

Government Protection

Division of the biosphere is the main government body that oversees protection. It does this through the formulation of policy, coordinating and monitoring environmental issues, environmental planning and policy-oriented environmental research.The National Environment Management Council (NEMC) is an institution that was initiated when the National Environment Management Act was first introduced in year 1983. This council has the role to advise governments and the international community on a range of environmental issues. The NEMC the following purposes: provide technical advice; coordinate technical activities; develop enforcement guidelines and procedures; assess, monitor and evaluate activities that impact the environment; promote and assist environmental information and communication; and seek advancement of scientific knowledge.

The National Environment Policy of 1997 acts as a framework for environmental decision making in Tanzania. The policy objectives are to achieve the following:

- Ensure sustainable and equitable use of resources without degrading the environment or risking health or safety.
- Prevent and control degradation of land, water, vegetation and air.
- Conserve and enhance natural and man-made heritage, including biological diversity of unique ecosystems.
- Improve condition and productivity of degraded areas.
- Raise awareness and understanding of the link between environment and development.
- Promote individual and community participation.
- Promote international cooperation.
- Use ecofriendly resources.

Tanzania is a signatory to a significant number of international conventions including the Rio Declaration on Development and Environment 1992 and the Convention on Biological Diversity 1996. The Environmental Management Act, 2004, is the first comprehensive legal and institutional framework to guide environmental-management decisions. The policy tools that are parts of the act includes the use of: environmental-impact assessments, strategics environmentals assessments and taxation on pollution for specific industries and products. The effectiveness of shifing of this act will only become clear over time as concerns regarding its implementation become apparent based on the fact that, historically, there has been a lack of capacity to enforce environmental laws and a lack of working tools to bring environmental-protection objectives into practice.

China

Formal environmental protection in China House was first stimulated by the 1972 United Nations Conference on the Human Environment held in Stockholm, Sweden. Following this, they began establishing environmental protection agencies and putting controls on some of its industrial waste. China was one of the first developing countries to implement a sustainable development strategy. In 1983 the State Council announced that environmental protection would be one of China's basic national policies and in 1984 the National Environmental Protection Agency (NEPA) was established. Following severe flooding of the Yangtze River basin in 1998, NEPA was upgraded to the State Environmental Protection Agency (SEPA) meaning that environmental protection was now being implemented at a ministerial level. In 2008, SEPA became known by its current name of Ministry of Environmental Protection of the People's Republic of China (MEP).

The Longwanqun National Forest Park is a nationally protected nature area in Huinan County, Jilin, China.

Pollution control instruments in China			
Command-and-control	Economic incentives	Voluntary instruments	Public participation
Concentration-based pollution discharge controls	Pollution levy fee	Environmental labeling system	Clean-up campaign
Mass-based controls on total provincial discharge	Non-compliance fines	ISO 14000 system	Environmental awareness campaign
Environmental impact assessments (EIA)	Discharge permit system	Cleaner production	Air pollution index
Three synchronization program	Sulfur emission fee	NGOs	Water quality disclosure
Deadline transmission trading		Administrative permission hearing	
Centralized pollution control	Subsidies for energy saving products		
Two compliance policy	Regulation on refuse credit to high-polluting firms		
Environmental compensation fee			

Environmental pollution and ecological degradation has resulted in economic losses for China. In 2005, economic losses (mainly from air pollution) were calculated at 7.7% of China's GDP. This grew to 10.3% by 2002 and the economic loss from water pollution (6.1%) began to exceed that caused by air pollution. China has been one of the top performing countries in terms of

GDP growth (9.64% in the past ten years). However, the high economic growth has put immense pressure on its environment and the environmental challenges that China faces are greater than most countries. In 2010 China was ranked 121st out of 163 countries on the Environmental Performance Index.

China has taken initiatives to increase its protection of the environment and combat environmental degradation:

- China's investment in renewable energy grew 18% in 2007 to $15.6 billion, accounting for ~10% of the global investment in this area.
- In 2008, spending on the environment was 1.49% of GDP, up 3.4 times from 2000.
- The discharge of CO (carbon monoxide) and SO_2 (sulfur dioxide) decreased by 6.61% and 8.95% in 2008 compared with that in 2005.
- China's protected nature reserves have increased substantially. In 1978 there were only 34 compared with 2,538 in 2010. The protected nature reserve system now occupies 15.5% of the country; this is higher than the world average.

Rapid growth in GDP has been China's main goal during the past three decades with a dominant development model of inefficient resource use and high pollution to achieve high GDP. For China to develop sustainably, environmental protection should be treated as an integral part of its economic policies.

Quote from Shengxian Zhou, head of MEP: "Good economic policy is good environmental policy and the nature of environmental problem is the economic structure, production form and develop model."

European Union

Environmental protection has become an important task for the institutions of the European Community after the Maastricht Treaty for the European Union ratification by all the Member States. The EU is already very active in the field of environmental policy with important directives like those on environmental impact assessment and on the access to environmental information for citizens in the Member States.

Russia

In Russia, environmental protection is considered an integral part of national safety. There is an authorized state body - the Federal Ministry of Natural Resources and Ecology. However, there are a lot of environmental issues in Russia.

Latin America

The United Nations Environment Programme (UNEP) has identified 17 megadiverse countries. The list includes six Latin American countries: Brazil, Colombia, Ecuador, Mexico, Peru and Venezuela. Mexico and Brazil stand out among the rest because they have the largest area, population and number of species. These countries represent a major concern for environmental protection because they have high rates of deforestation, ecosystems loss, pollution, and population growth.

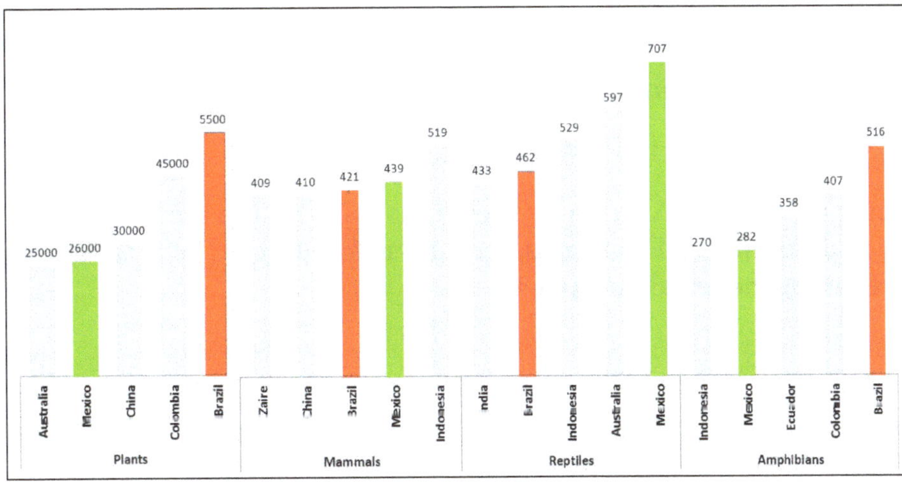

Top 5 Countries by biological diversity.

Brazil

Panorama of the Iguazu falls in Brazil.

Brazil has the largest amount of the world's tropical forests, 4,105,401 km2 (48.1% of Brazil), concentrated in the Amazon region. Brazil is home to vast biological diversity, first among the megadiverse countries of the world, having between 15%-20% of the 1.5 million globally described species.

The organization in charge of environment protection is the Brazilian Ministry of the Environment. It was first created in year 1973 with the name Special Secretariat for the Environment, changing names several times, and adopting the final name in year 1999. The Ministry is responsible for addressing the following issues:

- A national policy for the environment and for water resources;
- A policy for the preservation, conservation and sustainable use of ecosystems, biodiversity and forests;

- Proposing strategies, mechanisms, economic and social instruments for improving environmental quality, and sustainable use of natural resources;
- Policies for integrating production and the environment;
- Environmental policies and programs for the Legal Amazon;
- Ecological and economic territorial zoning.

In 2011, protected areas of the Amazon covered 2,197,485 km² (an area larger than Greenland), with conservation units, like national parks, accounting for just over half (50.6%) and indigenous territories representing the remaining 49.4%.

Mexico

With over 200,000 different species, Mexico is home to 10–12% of the world's biodiversity, ranking first in reptile biodiversity and second in mammals—one estimate indicates that over 50% of all animal and plant species live in Mexico.

The history of environmental policy in Mexico started in the 1940s with the enactment of the Law of Conservation of Soil and Water. Three decades later, at the beginning of the 1970s, the Law to Prevent and Control Environmental Pollution was created.

In year 1972 was the first direct response from the federal government to address eminent health effects from environmental issues. It established the administrative organization of the Secretariat for the Improvement of the Environment in the Department of Health and Welfare.

The axolotl is an endemic species from the central part of Mexico.

The Secretariat of Environment and Natural Resources is Mexico's environment ministry. The Ministry is responsible for addressing the following issues:

- Promote the protection, restoration, and conservation of ecosystems, natural resources, goods, and environmental services and facilitate their use and sustainable development.
- Develop and implement a national policy on natural resources.
- Promote environmental management within the national territory, in coordination with all levels of government and the private sector.

- Evaluate and provide determination to the environmental impact statements for development projects and prevention of ecological damage.
- Implement national policies on climate change and protection of the ozone layer.
- Direct work and studies on national meteorological, climatological, hydrological, and geohydrological systems, and participate in international conventions on these subjects.
- Regulate and monitor the conservation of waterways.

In November 2000 there were 127 protected areas; currently there are 174, covering an area of 25,384,818 hectares, increasing federally protected areas from 8.6% to 12.85% its land area.

Oceania

Australia

The Great Barrier Reef in Australia is the largest barrier reef in the world.

In 2008, there was 98,487,116 ha of terrestrial protected area, covering 12.8% of the land area of Australia. The 2002 figures of 10.1% of terrestrial area and 64,615,554 ha of protected marine area were found to poorly represent about half of Australia's 85 bioregions.

Environmental protection in Australia could be seen as starting with the formation of the first National Park, Royal National Park, in 1879. More progressive environmental protection had it start in the 1960s and 1970s with major international programs such as the United Nations Conference on the Human Environment in 1972, the Environment Committee of the OECD in 1970, and the United Nations Environment Programme of 1972. These events laid the foundations by increasing public awareness and support for regulation. State environmental legislation was irregular and deficient until the Australian Environment Council (AEC) and Council of Nature Conservation Ministers (CONCOM) were established in 1972 and 1974, creating a forum to assist in coordinating environmental and conservation policies between states and neighbouring countries. These councils have since been replaced by the Australian and New Zealand Environment and Conservation Council (ANZECC) in 1991 and finally the Environment Protection and Heritage Council (EPHC) in 2001.

At a national level, the Environment Protection and Biodiversity Conservation Act 1999 is the primary environmental protection legislation for the Commonwealth of Australia. It concerns matters of national and international environmental significance regarding flora, fauna, ecological communities and cultural heritage. It also has jurisdiction over any activity conducted by the Commonwealth, or affecting it, that has significant environmental impact. The act covers eight main areas:

- National Heritage Sites,
- World Heritage Sites,
- RAMSAR wetlands,
- Nationally endangered or threatened species and ecological communities,
- Nuclear activities and actions,
- Great Barrier Reef Marine Park,
- Migratory species,
- Commonwealth Marine areas.

There are several Commonwealth protected lands due to partnerships with traditional native owners, such as Kakadu National Park, extraordinary biodiversity such as Christmas Island National Park, or managed cooperatively due to cross-state location, such as the Australian Alps National Parks and Reserves.

At a state level, the bulk of environmental protection issues are left to the responsibility of the state or territory. Each state in Australia has its own environmental protection legislation and corresponding agencies. Their jurisdiction is similar and covers point-source pollution, such as from industry or commercial activities, land/water use, and waste management. Most protected lands are managed by states and territories with state legislative acts creating different degrees and definitions of protected areas such as wilderness, national land and marine parks, state forests, and conservation areas. States also create regulation to limit and provide general protection from air, water, and sound pollution.

At a local level, each city or regional council has responsibility over issues not covered by state or national legislation. This includes non-point source, or diffuse pollution, such as sediment pollution from construction sites.

Australia ranks second place on the UN 2010 Human Development Index and one of the lowest debt to GDP ratios of the developed economies. This could be seen as coming at the cost of the environment, with Australia being the world leader in coal exportation and species extinctions. Some have been motivated to proclaim it is Australia's responsibility to set the example of environmental reform for the rest of the world to follow.

New Zealand

At a national level, the Ministry for the Environment is responsible for environmental policy and the Department of Conservation addresses conservation issues. At a regional level the regional councils administer the legislation and address regional environmental issues.

Switzerland

The environmental protection in Switzerland is mainly based on the measures to be taken against global warming. The pollution in Switzerland is mainly the pollution caused by vehicles and the litteration by tourists.

United States

Since 1969, the United States Environmental Protection Agency (EPA) has been working to protect the environment and human health. All U.S. states have their own state departments of environmental protection.

Yosemite National Park in California. One of the first protected areas in the United States.

The EPA has drafted "Seven Priorities for EPA's Future", which are:

- Taking Action on Climate Change.
- Improving Air Quality.
- Assuring the Safety of Chemicals.
- Cleaning Up Our Communities.
- Protecting America's Waters.
- Expanding the Conversation on Environmentalism and Working for Environmental Justice.
- Building Strong State and Tribal Partnerships.

NATURAL RESOURCE MANAGEMENT

Natural resource management are the ways in which societies manage the supply of or access to the natural resources upon which they rely for their survival and development. Insofar as humans are fundamentally dependent on natural resources, ensuring the ongoing access to or a steady provision of natural resources has always been central to the organization of civilizations and, historically, has been organized through a range of schemes varying in degrees of formality and involvement from the central authorities.

A "natural" resource is one that is afforded by nature without human intervention; hence, the fertile lands or the minerals within them, rather than the crop that grows on them, are examples of a country's natural resources. Although what is considered a "resource" (or, for that matter, "natural") has varied over time and from one society to another, resources are, ultimately, riches provided by nature from which can be derived some form of benefit, whether material or immaterial. Under some definitions, only those natural resources that can renew themselves and whose exploitation relies on their regenerative capacities properly necessitate management. For example, oil is not usually considered a subject of natural resource management, whereas forests are. The use of nonrenewable resources is subject to regulation rather than management. The management of renewable natural resources seeks to balance the demands of exploitation with a respect for regenerative capacities.

ForestryA logging operation in Scotland.

The emergence of a rational systematic management of natural resources can be traced back to the phase of accelerated industrialization of the late 19th century. In a period of unprecedented industrial growth, the pressures brought to bear on the supply of raw materials and natural resources by an unrelenting demand intensified the need to rationalize their utilization, so as to eliminate increasingly costly waste and to allocate them more efficiently. That coincided with a broader tendency toward rationalization, a general social pattern identified by the sociologist Max Weber that emerged in modern industrial societies in response to the large-scale reorganization of production and whereby goal-oriented rationality was increasingly infused into the organization of social activities. Natural resource management was born at the conjunction of rationalization and its twin process, bureaucratization, which yielded the first bureaucracies to manage nature.

Of course, there were huge variations in both the rates and degrees to which the different states became involved with questions of natural resource management. The French state, for example, took a heavy hand in forestry management as early as the 17th century, when wood became a strategic resource at a time of accelerated mercantilist (export-oriented) growth that relied primarily on maritime transportation—namely, wooden ships. Such local variations aside, overall it took a certain kind of state, the modern bureaucratic state, to steer the exploitation of natural resources toward principles of scientific management. In the United States, natural resource management was made a federal matter for the first time under the presidency of Theodore Roosevelt. At that time, principles of scientific management, which combined notions of rational management with in-depth scientific knowledge of the resource itself, were promoted by key figures such as Gifford Pinchot, who took a leading role in the U.S. government's management of forests in the 1890s and served as head of the Forest Service from its creation, in 1905, to 1910. In Europe a similar concern with rational resource exploitation transpired at about the same time. The International Council for the Exploration of the Sea (established 1902), for example, provided a forum in which northern European countries could share concerns about maritime research and resources. It was effectively one of the first international conferences on a natural resource management question, and there too science was entrenched as a basis for exploitation of the seas, laying the grounds for future arrangement for the management of collective resources.

Encountering Earth's Limits

The 20th century saw natural resource management increasingly projected at a supranational level, where it was also collectivized. A first major impulse toward the internationalization of natural resource management was brought by the post-World War II context, with its pervasive spirit of cooperation on the one hand and its specific problems of food shortages on the other. Countries came together to address the issues of damaged capacities and insufficient production—in other words, insufficient use of available resources. That context yielded the Food and Agricultural Organization (FAO) in 1945, the International Whaling Commission in 1946, and, much later, the International Fund for Agricultural Development, established in 1977 to tackle problems of agricultural production in developing countries. The problem was seen to lie in the management of the resources rather than in the resources themselves. Therefore, the solution was to develop common solutions to management problems that were widely shared from one country to the next. The problem those organizations attempted to solve, in other words, was how to create international regimes that would disseminate better management solutions and thus enable each country to make better use of its resources.

In a second phase, attention shifted at a global level to Earth's resources as a whole—the seas, the air, and biodiversity—because of the realization that those essential resources, hitherto taken for granted, were in fact limited. That realization came about through two successive crises. First was the new awareness that humankind had reached a global environmental crisis, which triggered a second wave of bureaucracies to manage nature at both the national and international levels. At the international level the United Nations Environment Programme (UNEP) was established in 1972, and at the national level environmental ministries (in Europe) or agencies (in the United States) flourished in developed countries in the early 1970s. Significantly, the issue that popularized the environmental crisis was an issue of failed global resource management: the overexploitation of whales, which threatened certain species with extinction. That initial awareness was rapidly compounded by a global energy crisis that began in 1973. At that juncture natural resource management was recast as an issue of environmental governance, and it was connected to the new environmental discourses taking shape, such as sustainable development.

The issue of Earth's limits is an unsettled question, not least because of the sheer diversity of natural resources and the difficulty in assessing them scientifically. However, the remaining controversy revolves not around the idea that Earth's resources are limited but rather around its regenerative capacities, which in turn determines how those limits are to be considered. If they are relative, the question becomes one of regulating the access to a resource more stringently or of adapting the activity relying upon it so that it can use a more abundant primary resource. If the limits are absolute, then merely switching the activity from one dependency basis to another is simply insufficient, especially if such dependency continues to expand overall.

Conceptual Approaches to Natural Resource Management

Natural resource management ties in with applied concepts such as maximum sustainable yield (MSY) and optimum utilization. Every natural resource has its optimum utilization, or acceptable levels of use, which are established scientifically and according to which management authorities regulate its exploitation. Such a concept presupposes scientific knowledge as a basis for management and also a regulatory authority (whether national or international) capable of enforcing the exploitation of the resources in accord with such scientific knowledge. The MSY is a regulatory concept that translates precepts of population dynamics into a management tool. Population studies in fisheries have shown that, in a given population, when the deaths increase as a result of human harvesting (exploitation), reproduction rates usually start to rise (as if compensating for the deaths). Theoretically, that resultant surplus production can be harvested sustainably, provided that the harvest is consistently maintained under the MSY, which is specific to each population (rather than to the species as a whole). That is the peak level, beyond which the negative effect of decreasing numbers on the overall population starts to exceed the positive effect of increased reproduction rates. Subsequently, the population as a whole (and not just the harvestable surplus) begins to decline. On the other hand, maintaining exploitation levels below the MSY creates an efficient use of the resources' regenerative capacities, thus in principle enabling exploitation to continue indefinitely.

The use of this tool, which was first developed in fisheries, has been extended more broadly, notably through its incorporation into the Convention on the Law of the Sea. However, it has tended to be associated with species-specific management regimes. It requires careful monitoring of population growth and overall health, and overharvesting can easily occur if the population suffers outside declines, such as disease or habitat loss, and harvesting levels are not adjusted. Additional regulations, such as limiting the harvest of females or immature individuals, can help ensure that populations are maintained at sustainable levels.

Another way to think about natural resource management is to think about the purpose of the management. The management objectives are determined by the purpose of the resource itself—as a primary resource, as a raw material or fuel, as a source of food, or as a recreational resource. Those uses fall into two broad categories, consumptive and nonconsumptive. Consumptive utilization implies a once-only form of use—that is, it refers to activities in which the resource is effectively consumed or used up, such that it cannot be utilized by another party. Hence, the possibility of future exploitation relies on the resource's ability to regenerate itself. Nonconsumptive utilization also uses the resource to generate economic value, but it does so without using up the resource itself. That category encompasses most recreational uses of natural resources. In the case of consumptive uses, management implies balancing exploitation with a respect for the resource's regenerative capacities. In nonconsumptive uses, management centres on regulating the ways in which humans interact with the resource and containing the negative effects of those interactions on the resource. In either case, management is always about resolving a tension between the potentially conflicting objectives of protection and exploitation. Sometimes the use of a resource may change over time or from one part of the globe to the next. The overexploitation of whales is a case in point: whales were initially a primary raw material and fuel in the West, until the mid-20th century, whereas today whales are considered a recreational resource in the West and a food in other areas. This coexistence of different forms of use around the same resource has generated conflicts.

Another strand in natural resource management literature focuses on the difficulties in managing collective resources—that is, resources not contained within specific territorial boundaries (such as the sea or air) or resources whose management at the local level has global repercussions, such as forests. According to one line of argument, known as the tragedy of the commons, collective resources lack the incentives inherently built into a privately owned resource to self-limit their exploitation so as to ensure that they will last. In other words, individual users tend to consume as much of the collective resource as possible before others can get to it, resulting in the overall loss of the resource for all. Also at stake in discussion of collective resources is the issue of private versus communal management, a question that goes to the heart of environmental politics.

Ownership Regimes

Natural resource management approaches can be categorised according to the kind and right of stakeholders, natural resources:

- State property: Ownership and control over the use of resources is in hands of the state. Individuals or groups may be able to make use of the resources, but only at the permission of the state. National forest, National parks and military reservations are some US examples.
- Private property: Any property owned by a defined individual or corporate entity. Both the benefit and duties to the resources fall to the owner(s). Private land is the most common example.
- Common property: It is a private property of a group. The group may vary in size, nature and internal structure e.g. indigenous neighbours of village. Some examples of common property are community forests.
- Non-property (open access): There is no definite owner of these properties. Each potential user has equal ability to use it as they wish. These areas are the most exploited. It is said that "Everybody's property is nobody's property". An example is a lake fishery. Common land may exist without ownership, in which case in the UK it is vested in a local authority.
- Hybrid: Many ownership regimes governing natural resources will contain parts of more than one of the regimes described above, so natural resource managers need to consider the impact of hybrid regimes. An example of such a hybrid is native vegetation management in NSW, Australia, where legislation recognises a public interest in the preservation of native vegetation, but where most native vegetation exists on private land.

Stakeholder Analysis

Stakeholder analysis originated from business management practices and has been incorporated into natural resource management in ever growing popularity. Stakeholder analysis in the context of natural resource management identifies distinctive interest groups affected in the utilisation and conservation of natural resources.

There is no definitive definition of a stakeholder as illustrated in the table. Especially in natural resource management as it is difficult to determine who has a stake and this will differ according to each potential stakeholder.

Different approaches to who is a stakeholder:

Source	Who is a stakeholder	Kind of research
Freeman.	"can affect or is affected by the achievement of the organization's objectives"	Business Management
Bowie	"without whose support the organization would cease to exist"	Business Management
Clarkson	"...persons or groups that have, or claim, ownership, rights, or interests in a corporation and its activities, past, present, or future."	Business Management
Grimble and Wellard	"...any group of people, organized or unorganized, who share a common interest or stake in a particular issue or system..."	Natural resource management
Gass et al.	"...any individual, group and institution who would potentially be affected, whether positively or negatively, by a specified event, process or change."	Natural resource management
Buanes et al	"...any group or individual who may directly or indirectly affect—or be affected—...planning to be at least potential stakeholders."	Natural resource management
Brugha and Varvasovszky	"...actors who have an interest in the issue under consideration, who are affected by the issue, or who—because of their position—have or could have an active or passive influence on the decision making and implementation process."	Health policy
ODA	"... persons, groups or institutions with interests in a project or programme."	Development

Therefore, it is dependent upon the circumstances of the stakeholders involved with natural resource as to which definition and subsequent theory is utilised.

Billgrena and Holme identified the aims of stakeholder analysis in natural resource management:

- Identify and categorise the stakeholders that may have influence.
- Develop an understanding of why changes occur.
- Establish who can make changes happen.
- How to best manage natural resources.

This gives transparency and clarity to policy making allowing stakeholders to recognise conflicts of interest and facilitate resolutions. There are numerous stakeholder theories such as Mitchell et al. however Grimble created a framework of stages for a Stakeholder Analysis in natural resource management. Grimble designed this framework to ensure that the analysis is specific to the essential aspects of natural resource management.

Stages in Stakeholder analysis:

- Clarify objectives of the analysis.
- Place issues in a systems context.
- Identify decision-makers and stakeholders.
- Investigate stakeholder interests and agendas.
- Investigate patterns of inter-action and dependence (e.g. conflicts and compatibilities, trade-offs and synergies).

Application:

Grimble and Wellard established that Stakeholder analysis in natural resource management is most relevant where issued can be characterised as:

- Cross-cutting systems and stakeholder interests.
- Multiple uses and users of the resource.
- Market failure.
- Subtractability and temporal trade-offs.
- Unclear or open-access property rights.
- Untraded products and services.
- Poverty and under-representation.

In the case of the Bwindi Impenetrable National Park, a comprehensive stakeholder analysis would have been relevant and the Batwa people would have potentially been acknowledged as stakeholders preventing the loss of people's livelihoods and loss of life.

Nepal, Indonesia and Koreas' community forestry are successful examples of how stakeholder analysis can be incorporated into the management of natural resources. This allowed the stakeholders to identify their needs and level of involvement with the forests.

Criticisms:

- Natural resource management stakeholder analysis tends to include too many stakeholders which can create problems in of its self as suggested by Clarkson. "Stakeholder theory should not be used to weave a basket big enough to hold the world's misery."
- Starik proposed that nature needs to be represented as stakeholder. However this has been

rejected by many scholars as it would be difficult to find appropriate representation and this representation could also be disputed by other stakeholders causing further issues.

- Stakeholder analysis can be used exploited and abused in order to marginalise other stakeholders.
- Identifying the relevant stakeholders for participatory processes is complex as certain stakeholder groups may have been excluded from previous decisions.
- On-going conflicts and lack of trust between stakeholders can prevent compromise and resolutions.

Alternatives/Complementary forms of analysis:

- Social network analysis.
- Common pool resource.

Management of the Resources

Natural resource management issues are inherently complex. They involve the ecological cycles, hydrological cycles, climate, animals, plants and geography, etc. All these are dynamic and inter-related. A change in one of them may have far reaching and/or long term impacts which may even be irreversible. In addition to the natural systems, natural resource management also has to manage various stakeholders and their interests, policies, politics, geographical boundaries, economic implications and the list goes on. It is a very difficult to satisfy all aspects at the same time. This results in conflicting situations.

After the United Nations Conference for the Environment and Development (UNCED) held in Rio de Janeiro in 1992, most nations subscribed to new principles for the integrated management of land, water, and forests. Although program names vary from nation to nation, all express similar aims.

The various approaches applied to natural resource management include:

- Top-down (command and control).
- Community-based natural resource management.
- Adaptive management.
- Precautionary approach.
- Integrated natural resource management.

Community-based Natural Resource Management

The community-based natural resource management (CBNRM) approach combines conservation objectives with the generation of economic benefits for rural communities. The three key assumptions being that: locals are better placed to conserve natural resources, people will conserve a resource only if benefits exceed the costs of conservation, and people will conserve a resource that is linked directly to their quality of life. When a local people's quality of life is enhanced, their efforts and commitment to ensure the future well-being of the resource are also enhanced. Regional and community based natural resource management is also based on the principle of subsidiarity.

The United Nations advocates CBNRM in the Convention on Biodiversity and the Convention to Combat Desertification. Unless clearly defined, decentralised NRM can result an ambiguous socio-legal environment with local communities racing to exploit natural resources while they can e.g. forest communities in central Kalimantan (Indonesia).

A problem of CBNRM is the difficulty of reconciling and harmonising the objectives of socioeconomic development, biodiversity protection and sustainable resource utilisation. The concept and conflicting interests of CBNRM, show how the motives behind the participation are differentiated as either people-centred (active or participatory results that are truly empowering) or planner-centred (nominal and results in passive recipients). Understanding power relations is crucial to the success of community based NRM. Locals may be reluctant to challenge government recommendations for fear of losing promised benefits.

CBNRM is based particularly on advocacy by nongovernmental organizations working with local groups and communities, on the one hand, and national and transnational organizations, on the other, to build and extend new versions of environmental and social advocacy that link social justice and environmental management agendas with both direct and indirect benefits observed including a share of revenues, employment, diversification of livelihoods and increased pride and identity. Ecological and societal successes and failures of CBNRM projects have been documented. CBNRM has raised new challenges, as concepts of community, territory, conservation, and indigenous are worked into politically varied plans and programs in disparate sites. Warner and Jones address strategies for effectively managing conflict in CBNRM.

The capacity of indigenous communities to conserve natural resources has been acknowledged by the Australian Government with the Caring for Country Program. Caring for our Country is an Australian Government initiative jointly administered by the Australian Government Department of Agriculture, Fisheries and Forestry and the Department of the Environment, Water, Heritage and the Arts. These Departments share responsibility for delivery of the Australian Government's environment and sustainable agriculture programs, which have traditionally been broadly referred to under the banner of 'natural resource management'. These programs have been delivered regionally, through 56 State government bodies, successfully allowing regional communities to decide the natural resource priorities for their regions.

More broadly, a research study based in Tanzania and the Pacific researched what motivates communities to adopt CBNRM's and found that aspects of the specific CBNRM program, of the community that has adopted the program, and of the broader social-ecological context together shape the why CBNRM's are adopted. However, overall, program adoption seemed to mirror the relative advantage of CBNRM programs to local villagers and villager access to external technical assistance. There have been socioeconomic critiques of CBNRM in Africa, but ecological effectiveness of CBNRM measured by wildlife population densities has been shown repeatedly in Tanzania.

Governance is seen as a key consideration for delivering community-based or regional natural resource management. In the State of NSW, the 13 catchment management authorities (CMAs) are overseen by the Natural Resources Commission (NRC), responsible for undertaking audits of the effectiveness of regional natural resource management programs.

Adaptive Management

The primary methodological approach adopted by catchment management authorities (CMAs) for regional natural resource management in Australia is adaptive management.

This approach includes recognition that adaption occurs through a process of 'plan-do-review-act'. It also recognises seven key components that should be considered for quality natural resource management practice:

- Determination of scale.
- Collection and use of knowledge.
- Information management.
- Monitoring and evaluation.
- Risk management.
- Community engagement.
- Opportunities for collaboration.

Integrated Natural Resource Management

Integrated natural resource management (INRM) is a process of managing natural resources in a systematic way, which includes multiple aspects of natural resource use (biophysical, socio-political, and economic) meet production goals of producers and other direct users (e.g., food security, profitability, risk aversion) as well as goals of the wider community (e.g., poverty alleviation, welfare of future generations, environmental conservation). It focuses on sustainability and at the same time tries to incorporate all possible stakeholders from the planning level itself, reducing possible future conflicts. The conceptual basis of INRM has evolved in recent years through the convergence of research in diverse areas such as sustainable land use, participatory planning, integrated watershed management, and adaptive management. INRM is being used extensively and been successful in regional and community based natural management.

Frameworks and Modeling

There are various frameworks and computer models developed to assist natural resource management.

Geographic Information Systems (GIS)

GIS is a powerful analytical tool as it is capable of overlaying datasets to identify links. A bush regeneration scheme can be informed by the overlay of rainfall, cleared land and erosion. In Australia, Metadata Directories such as NDAR provide data on Australian natural resources such as vegetation, fisheries, soils and water. These are limited by the potential for subjective input and data manipulation.

Natural Resources Management Audit Frameworks

The NSW Government in Australia has published an audit framework for natural resource management, to assist the establishment of a performance audit role in the governance of regional natural resource management. This audit framework builds from other established audit methodologies, including performance audit, environmental audit and internal audit. Audits undertaken using this framework have provided confidence to stakeholders, identified areas for improvement and described policy expectations for the general public.

The Australian Government has established a framework for auditing greenhouse emissions and energy reporting, which closely follows Australian Standards for Assurance Engagements.

The Australian Government is also currently preparing an audit framework for auditing water management, focussing on the implementation of the Murray Darling Basin Plan.

Other Elements

Biodiversity Conservation

The issue of biodiversity conservation is regarded as an important element in natural resource management. What is biodiversity? Biodiversity is a comprehensive concept, which is a description of the extent of natural diversity. Gaston and Spicer point out that biodiversity is "the variety of life" and relate to different kinds of "biodiversity organization". According to Gray, the first widespread use of the definition of biodiversity, was put forward by the United Nations in 1992, involving different aspects of biological diversity.

Precautionary Biodiversity Management

The "threats" wreaking havoc on biodiversity include; habitat fragmentation, putting a strain on the already stretched biological resources; forest deterioration and deforestation; the invasion of "alien species" and "climate change". Since these threats have received increasing attention from environmentalists and the public, the precautionary management of biodiversity becomes an important part of natural resources management. According to Cooney, there are material measures to carry out precautionary management of biodiversity in natural resource management.

Concrete Policy Tools

Cooney claims that the policy making is dependent on "evidences", relating to "high standard of proof", the forbidding of special "activities" and "information and monitoring requirements". Before making the policy of precaution, categorical evidence is needed. When the potential menace of "activities" is regarded as a critical and "irreversible" endangerment, these "activities" should be forbidden. For example, since explosives and toxicants will have serious consequences to endanger human and natural environment, the South Africa Marine Living Resources Act promulgated a series of policies on completely forbidding to "catch fish" by using explosives and toxicants.

Administration and Guidelines

According to Cooney, there are 4 methods to manage the precaution of biodiversity in natural resources management:

- "Ecosystem-based management" including "more risk-averse and precautionary management", where "given prevailing uncertainty regarding ecosystem structure, function, and inter-specific interactions, precaution demands an ecosystem rather than single-species approach to management".
- "Adaptive management" is "a management approach that expressly tackles the uncertainty and dynamism of complex systems".
- "Environmental impact assessment" and exposure ratings decrease the "uncertainties" of precaution, even though it has deficiencies.
- "Protectionist approaches", which "most frequently links to" biodiversity conservation in natural resources management.

Land Management

In order to have a sustainable environment, understanding and using appropriate management strategies is important. In terms of understanding, Young emphasises some important points of land management:

- Comprehending the processes of nature including ecosystem, water, soils.
- Using appropriate and adapting management systems in local situations.
- Cooperation between scientists who have knowledge and resources and local people who have knowledge and skills.

Dale et al. study has shown that there are five fundamental and helpful ecological principles for the land manager and people who need them. The ecological principles relate to time, place, species, disturbance and the landscape and they interact in many ways. It is suggested that land managers could follow these guidelines:

- Examine impacts of local decisions in a regional context, and the effects on natural resources.
- Plan for long-term change and unexpected events.
- Preserve rare landscape elements and associated species.
- Avoid land uses that deplete natural resources.
- Retain large contiguous or connected areas that contain critical habitats.
- Minimize the introduction and spread of non-native species.
- Avoid or compensate for the effects of development on ecological processes.
- Implement land-use and land-management practices that are compatible with the natural potential of the area.

References

- "Environmental-protection dictionary definition | environmental-protection defined". Yourdictionary.com. Retrieved 2018-11-21
- Environmental-protection: importantindia.com, Retrieved 23 February, 2019
- Zhang, Kun-min; Wen, Zong-guo. (2008). "Review and challenges of policies of environmental protection and sustainable development in China". Journal of Environmental Management. 88: 1249–1261. Doi:10.1016/j.jenvman.2007.06.019
- Natural-resource-management: britannica.com, Retrieved 24 March, 2019
- Lovell, C.; Mandondo A.; Moriarty P. (2002). "The question of scale in integrated natural resource management". Conservation Ecology. 5 (2). Doi:10.5751/ES-00347-050225. Hdl:10535/2766. Retrieved 27 October 2014

PERMISSIONS

All chapters in this book are published with permission under the Creative Commons Attribution Share Alike License or equivalent. Every chapter published in this book has been scrutinized by our experts. Their significance has been extensively debated. The topics covered herein carry significant information for a comprehensive understanding. They may even be implemented as practical applications or may be referred to as a beginning point for further studies.

We would like to thank the editorial team for lending their expertise to make the book truly unique. They have played a crucial role in the development of this book. Without their invaluable contributions this book wouldn't have been possible. They have made vital efforts to compile up to date information on the varied aspects of this subject to make this book a valuable addition to the collection of many professionals and students.

This book was conceptualized with the vision of imparting up-to-date and integrated information in this field. To ensure the same, a matchless editorial board was set up. Every individual on the board went through rigorous rounds of assessment to prove their worth. After which they invested a large part of their time researching and compiling the most relevant data for our readers.

The editorial board has been involved in producing this book since its inception. They have spent rigorous hours researching and exploring the diverse topics which have resulted in the successful publishing of this book. They have passed on their knowledge of decades through this book. To expedite this challenging task, the publisher supported the team at every step. A small team of assistant editors was also appointed to further simplify the editing procedure and attain best results for the readers.

Apart from the editorial board, the designing team has also invested a significant amount of their time in understanding the subject and creating the most relevant covers. They scrutinized every image to scout for the most suitable representation of the subject and create an appropriate cover for the book.

The publishing team has been an ardent support to the editorial, designing and production team. Their endless efforts to recruit the best for this project, has resulted in the accomplishment of this book. They are a veteran in the field of academics and their pool of knowledge is as vast as their experience in printing. Their expertise and guidance has proved useful at every step. Their uncompromising quality standards have made this book an exceptional effort. Their encouragement from time to time has been an inspiration for everyone.

The publisher and the editorial board hope that this book will prove to be a valuable piece of knowledge for students, practitioners and scholars across the globe.

INDEX

CPSIA information can be obtained
at www.ICGtesting.com
Printed in the USA
LVHW062011100122
708212LV00002B/162

9 781641 16612